STUDIES IN BIOETHICS

SHOULD THE BABY LIVE?
The Problem of Handicapped Infants

STUDIES IN BIOETHICS

General Editor *Peter Singer*

Studies in Bioethics is a series aimed at introducing more rigorous argument into the discussion of ethical issues in medicine and the biological sciences.

Already published

Helga Kuhse and Peter Singer   *Should the Baby Live? The Problem of Handicapped Infants*
Peter Singer and Deane Wells   *The Reproduction Revolution: New Ways of Making Babies*

Forthcoming

Michael Lockwood (ed.)   *Moral Dilemmas in Modern Medicine*
James Rachels   *The End of Life: Euthanasia and Morality*

SHOULD THE BABY LIVE?

The Problem of Handicapped Infants

HELGA KUHSE and
PETER SINGER

Oxford   New York   Melbourne
OXFORD UNIVERSITY PRESS
1985

Oxford University Press, Walton Street, Oxford OX2 6DP

Oxford New York Toronto
Delhi Bombay Calcutta Madras Karachi
Kuala Lumpur Singapore Hong Kong Tokyo
Nairobi Dar es Salaam Cape Town
Melbourne Auckland

and associated companies in
Beirut Berlin Ibadan Mexico City Nicosia

Oxford is a trade mark of Oxford University Press

British Library Cataloguing in Publication Data

Kuhse, Helga
Should the baby live?: the problem of
handicapped infants.— (Studies in bioethics)
1. Medical ethics   2. Infants (Newborn)
I. Title   II. Singer, Peter   III. Series
174'.24   R725.5
ISBN 0-19-217745-1
ISBN 0-19-286062-3 Pbk

Library of Congress Cataloging in Publication Data

Kuhse, Helga.
Should the baby live?
(Studies in bioethics)
Includes bibliographical references and index.
1. Infants—Diseases—Treatment—Moral and ethical
aspects. 2. Euthanasia—Moral and ethical aspects.
3. Infanticide—Moral and ethical aspects.
I. Singer, Peter.   II. Title.   III. Series.
RJ59.S53 1985   174'.24   85-3017
ISBN 0-19-217745-1
ISBN 0-19-286062-3 (pbk.)

Set by Hope Services
Printed in Great Britain by
Billing & Sons Ltd., Worcester

PREFACE

This book contains conclusions which some readers will find disturbing. We think that some infants with severe disabilities should be killed. This recommendation may cause particular offence to readers who were themselves born with disabilities, perhaps even the same disabilities we are discussing. We therefore consider it necessary to state, right at the outset and in the plainest possible terms, that nothing in the views we express in this book in any way implies a lack of concern for disabled people in our community. On the contrary, it is our view that affluent nations should be spending far more than they presently allocate to assist disabled people to live fulfilling, worthwhile lives, and to enable people with disabilities to develop their potential to the utmost. We should commit ourselves to transforming the often deplorable standards of institutional care, and to providing the services needed for disabled people to move out of institutions and into the community.

If a hasty reading of our book gives an impression that we hold other views, it is probably a result of failing to bear in mind that our subsequent discussion refers to disabled *infants*. For reasons given in later chapters of this book, decisions whether infants should live or die are very different from life and death decisions in the case of people who can understand, or once were capable of understanding, at least some aspects of what a decision to live or die might mean. To put it even more bluntly: it is one thing to say, before a life has properly begun, that such a life should not be lived; it is quite different to say that, once a life is being lived, we need not do our best to improve it. We are sometimes prepared to say the former: we are never prepared to say the latter.

* * *

It is our pleasure to acknowledge the assistance of the Australian Research Grants Scheme, which has supported the research project on which this book is based. We also thank the members of the Committee of the Centre for Human Bioethics, at Monash University, for their support and encouragement. Dr Cora Singer applied her considerable medical experience and sympathetic understanding to the delicate task of interviewing paediatricians and obstetricians on their treatment of severely handicapped infants; her reports yielded valuable new information and led to many fruitful discussions. We are grateful to the Australian College of Obstetricians and Gynaecologists for their co-operation in this matter. We learnt much from discussions with other doctors and with nursing staff; although we cannot thank them all individually, we must mention in particular Dr Bernard Neal, Dr John Drew, and Sister Kate Collins. For assistance with the anthropological material we thank Dr G. B. Silberbauer.

We ˜also had assistance from many people overseas. In England, Professor Alister Campbell, Professor John Lorber, and Professor Robert Zachary were kind enough to be interviewed by one of us, while Jonathan Glover and Dr Peter Dunn provided us with material on the trial of Dr Leonard Arthur. We also thank Alison Davis for corresponding with us, and for permission to quote from her letter in this book. In the United States Dr William Silverman has been a great friend, while we must also thank Helen Harrison and John and Susan West for sharing with us their experiences with their own disabled children and for giving us access to the materials they have on this topic. Both the American Academy of Pediatrics and the American Medical Association have kindly provided us with documents concerning the 'Baby Doe' rules and the litigation which followed. One of us (PS) presented sections of the book to a graduate class at the University of Colorado, Boulder, and he wishes to thank both students and staff for the stimulating comments received, and the philosophy department for the congenial atmosphere in which he could work on the final chapter of the book.

There have been many previous occasions on which we have had to thank Jean Archer for her typing, and even more for capably handling so many different secretarial and administrative tasks. Because of her impending retirement, this will be the last book in which we will acknowledge her help, and so this time we do so with a sharpened sense of what we are about to lose. Thank you, Jean.

Melbourne, January 1985   H.K.
                                                            P.S.

For Cora and Klara

CONTENTS

1 TWO BABIES

In this chapter we tell the stories of two babies. The first is John Pearson, born in the English industrial city of Derby on 28 June 1980. The second baby was born in Bloomington, Indiana, an American university town, on 9 April 1982. This baby's name has not been released: it is known to the public by its legal pseudonym, 'Baby Doe'.

The stories of these two infants are similar in several respects: both were born with Down's syndrome, a condition which involves permanent mental retardation. Because of this condition, the parents of both infants did not wish them to survive. Both were treated by doctors who sympathized with the attitudes of the parents, and therefore did not seek to prolong the lives of the infants. Both infants died within a few days of birth. Obviously the lives and deaths of these babies raise far-reaching ethical questions. It is not, however, because of these features alone that we have picked out these two cases, for the features we have mentioned do not distinguish the short lives of John Pearson and Baby Doe from those of many other infants born with Down's syndrome and rejected by their parents. What is distinctive about John Pearson and Baby Doe is that their deaths had, in different ways, legal and political consequences of considerable significance. Hence their stories can serve as an introduction to the recent controversies over the treatment of infants born with major handicaps.

John Pearson

At 7.55 a.m. on Saturday 28 June 1980, in Derby General Hospital, Molly Pearson gave birth to a boy, John. It was a normal birth, but on seeing the infant the midwife immediately recognized Down's syndrome. When told of the child's condition the mother wept, and one sister heard her say to her husband: 'I don't want it, Duck.'

At noon on the same day, John Pearson was examined by Dr Leonard Arthur, a senior consultant paediatrician employed by the hospital. He found that the baby had the facial features which have led to people with Down's syndrome being referred to as 'mongols'—slanting eyes, a broad, flattened nose, a large tongue, and a broad, short head. Often Down's syndrome babies have other abnormalities—heart problems, or a blockage somewhere in the stomach or intestine—but Dr Arthur's notes indicate that he found no such problems. Undoubtedly John Pearson was a Down's syndrome baby, but in other respects he seemed healthy.

John Pearson's parents were present during Dr Arthur's examination. There is no record of the conversation that must have taken place, but the substance of what passed between the parents and the doctor is apparent from the brief note Dr Arthur put in John Pearson's records: 'Parents do not wish baby to survive. Nursing care only.' Dr Arthur also prescribed a strong pain-killing drug, DF 118, at a dosage of 5 milligrams, to be administered 'as required', at the discretion of the nurse in charge, but not more than every four hours.

DF 118 is not a drug recommended for administration to infants. Moreover Down's syndrome is not a painful condition. If a healthy Down's syndrome infant was being adequately fed and looked after, it would not normally require pain-killing drugs.

Between noon and 2 p.m., the attending midwife thought John Pearson was 'poorly'. It may be that he then received his first 'feed', consisting only of water and DF 118, but the hospital records do not specify when and how often John Pearson was 'fed'.

During the afternoon, the child was checked regularly and was found to be quiet, clean, and comfortable. By evening, however, the infant was 'going grey and its breathing was becoming laboured'. At 9.30 p.m., when the night nurse came on duty, she found the baby 'quite blue in its extremities and its face was grey'. John Pearson appears to have been given water and DF 118 again at 10 p.m., 2 a.m., and 6 a.m. On the last of these occasions he had difficulties in sucking, and vomited part of his 'feed' back. His breathing was becoming more laboured.

During Sunday, the baby's condition worsened. He continued to have four-hourly 'feeds', but he vomited again, or would not suck. His breathing became more rattly, and he became limp. By 9 p.m. one nurse thought John Pearson was likely to die soon, and arranged for him to be baptized.

By Monday John Pearson could no longer feed from a bottle, so he was given his water and pain-killer through a tube into his stomach. He was very restless and struggling to breathe. He continued in this state throughout the night. At 5.10 a.m. on Tuesday 1 July, John Pearson died in the arms of a nurse.

There is little doubt that John Pearson was not the first Down's syndrome infant to be rejected by its parents and treated in the manner employed by Dr Arthur. His death, like that of others before him, might have remained a private episode between his parents and the doctors and nurses who attended him. It did not, because a member of the hospital staff reported the circumstances to an organization called 'Life'. Life is principally an anti-abortion association, but it sees its aim more broadly as the protection of innocent human life. Life went to the police with the information they had obtained, and as a result, Dr Arthur was prosecuted.

Initially, the charge was murder. The prosecution claimed that: (1) Dr Arthur had ordered the administration of the drug DF 118 with the intention of bringing about the baby's death; and (2) the fact that Dr Arthur had ordered 'nursing care only' showed that he had intended the infant to die.

The trial was held before Justice Farquharson, at Leicester, in November 1981. On the basis of the facts we have already presented, it might seem that the prosecution had a strong case. This case was further strengthened when evidence was given about the results of an autopsy on John Pearson. The court was told that 7.4 micrograms of DF 118 were found in John Pearson's blood, and 4.3 micrograms in his liver. One prosecution witness, Dr Toseland, said that the highest level he had found in a patient's blood in cases where the drug was administered for therapeutic reasons was 0.7 micrograms. Dr Toseland said that he regarded 2.5 micrograms as the toxic level. A second witness, Dr Ossleton, said that the level of DF 118 found in the liver of John Pearson was consistent with fatal poisoning.

Perhaps the most important Crown witness, however, was Professor Alan Usher, an eminent pathologist who served as a consultant to the British Government. Professor Usher conducted a post-mortem examination of John Pearson four days after the baby's death. He certified that the infant had died of bronchial pneumonia, caused by inactivity of the lungs. This inactivity was in turn, he said, due to poisoning by DF 118. This drug is not recommended for use in infants, he added, because it can cause depressed or reduced breathing activity, and new-born infants are particularly susceptible to this condition. Professor Usher also pointed out that uncomplicated Down's syndrome is not a painful condition, and there is no reason to administer a pain-killer in such a case.

This expert evidence looked damning. The prosecution's case began to go wrong, however, when the defence called as its own expert witness another eminent pathologist, Professor John Emery. Professor Emery had one advantage over Professor Usher, in that he specialized in the pathology of children. Professor Emery testified that he had found John Pearson to have several abnormalities in addition to Down's syndrome, including abnormalities of the lung, heart, and brain. The thrust of Professor Emery's evidence was that John Pearson may have developed pneumonia naturally, and died of natural causes.

Following Professor Emery's evidence, Professor Usher was recalled to the witness stand. On viewing the evidence presented by his colleague, he agreed that his own initial findings had been incomplete and inaccurate, and that the conditions now found would have rendered John Pearson more susceptible to pneumonia than an ordinary infant. He nevertheless maintained his view that the treatment regime ordered by Dr Arthur 'made the development of pneumonia virtually inevitable' and that if pneumonia had developed naturally, 'Dr Arthur's regime would have hastened death'. He concluded: 'I don't wish to alter my opinion that this is a fatal poisoning.'

At this point the judge intervened. Since Professor Usher had conceded that his initial evidence was incomplete and inaccurate, and since there was a possibility that the child had developed pneumonia naturally rather than as a consequence of what Dr Arthur had done, Mr Justice Farquharson ordered that the charge of murder be withdrawn, and substituted for it a charge of attempted murder.

It may seem odd to change a charge from murder to attempted murder when the alleged victim is undoubtedly dead. The reasoning behind the alteration, however, was that for a charge of murder it would need to be shown that what Dr Arthur had done actually brought about the death of John Pearson; and this, in the light of the admission by the chief expert witness for the prosecution, was uncertain. It might still be the case, however, that what Dr Arthur had done amounted to an attempt to bring about John Pearson's death, even though natural causes intervened. (If a man was seeking to get rid of his wife and put a lethal dose of poison in her tea, but she was run over by a bus before the poison could take effect, he would be guilty of attempted murder, but not of murder.)

With the alteration in the charge, the focus of the trial switched to the question of what Dr Arthur had intended to achieve by the treatment he prescribed. Justice Farquharson later remarked to the jury that an answer to the question of what Dr Arthur's intention was at the time 'would have best come from him'. Neither Dr Arthur, nor John Pearson's parents, however, gave evidence at the trial.

The only indication we have of what Dr Arthur might have said in his defence comes from a statement he gave to the police. In it he said that 'the sole intention' he had had in prescribing DF 118 'was to reduce any suffering on the part of the infant'. Yet Dr Arthur's professional training must have told him that the dosage he prescribed was likely to be lethal. And there is still the question why Dr Arthur should have prescribed a strong narcotic pain-killer without any apparent reason: for we know from Dr Arthur's records that he believed, at the time, that John Pearson was born healthy apart from his (painless) Down's syndrome. So what suffering was there to be reduced?

The only plausible answer seems to be that suffering is likely to arise from the directive to give 'nursing care only'. Let us pause for a moment to ask exactly what this directive meant. Some evidence about this was given at the trial. According to Sister Mahon, the midwife who delivered the baby, 'nursing care only' means 'keeping the baby comfortable and feeding it with water'.

For the houseman, Dr Fryatt, the term includes nourishment but excludes treatment, should an infection develop. And for Sister Simcox, it means the following:

Nursing care only, if it appears on the sheet of the mother and the baby, [means] the child goes to a different ward. The nurses would cherish him and remain in the ward until he died. If 'nursing care only' is prescribed, it depends on the context whether the patient survives, but in the cases of the severely deformed child, this has never happened in that hospital.

While there is some disagreement about whether 'nursing care only' includes feeding, no one disputes that if the child develops an infection, such as pneumonia, it will not be treated, but will be left to die. This is, of course, what happened to John Pearson. Now one can readily agree that if an infant is being left to die, whether from lack of food or from an infection, there will be suffering, and it would be humane to relieve this suffering by prescribing a pain-killer. Yet could *this* reason for giving John Pearson DF 118 have helped Dr Arthur's defence? Would it not have led straight to the second prong of the prosecution's case, that Dr Arthur's policy of non-treatment showed that he had intended the infant to die? Since John Pearson had in fact died, and since it would seem to have been open to the jury to find that he died because he was not treated, we might wonder if Justice Farquharson did not act hastily in withdrawing the charge of murder. Even if there were room for doubt about whether the administration of DF 118 caused the pneumonia from which John Pearson died, the baby's death may still have been a consequence of Dr Arthur's intentional withholding of antibiotics—and at law, murder does not always require an act. Murder can be committed by an omission, if the accused is under a legal duty of care, as doctors are in respect of their patients. So it seems strange that the judge did not allow the jury to consider the prosecution's case that Dr Arthur had murdered John Pearson by ordering 'nursing care only'.

One possible reason is suggested by a close reading of Justice Farquharson's summing-up to the jury, in which he drew a sharp distinction between murder, and the mere 'setting of conditions' in which death may occur. He did not deny that an omission can, in the right circumstances, amount to murder: the law is clear that it can. Nevertheless he told the jury that the distinction between murder and the setting of conditions in which death is allowed to occur is important; it demarcates, he said, the line between unlawful homicide and the proper practice of medicine. To assist the jury in appreciating this difference he gave four examples:

Example 1

A Down's syndrome child is born with an intestinal obstruction. If the obstruction is not removed, the child will die. Here, Justice Farquharson said, the surgeon might say: 'As this child is a mongol . . . I do not propose to operate; I shall allow nature to take its course.' And Justice Farquharson continued, 'No one could say that the surgeon was committing an act of murder by declining to take a course which would save the child.'

Example 2

A severely handicapped child, who is not otherwise going to die, is given a drug in such amounts that the drug itself will cause death. If the doctor acts intentionally, Justice Farquharson said, then 'it would be open to the jury to say: yes, he was killing, he was murdering that child'.

Example 3

A patient is afflicted with terminal cancer and is suffering great pain. Increasing doses of pain-killing drugs are required to alleviate the patient's distress. The point will be reached where the pain-killing drug will cause the patient's death. This is a case, Justice Farquharson suggested, which 'could never be murder. That was a proper practice of medicine.'

Example 4

A child afflicted with an irreversible handicap and rejected by its mother contracts pneumonia. If in this case the doctor withheld antibiotics and 'by a merciful dispensation of providence' the child died, then, Justice Farquharson suggested, 'it would be very unlikely . . . that you (or any other jury) would say that the doctor was committing murder'.

Given these examples, it would have been easy for the jury to decide that the 'nursing care only' order merely 'set the conditions' for John Pearson's death. That aspect of Dr Arthur's treatment, after all, closely resembled Justice Farquharson's fourth example, and the judge had told them that he thought it unlikely that any jury would convict in these circumstances. (Note, though, Justice Farquharson's carefully chosen words: he did not say that the doctor was not, in law, guilty of murder. A prediction about what a jury will do is very different from a statement of the law.)

The jury may also have been influenced by the eminent medical practitioners who testified, in Dr Arthur's defence, that 'nursing care only' orders are normal medical practice. Professor Alister Campbell, Professor of Child Health at the University of Aberdeen, stated that he had, on a number of occasions, put an infant on 'nursing care only', with the intention that it should not survive. A second witness, Dr Dunn, said that if he had been in charge of the treatment of John Pearson, he would have hoped that the infant 'had contracted pneumonia . . . or had some defect'. He also stated that in cases such as this, food would be withheld 'in the hope that complications would develop which would lead to death by natural causes'. A similar view was expressed by Sir Douglas Black, who held the prestigious position of President of the Royal College of Physicians. According to Sir Douglas, 'it would be ethical to put a rejected child upon a course of management that would end in its death . . . I say that it is ethical that a child suffering from Down's syndrome . . . should not survive.'

Dr Arthur's trial thus revealed that deliberately letting handicapped infants die is common medical practice, and is endorsed by some of the most respected members of the medical community. The testimony of these doctors was given added weight by Justice Farquharson in his summing-up. Though it is not impossible, the judge pointed out, that such highly respected men were committing crimes, he imagined that the jury would 'think long and hard before deciding that doctors of the eminence we have heard . . . have evolved standards which amount to committing crime'.

This then was the defence to the claim that Dr Arthur

murdered, or attempted to murder, John Pearson by ordering 'nursing care only'. This was, as we have seen, only the second prong of the prosecution's case; the first prong was the claim that Dr Arthur attempted to bring about the baby's death by administering DF 118. But note that if the defence to the second prong is accepted, and it is held that Dr Arthur was entitled to 'set the conditions' for John Pearson to die, then—and only then—can Dr Arthur plausibly maintain that he prescribed DF 118 in order 'to reduce any suffering on the part of the infant'. For there is no doubt that if John Pearson was going to die from an infection, or from the withholding of food, it would be desirable to give a pain-killer to reduce the suffering involved in such a death. If 'nursing care only' is an allowable procedure, the administration of a pain-killer makes sense.

Still, the jury would have had to consider the evidence about the amount of DF 118 found in John Pearson's body. Even if there was good reason to give a pain-killer, and Dr Arthur prescribed doses that he knew were likely to kill the child, must he not be guilty at least of attempted murder?

Here the jury may have looked for guidance to Justice Farquharson's third example: the case of the patient with terminal cancer, who requires increasing doses of pain-killing drugs. Even though the point will be reached where the pain-killing drugs cause the patient's death, this 'could never be murder', the judge had said. It was 'a proper practice of medicine'.

At first glance, of course, it may have seemed that the case before the jury was more like the judge's second example than like the third. The second example was that of a severely handicapped child who is not otherwise going to die, and is given a drug in such amounts that the drug itself will cause death. If the doctor acts intentionally, the judge had said, the jury could say that this was a case of murder. John Pearson, of course, was not suffering from terminal cancer. At birth, he was a severely handicapped child, but as far as Dr Arthur could tell, he would not die if he were given food and normal care. But once it is accepted that 'nursing care only' is proper medical practice—and especially once John Pearson had contracted pneumonia, for which he was not going to be given any antibiotics—then John

Pearson *was* going to die. He was, the jury may have thought, suffering from the 'terminal condition' of pneumonia combined with 'nursing care only'. If this is the view the jury took, the case before it was closer to the judge's third example than to his second. Therefore, in accordance with what the judge had said, even if Dr Arthur knew that the doses he was prescribing would lead to the death of the patient, and they did, he would not be guilty of murder.

Whether, in setting out the examples, Justice Farquharson properly stated the law is a question we shall not discuss. We shall, however, return to the question of whether the law, if it was properly stated, makes sound moral distinctions between what is 'proper practice of medicine' and what is homicide. As for the question of whether the jury followed the path of reasoning just outlined, that is something we shall never know. All we do know is that after the judge's summing-up, the jury retired and deliberated for two hours. They then returned a verdict of 'not guilty'.

In the courtroom, Dr Arthur's acquittal was greeted with scenes of public rejoicing. *The Times* announced the verdict with the headline: 'Women cry "Thank God" as Dr Arthur is cleared.' This response apparently reflected the feelings of the majority of British citizens. An opinion poll conducted for the BBC at the time of the trial asked two thousand adults whether they thought a doctor should be found guilty of murder if, with the parents' agreement, 'he sees to it that a severely handicapped baby dies'. Considering the controversial nature of the issues, the result was astonishingly clear-cut: 86 per cent said that in these circumstances the doctor should not be found guilty of murder; only 7 per cent said he should.

The verdict also met with general approval from the medical profession. Dr Peter Dunn, an eminent Bristol paediatrician who had testified on behalf of Dr Arthur, said that the verdict would bring 'tremendous relief' to the medical profession, particularly to those in paediatrics. He also criticized the unknown informer who had reported the case to Life, asking if such people realize what 'terrible harm' they do to the relationships of confidentiality and trust which exist between patients and doctors. Dr John Lorber, former Professor of Paediatrics at Sheffield University, said that doctors would no longer have to look over their shoulders for spies; and Dr John Havard, secretary of the British Medical Association, expressed the hope that the Director of Public Prosecutions 'will now realize that it is not appropriate to bring criminal proceedings against eminent and distinguished paediatricians'.

There was, of course, one section of the community that was not at all pleased with the verdict. The prosecution came about, as we saw, because a member of the hospital staff had contacted the anti-abortion group Life. Following Dr Arthur's acquittal, Nuala Scarisbrick, the Honorary Administrator of the organization, commented: 'The verdict gives *carte blanche* to doctors to give treatment to patients who are unwanted or handicapped or both, that will result in their death. Now to be unwanted is to be guilty of a capital offence.'

Baby Doe

On the evening of Friday 9 April 1982, a baby was born in Bloomington Hospital, Indiana. To protect the parents from publicity, the baby is referred to in court records as 'Baby Doe', and the parents as 'John Doe' and 'Mary Doe'. As in the case of John Pearson, the birth itself was uneventful, but the baby was found to have Down's syndrome. Unlike the English baby, however, Baby Doe had additional problems; the major one was that the passage from the mouth to the stomach—the oesophagus—was not properly formed. This meant that any attempt to feed the child in the normal way would fail; anything taken through the mouth would be taken into the lungs, and Baby Doe would probably suffocate; even if it didn't, it would not obtain sufficient nourishment.

Complications of this sort are more common among Down's syndrome infants than in the population as a whole, but they do occur in children with no other disability. The usual procedure is immediate surgery. Operating on new-born infants always involves some risk, but the prospects for removing a blockage or for a successful restructuring of the malformed passage are good. In the majority of cases in which surgery is attempted, the child is subsequently able to eat normally. Of course, if the child has

Down's syndrome, its mental handicap remains unaffected by the operation.

Baby Doe's condition was noticed by the obstetrician, Dr Walter Owens. He called in a paediatrician, Dr James Schaffer, who then consulted with another paediatrician, Dr Paul Wenzler. Dr Schaffer and Dr Wenzler recommended that since Bloomington Hospital was not equipped for surgery of this type, the baby should be transferred to Riley Hospital in nearby Indianapolis, where the corrective surgery could be performed. Dr Owens, on the other hand, recommended that Baby Doe stay at Bloomington Hospital and be kept comfortable and free of pain. In this recommendation he was supported by two other Bloomington obstetricians. All three obstetricians were, of course, aware that if the baby stayed at Bloomington Hospital it would die within a short time, either from a combination of dehydration and starvation, or because stomach acids reaching the lungs would lead to pneumonia.

Dr Owens then went to Mr and Mrs Doe and told them of the two conflicting sets of medical opinions. The paediatricians also went to the parents and discussed their recommendation.

Mr Doe later told the Monroe County Circuit Court that he was a schoolteacher and had sometimes worked closely with Down's syndrome children. He said that he and his wife were of the opinion that such children never had a minimally acceptable quality of life. They therefore decided that it was in the best interests of Baby Doe, and also of their family as a whole—they had two other children—to follow the course of treatment recommended by Dr Owens.

So on the afternoon of 9 April in the presence of witnesses, John and Mary Doe signed a statement saying that they understood the proposals made to them by the various doctors for the treatment of their child, and 'that the course of treatment shall proceed as directed by Dr Walter Owens, MD, who does not have privilege to practice pediatrics at Bloomington Hospital'.

At this point the management of Bloomington Hospital intervened. They contacted the local Monroe County Court, and informed Judge John Baker that there was an extreme emergency. Judge Baker ordered an immediate hearing. The hearing took place in Bloomington Hospital, at 10.30 p.m. on

9 April. Legal counsel for Bloomington Hospital said that the hospital's primary function was 'to reduce morbidity and mortality' and that since the hospital did not have the knowledge or authority to prescribe treatment, it was requesting the Court to make a ruling.

Evidence was taken from the doctors and from John Doe. The account we have just given is a summary of that evidence. Mary Doe was said to be physically unable to attend; John Doe was described as 'lucid and able to make an intelligent, informed decision'.

After a recess, Judge Baker gave his judgement. The issue, he said, was whether Mr and Mrs Doe, as the natural parents of Infant Doe, have the right, after being fully informed of the consequences, to determine the appropriate course of treatment for their child, who is legally a minor. His conclusion was that they do have the right to choose 'a medically recommended course of treatment for their child in the present circumstances'. He therefore directed Bloomington Hospital to allow the course of treatment prescribed by Dr Owens for Infant Doe. At the same time, however, he appointed the Monroe County Department of Public Welfare as guardian of Infant Doe for the specific purpose of determining whether there should be an appeal to a higher court.

With Baby Doe three days old, Monroe County Welfare officials decided not to appeal against Judge Baker's ruling. On the following day, however, the Monroe County prosecutor's office took action. The prosecution asked another judge to order intravenous feeding, so that Baby Doe could be kept alive at least on a temporary basis. The judge refused. The next day, Wednesday 13 April, the prosecutor's office went to the Indiana State Supreme Court and again asked for intervention. After listening to two hours of arguments, the Indiana Supreme Court decided by a 3 to 1 vote not to overturn the ruling of the lower court.

After the court's ruling became known, a number of families called the hospital offering to adopt the baby. On Thursday 14 April, as a Monroe County deputy prosecutor flew to Washington, DC seeking emergency intervention by the United States Supreme Court, Baby Doe died.

Public reaction began with outraged protests from the right to life movement, but soon spread beyond these circles. On 18 April the influential *Washington Post* published an editorial headed 'The Bloomington Baby' which asserted that life for a Down's syndrome child, even with a repaired digestive system, 'can be a life very much worth living'. The editorial went on to deplore the decision 'to allow a helpless Down's syndrome infant to starve to death'. The following week the *New York Times* added the considerable weight of its editorial column to a similar point of view. The letters columns of newspapers around the country discussed the case, the majority deploring the decisions of the parents and the courts. Letters of protest began to flow in to Congress and the White House.

The White House responded with unusual speed. In a memorandum dated 30 April 1982, President Reagan ordered Richard Schweiker, Secretary for Health and Human Services, to ensure that federal laws protecting the rights of handicapped citizens were being adequately enforced. In particular, the President instructed Secretary Schweiker to notify all who provide health care that section 504 of the Rehabilitation Act of 1973 forbids recipients of federal funds to withhold from handicapped citizens, simply because they are handicapped, any benefit or service that would ordinarily be provided for people without handicaps. Regulations under this law, the President continued, prohibit hospitals which receive federal assistance from discriminating against the handicapped. President Reagan then instructed the Attorney General to report on constitutional and legal means of preventing the withholding from the handicapped of potentially life-saving treatment. His memorandum concluded with the following words:

Our Nation's commitment to equal protection of the law will have little meaning if we deny such protection to those who have not been blessed with the same physical or mental gifts we too often take for granted. I support Federal laws prohibiting discrimination against the handicapped, and remain determined that such laws will be vigorously enforced.

In a later chapter, we shall examine the reasoning behind President Reagan's memorandum, and follow the chain of complex developments that flowed from this presidential directive. Meanwhile, to conclude this chapter, we shall look at two conflicting opinions about the death of Baby Doe.

The first view is that of George Will, a syndicated columnist who writes for papers such as the *Washington Post* and the *Los Angeles Times*. Will's essay, 'The Killing Will Not Stop', appeared in these newspapers a week after Baby Doe's death. After briefly describing what happened, Will says that the case is one of homicide. Nor are such homicides aberrations, or culturally incongruous; they are 'part of a social program to serve the convenience of adults by authorizing adults to destroy inconvenient young life'. He is referring, of course, to abortion, and he sees what happened to Baby Doe as an extension of the 'right to kill fetuses' granted by the 1973 decision of the United States Supreme Court. Critics of this decision, Will points out, were alarmed because the Court offered no intelligible reason why birth should be the point at which 'discretionary killing' stops. As Will puts it: 'Critics feared what the Indiana homicide demonstrates: the killing will not stop.'

Will also attacks statements in the press that the baby would have been 'severely retarded'. Only 'a small fraction' of Down's syndrome children, he says, are 'severely retarded'. The degree of handicap cannot be known at birth, and 'such children are dramatically responsive to infant stimulation and other early interventions'.

Will then concludes his article by admitting a direct personal interest in the issue:

Jonathan Will, 10, fourth-grader and Orioles fan ... has Down's syndrome. He does not 'suffer from' (as newspapers are wont to say) Down's syndrome. He suffers from nothing, except anxiety about the Orioles lousy start ... He can do without people like Infant Doe's parents, and courts like Indiana's asserting by their actions the principle that people like him are less than fully human. On the evidence, Down's syndrome citizens have little to learn about being human from the people responsible for the death of Infant Doe.

There were others who, like Will, spoke from personal experience, but took a very different view. The appearance of Will's article in the *Los Angeles Times* prompted a reply from a

Santa Barbara couple, John and Susan West. The Wests reject Will's premise that children like Baby Doe are allowed to die because they are an 'inconvenience'. If that were the case, say the Wests, the parents would hand the children over to institutions. Rather, the decisions are made 'out of love and compassion for the severely afflicted child'. To choose death does not mean that the child is not loved: 'On the contrary, the person is loved enough to be "let go" instead of being forced to continue with very probably pain, suffering and severely limiting handicaps.'

Then the Wests speak of their own experiences

We identify closely with the Bloomington parents. Our baby was born 18 months ago with Down's syndrome and esophageal atresia. In our baby's case, there was absolutely no portion of the esophagus between the back of the mouth and the stomach. After much agonizing thought, prayer and discussion with family, friends, clergymen and other doctors, we made the same painful decision that the Bloomington parents made.

The authorities at the hospital stated that they knew how to surgically replace the missing esophagus. It would be a difficult operation, and there were many side-effects and problems that were likely to occur. We were told that they were going to proceed with the surgery with or without our consent.

Parental permission was *not* given, a court order was obtained, and surgery was performed after a long and complicated course of medical problems. Our baby has endured a great deal of pain, suffering and misery during his 18 months on Earth, due to the nature of his deformities, surgical procedures, and complications arising from them.

He is not well today and is unable to eat orally. The doctors have told us there is a good probability that our son will suffer from lifelong problems because the operation to replace the missing esophagus is not totally effective. So far, the complications the doctors described, as well as some that were not anticipated, have been happening. It is indeed difficult to stand by and watch this occur.

If the deaths of John Pearson and Baby Doe raise difficult ethical questions, so too does the life of the child of John and Susan West. Here are some of the questions we now have before us:

• Is it right to do less to prolong the life of a handicapped infant than one would do for a normal baby? If so, how severe must the handicap be? Is all human life equally worthy of our striving to extend it, or does the quality of life count?

- Who should make the decision? The parents? The doctors? The courts?

- In making such a decision, whose interests should be considered? Only those of the baby? Or also the interests of the parents and any other children they might have? Should any weight be given to the considerable cost to society of institutional care and extensive medical treatment?

- If it is ethically defensible to refuse consent for life-saving surgery—as in the case of Baby Doe—can it also be defensible to give no nourishment, as in the case of John Pearson?

- Could it really be ethically defensible to refuse consent to life-saving surgery, knowing that as a result the infant will die slowly, and yet ethically indefensible to give the same infant a lethal injection?

In the pages that follow, we shall try to answer these questions. We begin with the fundamental issue of whether all human life is of equal worth.

2 IS ALL HUMAN LIFE OF
   EQUAL WORTH?

When we are confronted with complex ethical questions like those we have just raised, it is tempting to look for a simple answer; and in this case, a simple answer seems to be available: that all human life is of equal worth. According to this view, the life of a Down's syndrome baby is no less valuable than the life of a normal baby, or of any other patient. Since all human life is of equal worth, it is as wrong to let a Down's syndrome baby die, when it could be kept alive, as it would be to let any other patients die when they could be kept alive.

The sanctity of human life

The simple answer gains support from two quite distinct sources. One is the traditional doctrine of the sanctity of human life. Those who speak of 'the sanctity of life' hold a cluster of related ideas, rather than a single doctrine; nevertheless they agree in rejecting claims that one human life is more valuable than another. In a later chapter we shall examine the origins of this view in the Judaeo-Christian religious tradition. For the moment it is enough to note that it has had a dominant influence on both morality and law in Western civilization. The central idea is well expressed by Sanford Kadish, writing on the view of human life taken by Anglo-American law:

> all human lives must be regarded as having an equal claim to preservation simply because life is an irreducible value. Therefore, the value of a particular life, over and above the value of life itself, may not be taken into account.

Here the key claim is that life is an irreducible value—that is, the value of life cannot be reduced to anything else, such as the happiness, self-consciousness, rationality, autonomy, or even simple consciousness, that life makes possible. Life is not valuable because of the qualities it may possess; it is valuable in itself. It is easy to see how this claim leads to the conclusion that all human life is of equal value.

The traditional sanctity of life doctrine is also sometimes supported by the claim that human life is of *infinite* value. The Chief Rabbi of Great Britain, Rabbi Immanuel Jakobovits, has referred to this idea as the ground for opposition to euthanasia:

The basic reasoning behind the firm opposition of Judaism to any form of euthanasia proper is the attribution of *infinite* value to every human life. Since infinity is, by definition, indivisible, it follows that every fraction of life, however small, remains equally infinite so that it makes morally no difference whether one shortens life by seventy years or by only a few hours, or whether the victim of murder was young and robust or aged and physically or mentally debilitated.

Dr Moshe Tendler, a professor of Talmudic law, confirms this position.

human life is of infinite value. This in turn means that a piece of infinity is also infinity, and a person who has but a few moments to live is no less of value than a person who has 60 years to live . . . a handicapped individual is a perfect specimen when viewed in an ethical context. The value is an absolute value. It is not relative to life expectancy, to state of health, or to usefulness to society.

The Protestant theologian Paul Ramsey, Professor of Religion at Princeton University, takes a similar view:

there is no reason for saying that [six months in the life of a baby born with the invariably fatal Tay Sachs disease] are a life span of lesser worth to God than living seventy years before the onset of irreversible degeneration. A genuine humanism would say the same thing in other language. It is only a reductive naturalism or social utilitarianism that would regard those months of infant life as worthless because they lead to nothing on a time line of earthly achievement. All our days and years are of equal worth whatever the consequence; death is no more a tragedy at one time than at another time.

A value might be irreducible without being infinite, and if human life is of irreducible rather than infinite value, there may not be great value in prolonging human existence by a few moments. On the other hand, if human life is of infinite value, every second of prolonged life would be as valuable as a lifetime. This is, on the face of it, implausible: most of us are indifferent to the prospect of our life being shortened by one second, but we are very far from indifferent to the thought that our life might be cut short by thirty years. As far as the treatment of John Pearson and Baby Doe is concerned, however, the difference between irreducible value and infinite value does not matter. Both babies could, with appropriate care, have lived for many years, possibly a near-normal lifespan. (The life expectancy of people with Down's syndrome is less than normal, but some do live into their forties or even fifties.) So if human life is in itself a value, irrespective of the quality of the particular life, the presence of Down's syndrome is not relevant to the value a life has.

Human rights

Whereas the traditional doctrine of the sanctity of human life has its roots in ancient times, the second source of support for the view that all human life is of equal worth is relatively recent. It is the acceptance of the belief that there are human rights, and that all humans share these rights equally. Public support for this belief goes back no further than the eighteenth century and the 'Declarations of Rights' that figured so prominently in the American and French revolutions. Today the human rights movement is a major force against the violations of individual rights by repressive regimes. In the struggle against discrimination, too, it has been important to insist that human rights are possessed equally by all humans. The idea of equal human rights stands as a barrier against those who use some irrelevant or totally spurious ground, such as a difference of race or sex, as an excuse for denying the rights of those who do not belong to their own group.

It is not difficult to see how belief in equal human rights can lead to the view that every human life is of equal worth. The right to life was the first right mentioned in the American Declaration of Independence. It is the most basic of all rights, for if one's right to life is violated, one cannot enjoy any other rights. The idea that all humans are entitled to the same rights thus can be used against making distinctions between the rights to life of different categories of human beings.

This is precisely what happened in the United States, in the aftermath to the Baby Doe case. We saw in the previous chapter that, barely two weeks after Baby Doe's death, President Reagan sent a memo to his Secretary for Health and Human Services instructing him to ensure that laws prohibiting discrimination against the handicapped were 'vigorously enforced'. Reagan was referring to Section 504 of the Rehabilitation Act of 1973. This section states that:

No otherwise qualified handicapped individual shall, solely by reason of handicap, be denied the benefits of, or be subjected to discrimination under, any program or activity receiving Federal financial assistance.

The language of this statute is similar to that of other United States civil rights legislation. In a subsequent court case, Judge Gerhard Gesell pointed out that when the section was passed, debate in Congress focused on discrimination against adults and older children, and the denial of access of some handicapped people to federal government programmes. As Judge Gesell said:

As far as can be determined, no congressional committee or member of the House or Senate ever even suggested that section 504 would be used to monitor medical treatment of defective newborn infants or establish standards for preserving a particular quality of life.

The section, in other words, was an extension to the handicapped of the movements to protect the civil rights of blacks and women. It was based on the principle of human equality, and opposition to discrimination on irrelevant grounds. It is so broad, however, that it can be invoked to support the view that all human life is of equal worth, irrespective of the characteristics of the particular life. This is what the Secretary for Health and Human Services did when, in accordance with the President's instructions, he sent 6,800 American hospitals a 'Notice to Health Care Providers'. The notice reminded hospital administrators that it was

unlawful for a recipient of Federal financial assistance to withhold from a handicapped infant nutritional sustenance or medical or surgical treatment required to correct a life-threatening condition if

(1) the withholding is based on the fact that the infant is handicapped; and

(2) the handicap does not render treatment or nutritional sustenance contra-indicated.

Hospital administrators were told that they would have federal government funds cut off if they allowed handicapped infants to die when non-handicapped infants in similar circumstances would be saved. The notice said, in effect, that no matter how severe an infant's handicap might be, the efforts made to preserve its life must be no less than the efforts that would be made to preserve the life of a non-handicapped infant in an otherwise similar condition.

Hard cases for the simple answer

The view that all human life is of equal worth may well be the simplest way of answering questions about the treatment of infants born with major handicaps; but there are two questions that need to be asked about this simple answer. First, does it give us acceptable practical guidance? Second, does it have a sound ethical basis? For the moment we shall focus on the first question, leaving the theoretical issues for a later chapter.

The question of whether the simple answer gives adequate practical guidance was raised very directly by the 'Notice to Health Care Providers' issued by the Reagan administration, and it is interesting to examine it in this context. First, however, we need to take the story a step further. Strong as its language might seem, the 'Notice' was not sufficient for the White House. In March 1983 the Department of Health and Human Services therefore issued a more forceful follow-up regulation. Officially, the new regulation carried the contradictory title 'Interim Final Rule', but it has become known as the 'Baby Doe Guidelines'. These guidelines specified that a poster was to be conspicuously displayed in each delivery ward, maternity ward, paediatric ward, and intensive care nursery. The poster was to read as follows:

NOTICE

Department of Health and Human Services Office for Civil Rights
DISCRIMINATORY FAILURE TO FEED AND CARE FOR
HANDICAPPED INFANTS IN THIS FACILITY IS PRO-
HIBITED BY FEDERAL LAW. SECTION 504 OF THE
REHABILITATION ACT OF 1973 STATES THAT

"NO OTHERWISE QUALIFIED HANDICAPPED
INDIVIDUAL SHALL, SOLELY BY REASON OF
HANDICAP, BE EXCLUDED FROM PARTICI-
PATION IN, BE DENIED THE BENEFITS OF, OR BE
SUBJECTED TO DISCRIMINATION UNDER ANY
PROGRAM OR ACTIVITY RECEIVING FEDERAL
FINANCIAL ASSISTANCE."

Any person having knowledge that a handicapped infant is being
discriminatorily denied food or customary medical care should
immediately contact:

Handicapped Infant Hotline
US Department of Health and Human Services
Washington, D.C. 20201
Phone 800-368-1019
(available 24 hours a day) TTY Capability
In Washington, D.C. call 863-0100
OR
Your State Child Protective Agency.

Federal Law prohibits retaliation or intimidation against any
person who provides information about possible violations of the
Rehabilitation Act of 1973.

Identity of callers will be held confidential.

Failure to feed and care for infants may also violate the criminal
and civil laws of your state.

The Baby Doe Guidelines incensed many of the nation's most
senior paediatricians—not surprisingly, since it invited all and
sundry to make confidential complaints about the way those
doctors treated their patients. As a result the American Academy
of Pediatrics, an association of 24,000 paediatricians, joined
with the National Association of Children's Hospitals and the

Children's Hospital National Medical Center, in Washington, DC, to contest the regulations in the courts.

Among the grounds for opposition to the guidelines was the question of their scope. The American Academy of Pediatrics submitted affidavits describing medical conditions in new-borns which are, it said, 'simply not treatable'; should efforts still be made to prolong the lives of these infants, as they would be, of course, if the infants did not have the conditions in question? In other words,the academy was asking, are doctors now supposed to do everything in their power to prolong all infant lives, no matter what the prospects?

The affidavits referred to three conditions. The first is anencephaly. This means 'no brain' and refers to a condition which occurs approximately once in every two thousand births. The infant is born with most or all of the brain missing. Many of these babies die at birth or very soon after, but some have lived for a week or two, and it would be possible, with modern artificial support systems, to keep them alive even longer. The absence, or virtual absence, of a brain means that even if such infants could be kept alive indefinitely, they would never become conscious or respond in any way to other human beings.

The second condition is an intra-cranial haemorrhage—less technically, a bleeding in the head. Dr Robert Parrott, Director of the Children's Hospital National Medical Center, described some cases of 'infants who have such severe bleeding in their heads that they will never breathe without mechanical respiratory assistance yet [*sic*] never will have the capacity for cognitive behaviour'.

The third condition is one in which an infant lacks a substantial part of its digestive tract, for instance its intestine and bowels. The infant cannot be fed by mouth, for it will not obtain anything of nutritional value. It is not possible to correct the condition by surgery. Feeding such infants by means of a drip directly into the bloodstream will keep them alive, but nutritional deficiencies are likely and the long-term prospects are poor.

In mentioning these three conditions, the Academy was suggesting that the guidelines were, at best, unclear whether in these cases infants might be allowed to die without receiving life-sustaining treatment; or, at worst, the guidelines would direct that such life-sustaining treatment be given, despite the apparent futility of such treatment.

At the hearing before Judge Gerhard Gesell, the Department of Health and Human Services denied that the Interim Final Rule would compel doctors to provide life-sustaining treatment in these extreme cases. The chief spokesman for the Department's position was Dr C. Everett Koop, Surgeon General of the United States and an experienced paediatric surgeon. Dr Koop told the court that he had been involved in the decision to issue the 'Notice to Health Care Providers', and the subsequent formulation of the Interim Final Rule. Referring to the case of a child having 'essentially no intestine', Dr Koop said:

these regulations never intended that such a child should be put on hyper-alimentation [i.e., be artificially nourished] and carried for a year and a half.

Incidentally, I was the first physician that ever did that, so I know whereof I speak. And we would consider customary care in that child the provision of a bed, of food by mouth, knowing that it was not going to be nutritious, but not just shutting off the care of that child ... nor do we intend to say that this child should be carried on intravenous fluids for the rest of its life.

Dr Koop made a similar remark about one of the other cases mentioned by the Academy:

When you talk about a baby born without a brain, I suspect you meant an anencephalic child and we would not attempt to interfere with anyone dealing with that child. We think it should be given loving attention and would expect it to expire in a short time.

To Dr Koop, it was apparently plain common sense that one did not attempt to prolong the lives of infants born with such serious conditions. We agree. But is not this 'plain common sense' at odds with the view that all human lives are of equal worth? Can it be squared with an insistence that a handicapped infant must not be refused life-sustaining treatment which would be offered to an infant without the handicap?

Certainly the non-treatment of these infants must be incompatible with the idea that all human life is of infinite value. Anyone who believed this would have to say that the life of an anencephalic infant is also of infinite value. Moreover, since any part of infinity is, as Chief Rabbi Jakobovits said, still infinite, one would have to hold that prolonging the life of an anencephalic infant by a single day—or even a second—would still be of infinite value. Since it clearly is possible, by means of artificial feeding and respiration, to prolong the lives of anencephalic infants by several days, perhaps even weeks or months, anyone who believes that all human life is of infinite value would have to consider it wrong to decide not to take any steps to prolong life in these cases.

What of those who, without necessarily believing that all human life has infinite value, support the principle that all human lives are of equal worth, irrespective of their quality? Those who hold this view would also seem to be committed to advocating life-sustaining measures for infants born without brains or without intestines. For example, in the passage quoted above, Dr Koop referred to the possibility of 'carrying' an infant without an intestine for 'a year and a half'; yet Dr Koop did not advocate that infants born without an intestine should be kept alive for as long as possible. (In fact it is possible for children being artificially fed to survive considerably longer than this, but the precise period is not relevant here.) Why does Dr Koop not think such infants should be kept alive as long as possible? Would he not think an eighteen-month extension of life worthwhile for a normal child? Would he not think it worthwhile for a normal adult? If he would, the obvious explanation for his different view in the first case is that he does not regard the life of an artificially nourished infant as being of the same worth as that of a normal infant or a normal adult.

Getting around the hard cases

'Medical decisions'

Is there any other possible explanation for the views expressed by Dr Koop? The Department of Health and Human Services soon had a second chance to explain its stance on the type of case we have been considering. Judge Gerhard Gesell found in favour of the Academy of Pediatrics and its co-plaintiffs on the ground that the Department had, by issuing the regulation without allowing a period for public comment, failed to comply with the requirements of the Administrative Procedure Act, an act designed to curb bureaucratic actions taken without consultation with, and notice to, those affected. The Department therefore issued, on 5 July 1983, a new 'Proposed Rule'. The new rule was essentially similar to the ill-fated 'Interim Final Rule', but it was issued with considerably more information on the circumstances in which it was to apply. In particular, it was stated that:

Section 504 does not compel medical personnel to attempt to perform impossible or futile acts or therapies. Thus, Section 504 does not require the imposition of futile therapies which merely temporarily prolong the process of dying of an infant born terminally ill, such as a child born with anencephaly or intra-cranial bleeding. Such medical decisions, by medical personnel and parents, concerning whether to treat, and if so, what form the treatment should take, are outside the scope of Section 504. The Department recognizes that reasonable medical judgments can differ when evaluating these difficult, individual cases.

Here the Department takes the commonsensical view that it is not obligatory to keep alive infants with anencephaly or intra-cranial bleeding. It is interesting to see how the Department tries to take this view without basing it on the fact that infants with these conditions have no prospect of a reasonable quality of life. What the Department suggests is that in these cases treatment is 'futile' and will 'merely temporarily prolong the process of dying' of an infant born terminally ill. Whether treatment is futile in this way is, the Department states, a 'medical decision' and 'reasonable medical judgments can differ' in these cases. The Department seems to be saying that it does not wish to interfere in these 'medical decisions'.

This will not do. As we have seen, sophisticated modern medical techniques could indefinitely prolong the lives of children with anencephaly or intra-cranial bleeding. The judgement that someone whose life could be indefinitely prolonged by available medical means is 'terminally ill' and therefore should not have his or her life prolonged is not a *medical* judgement; it is an ethical judgement about the desirability of prolonging that particular life.

Could the Department defend its view by saying that whether a patient is dying is a medical judgement, based on the fact that the patient can survive only with the help of medical treatment? Such a test would be far too broad. By this standard, a patient suffering from diabetes would be 'terminally ill' and it would not be required to provide 'futile' insulin therapy. The fact that no one in their right mind would regard insulin therapy for a diabetic as 'futile' should make us realize that judgements about the futility of treatment are not purely medical judgements based on the prospect of the underlying condition being cured. It is no more possible to cure diabetes by administering insulin than it is to cure anencephaly, a brain destroyed by intra-cranial bleeding, or the absence of an intestine. In all these conditions, the patient must currently expect to remain, for his or her entire life, dependent for survival on continuing medical treatment. The difference between diabetes and the other three conditions is, of course, that the diabetic will be able to enjoy a near-normal life, while no matter how much we prolong the life of the infant with massive intra-cranial bleeding, for instance, the infant's life will always remain devoid of everything that we regard as making life worth while.

As we read on through the 'supplementary information' issued by the Department of Health and Human Services it becomes still clearer that, despite protestations to the contrary, the Department's position is based on thinly-veiled judgements that some lives are not worth living. The Department's statement continues:

Section 504 simply preserves the decision-making process customarily undertaken by physicians in any treatment decision: will the treatment be medically beneficial to the patient and are those benefits outweighed by any medical risk associated with the treatment? It is only when non-medical considerations, such as subjective judgments that an unrelated handicap makes a person's life not worth living, are interjected in the decision-making process that the Section 504 concerns arise.

The problem with this way of putting it is that we need to decide what treatments are 'medically beneficial to the patient'. The simple answer, and the only answer that is consistent with the idea that all human life is of equal worth, is that all treatments which prolong life are beneficial. Yet this is clearly not the answer the Department would give: it does not regard it as beneficial to prolong the lives of infants born with virtually no brain, or who have suffered intra-cranial bleeding. Why is this not 'medically beneficial to the patient' in the same way that giving insulin is medically beneficial to the diabetic? Once again, the answer must be that it is not medically beneficial to prolong the lives of infants who will never experience anything, and will remain alive but in a state without feelings or awareness, unable to enjoy their lives in any way. Plainly, the prolongation of such a life is not 'medically beneficial' because it is not beneficial in any sense. Karen Ann Quinlan, the New Jersey woman who has been in an irreversible coma since 1975, has not benefited from the fact that her life has been prolonged for many years. She has not been aware of the extra years of life she has had, and has had no benefit from them. Similarly, prolonging the life of an infant without a brain does the infant no good because it is not possible for the infant to benefit from the additional period of life. This is not, however, a medical judgement. It is, quite obviously, a 'non-medical consideration' based on the judgement that the handicap —in this case, the virtual absence of a brain—'makes a person's life not worth living'. The Department seems to think that such judgements are 'subjective' and must not be 'interjected in the decision-making process'; yet its own position is based on just this type of judgement.

Admittedly, the Department does refer to judgements about 'an unrelated handicap', and in criticizing its position we have not taken account of the stipulation that the judgement be about a handicap that is 'unrelated'. But it is difficult to see exactly what this means or how it can make a difference. Presumably it is supposed to be wrong to take account of a handicap unrelated to the treatment needed to keep the infant alive; but how do we define what the handicap is? This may seem clear enough in a case like a Down's syndrome baby with a blocked intestine, where Down's syndrome is the reason for not operating on the blockage; but what about the case of, say, an intra-cranial bleeding? The treatment needed to keep the infant alive might be artificial respiration. A baby who was having breathing problems, but was otherwise normal, would certainly be put on a respirator; the baby who, as Dr Parrott put it, 'never will have the capacity for cognitive behaviour', would not be put on a respirator. If the lack of any 'capacity for cognitive behaviour' is a factor in the decision not to put it on the respirator, this would have to be a 'subjective judgment that an unrelated handicap makes a person's life not worth living'. As such, it should give rise to what the Department calls 'Section 504 concerns'. Yet apparently the Department does not think it does. On the other hand, the Department presumably would think that 'Section 504 concerns' arise even in some cases where the decision not to sustain life is made because of a handicap that *is* directly related to the form of treatment—for instance, if a doctor did not give insulin to a diabetic patient because in the doctor's judgement diabetes is a handicap that makes life not worth living. Thus, whether the life-sustaining treatment is or is not related to the patient's handicap cannot be, even in the Department's view, a crucial factor in whether a decision not to prolong life is a case of discriminating against the handicapped.

Extraordinary means

There is another frequently used tactic by which those who wish to uphold the tenet of the equal worth of all human lives can still try to argue that we do not always have to prolong life in cases like those we have been discussing. This is the claim that there is no moral requirement to use 'extraordinary' means of treatment; our obligations extend only to the provision of 'ordinary' means of prolonging life. Since 'extraordinary' means would be needed to keep alive an infant with virtually no brain, with very severe bleeding in the brain, or without an intestine, it is ethically acceptable to provide only 'ordinary' care, and allow the infants to die.

This view was the basis of testimony by a Roman Catholic bishop, Bishop Lawrence Casey, in the much-publicized case of Karen Quinlan. Bishop Casey supported the request by Karen Quinlan's parents to have artificial means of life support removed from their comatose daughter. He told the court:

The continuance of mechanical (cardiorespiratory) supportive measures to sustain continuation of her body functions and her life constitute extraordinary means of treatment. Therefore the decision of Joseph . . . Quinlan to request the discontinuation of treatment is, according to the teachings of the Catholic Church, a morally correct decision.

Consistently with this teaching, when Karen Quinlan was taken off the respirator and, to everyone's surprise, continued to breathe, her parents did not seek to discontinue artificial feeding. Providing nourishment they presumably regarded as an 'ordinary' means and hence one that could not be withdrawn.

In a recent 'Declaration on Euthanasia' issued by the Vatican, the Roman Catholic Church has reaffirmed its view that the principle of the 'extraordinary means' criterion 'still holds good', despite the imprecision of the term and the progress made in the treatment of sickness. The American Medical Association has also invoked the principle in a much-discussed attempt to distinguish 'the cessation of the employment of extraordinary means', which it allows, from 'the intentional termination of the life of one human being by another', which it describes as 'mercy killing' and 'contrary to that for which the medical profession stands'.

The distinction between 'ordinary' and 'extraordinary' means is so frequently invoked that it may seem surprising that the Department of Health and Human Services did not refer to it in its explanation of why Section 504 does not require doctors to keep alive infants without brains. Although the Department did not use the terms 'ordinary' and 'extraordinary', it appeared to be appealing to a version of the distinction when it included a reference to 'customary medical care' in the key sentence of the notice to be posted in hospitals, telling people to contact the Handicapped Infant Hotline if they have knowledge that a handicapped infant 'is being denied food or customary medical care'. Presumably whatever is 'customary' cannot be 'extraordinary', and so the Department is saying in its own terminology, that only 'ordinary' care is required. This reference to 'customary medical care' was subjected to close questioning by Judge Gerhard Gesell, and we shall examine it after we have looked at the more widely used distinction between 'ordinary' and 'extraordinary' means.

The first question to ask about the distinction is how we are to decide which means are 'ordinary' and which are 'extraordinary'. To get this straight may seem a mere matter of terminological precision: it turns out, however, to be a difficulty that threatens the usefulness of the distinction itself. The problem is not merely to differentiate 'ordinary' from 'extraordinary' means, but to do so in a manner that is morally relevant. If we are going to say that ordinary means of saving life must be employed, but extraordinary means need not be, the distinction must be one in which we can find moral significance.

The most natural understanding of the distinction is that ordinary means are those most commonly used, whereas extraordinary means are unusual ones. This is the sense to which the Department of Health and Human Services appears to appeal: 'customary medical care' is the care that is commonly given. The means one is not obliged to use, then, are the non-standard treatments, the techniques that are new and rare.

An alternative interpretation is that ordinary care is simple and straightforward, while extraordinary means are those that involve high technology medicine, or are elaborate and demanding in terms of effort and resources.

These two interpretations will agree in some cases and disagree in others. On either interpretation, for instance, the use of antibiotics to combat a life-threatening infection would, nowadays, be ordinary treatment. Antibiotics are very commonly used, and they are a simple form of treatment. On the other hand, putting an infant on artificial respiration is no longer a rare or non-standard form of treatment; it is, however, still a form of treatment that uses complex and quite expensive equipment.

Obviously, whichever interpretation we adopt, there will be borderline cases. Neither the distinction between 'usual' and 'unusual', nor that between 'simple' and 'complex' is marked by clear boundaries. The real problem, however, is not the borderline cases: it is that whether treatment is usual or unusual, simple or complex, is *in itself* totally irrelevant to morally important issues, such as the risk associated with the treatment. Unusual treatment may be more risky than usual treatment; but if it is, then it is *this* difference that is morally relevant in deciding for or against treatment. Or again, complex treatment may be more costly than a simple one. Given limited medical resources, this may be relevant to deciding whether to use it; but again, it is the difference in cost, combined with the needs of other patients when we do not have the resources to treat them all, that is relevant here. The crucial point is that there is no perfect correlation between the obviously relevant features of risk and cost, and the

usual/unusual or the simple/complex distinctions. To the extent
that this correlation is lacking, it is clear that the distinctions
themselves are not morally relevant.

Suppose that Baby A's life can be prolonged by using some
common means of treatment, but Baby B will die unless we use
an unusual treatment. If there is *no* difference in the safety and
efficacy of the two treatments, what is the relevance of the fact
that one is more commonly used than the other? If the cases are
otherwise similar, it is surely just as obligatory to treat B as it is to
treat A. Or suppose that the treatment for Baby A is simple, but
that for Baby B is complex and requires high technology: if there
are ample resources available to employ both treatments, can the
difference in complexity affect the obligation to treat the babies?

Those who use the ordinary/extraordinary distinction do not
attempt to defend the claim that rarity or complexity are in
themselves grounds for withholding a means of treatment.
Instead they seek to redefine the terms 'ordinary' and 'extraordinary' so that they mean something quite different.

In the ethical analyses of the theologians, philosophers, and
doctors who invoke the distinction, 'ordinary' means neither
'usual' nor 'simple', and 'extraordinary' means neither 'unusual'
nor 'complex'. Consider, for example, the definitions employed in
a book entitled *Medico-Moral Problems*, written by the Jesuit
theologian Gerald Kelly and published by the Catholic Hospital
Association. According to Father Kelly, ordinary means are all

medicines, treatments and operations, which offer a reasonable hope of
benefit for the patient and which can be obtained and used without
excessive expense, pain or other inconvenience.

Extraordinary means, on the other hand, include

all medicines, treatments and operations which cannot be obtained
without excessive expense, pain or inconvenience, or which, if used,
would not offer a reasonable hope of benefit.

Note here the reference, in both definitions, to 'a reasonable hope
of benefit'. In the light of our earlier discussion of the use of the
expression 'medically beneficial' by the Department of Health
and Human Services, it is easy to see what is going on here:
quality of life judgements are again being made. Otherwise, how

are we to decide when treatment offers 'a reasonable hope of benefit'? If quality of life does not enter into it, every treatment that offers a reasonable hope of prolonging life would be treatment that offers a reasonable hope of benefit; but this is not what those who appeal to the ordinary/extraordinary distinction have in mind.

For a clear example of a quality of life judgement disguised as an appeal to the ordinary/extraordinary distinction, let us look once more at the testimony of Bishop Lawrence Casey in the case of Karen Quinlan. We saw earlier that Bishop Casey testified that the artificial life-support systems thought to be keeping Karen Quinlan alive constituted extraordinary means of treatment and therefore could legitimately be discontinued. What we have not noted, up to now, is that Bishop Casey prefaced his opinion by saying that Karen Quinlan 'has no reasonable hope of recovery from her comatose state by the use of any available medical procedure'. What is the significance of this sentence, which immediately precedes the classification of the artificial life-support system as 'extraordinary means'? Obviously it implies that if Karen Quinlan did have some hope of recovery from her comatose state, the use of artificial life-support systems would *not* be 'extraordinary'.

Why would this be so? Is it simply that the medical procedures offered Karen Quinlan no hope of *recovery*? But there are no available medical procedures which offer a diabetic any hope of recovery; and yet Bishop Casey would surely not say that the administration of insulin to a diabetic is an extraordinary means, and that it would therefore be morally correct to request that it be discontinued. So it must be the fact that the medical procedures offered Karen Quinlan no hope of recovery *from her comatose state* which is decisive in Bishop Casey's classification of the procedures as 'extraordinary'. Since the procedures could have indefinitely prolonged Karen Quinlan's life, and since they would not have been extraordinary if that life were the life of a person not in a permanently comatose state, we must conclude that it is the difference in quality of life between being in an irreversible coma and not being in an irreversible coma that is the basis for Bishop Casey's judgement.

Because the terms 'ordinary means' and 'extraordinary means' *appear* to mark a distinction in the nature of the means used, but *in practice* reflect judgements about the desirability of prolonging a particular patient's life, the distinction has given rise to some bizarre statements. Prominent among them is a remark by Judge John Ferris, who presided over a Florida trial in which a dying 76-year-old man was requesting the cessation of life-sustaining treatment, including artificial respiration. The patient's physician testified that the use of a respirator is 'standard procedure' and said: 'I deal with respirators every day of my life.' To this the judge responded:

I understand that he deals with them every day, but in the sense of ordinary as against extraordinary, I believe it to be extraordinary.

In order to shed light on the way doctors use the terms 'ordinary' and 'extraordinary' we asked 87 obstetricians and 111 paediatricians if they thought it important to distinguish between 'ordinary' and 'extraordinary' means of prolonging life. Nearly 80 per cent said they did. We then asked the doctors to give us examples of each type of means of prolonging life. Although the responses indicated that 'extraordinary means' is often applied to intensive care or the use of sophisticated and expensive technology, 24 doctors regarded antibiotics as 'extraordinary', despite the fact that they are simple, inexpensive, and in everyday use. Three doctors said that they regarded *everything* as extraordinary, except warmth, fluid, demand feeding, and sedatives if necessary. Other doctors, however, classified not only antibiotics, but also pacemakers and humidicribs as 'ordinary'.

We also asked our sample a more general question: 'Under what circumstances do you consider that less than a maximum effort should be made to preserve the life of the infant?' The question was open-ended and answers varied, but one common response, given by more than half of the obstetricians and nearly 20 per cent of paediatricians, was that less than maximum efforts should be made when an infant's condition is such that it is 'incompatible with reasonable and independent life'. If we view this response in the light of the fact that most of the doctors had said they thought it important to distinguish between ordinary and extraordinary means, it seems likely that when there is no prospect of an infant leading a reasonable and independent life, some doctors will regard as 'extraordinary' the same means of treatment which they would regard as 'ordinary' if the infant's prospects were better. Thus the quality of life prospects of the infant, rather than any objective criteria of the 'extraordinariness' of the medical treatment, is the significant factor in the doctors' decisions to treat or not to treat.

There is now increasing recognition of the fact that the distinction between ordinary and extraordinary means serves no good purpose. Robert Veatch, in *Death, Dying and the Biological Revolution*, goes through some of the confused and conflicting interpretations of the distinction and concludes that the language of ordinary and extraordinary means should 'be banned from further use'. The Law Reform Commission of Canada, in its Working Paper entitled *Euthanasia, Aiding Suicide and Cessation of Treatment*, says that the distinction is 'too ambiguous to serve as a solid basis for any precise description of the scope of the physician's legal duty to his patient and therefore to serve as a good basis for reform'.

The Editor of the *Journal of Medical Ethics*, the leading British journal in the field, has described the distinction as 'dangerously deceptive' and said that 'once the actual criteria of decision are specified the misleading labels "ordinary means" and "extraordinary means" become superfluous and may be safely allowed to "drop out of the picture" by those who have no special reason to retain them'.

Most damning of all, however, is the opinion of the United States President's Commission for the Study of Ethical Problems in Medicine and Biomedical and Behavioral Research. This Commission, appointed by President Carter, wrote a 545-page report entitled *Deciding to Forego Life-Sustaining Treatment*. The report was issued on 21 March 1983—coincidentally, the very day of the hearing before Judge Gerhard Gesell on the Baby Doe Guidelines. After a careful discussion of the various ways in which people have attempted to draw the distinction between ordinary and extraordinary means, the Commission found that the only form of the distinction that has moral significance is when it is understood in terms of the 'usefulness and burdensomeness of a particular therapy'. The Commission then continued:

This line of reasoning suggests that extraordinary treatment is that which, in the patient's view, entails significantly greater burdens than benefits and is therefore undesirable and not obligatory, while ordinary treatment is that which, in the patient's view, produces greater benefits than burdens and is therefore reasonably desirable and undertaken. The claim, then, that the treatment is extraordinary is more of an expression of the conclusion than a justification of it.

After thus pointing out that, in its most plausible usage, the distinction is doing no work except to serve as the expression of a conclusion reached on other grounds, the Commission sums up:

> Despite its long history of frequent use, the distinction between ordinary and extraordinary treatments has now become so confused that its continued use in the formulation of public policy is no longer desirable . . . Clarity and understanding in this area will be enhanced if laws, judicial opinions, regulations, and medical policies speak instead in terms of the proportionate benefit and burdens of treatment as viewed by particular patients.

Thus the President's Commission confirms the conclusion suggested by our examination of Bishop Casey's testimony, and also the view we formed as a result of our survey of obstetricians and paediatricians. In each case, the conclusion is that even though the decision to give or withhold treatment appears at first to be based on some fact about the nature of the means of treatment, the decision is really being taken on quite different grounds: an evaluation of the kind of life the patient is expected to lead. Thus the distinction between ordinary and extraordinary means cannot assist anyone wishing both to preserve the view that all human life is of equal value, and to explain why we are not required to keep alive a baby born without a brain. Those who invoke the distinction only explain why we are not obliged to prolong life in such a case because they covertly take account of the poor quality of such a life and the consequent uselessness, or absence of benefit, of such a treatment. In doing so, those who invoke the distinction are abandoning the view that all human life is of equal worth.

'Customary medical care'

In its original 'Notice to Health Care Providers' of 18 May 1982, the Department of Health and Human Services informed hospitals receiving federal funds that it was unlawful for them to withhold from a handicapped infant 'nutritional sustenance or medical or surgical treatment required to correct a life-threatening condition' if the withholding was based on the fact that the infant was handicapped, and the treatment was not 'medically contra-indicated'. This very sweeping terminology was widely criticized; it seemed to require every form of treatment that could prolong life, even for the most hopeless cases like infants born without brains. So ten months later, in issuing its Interim Final Rule, the Department modified its position by referring to 'infants discriminatorily denied food or customary medical care'.

'Customary medical care' is, as we have seen, very close to one of the senses of 'ordinary' suggested by the ordinary/extraordinary distinction. If the Department thought that by using this term it could avoid the ambiguities and difficulties of that distinction, however, it soon received a rude awakening.

Any attempt to vest ethical significance in custom is problematic: what we customarily do is not always the best thing to do. For the Department of Health and Human Services the appeal to 'customary medical care' posed a special problem which it really ought to have foreseen. The problem was that the Department, in documenting the need for new guidelines on the treatment of handicapped infants, had clearly established that the treatments it was attempting to make compulsory were *not* customary.

The difficulty the Department was in emerged very clearly at the hearing before Judge Gerhard Gesell. As we have seen, the chief witness for the Department at that hearing was Dr C. Everett Koop, Surgeon General of the United States, and a key person in the drawing-up of the Interim Final Rule. Judge Gesell asked Dr Koop whether there was documentation of the problems they were discussing. Dr Koop gave a lengthy reply which included the following passages:

there was a very telling survey done by the surgical section of the Academy of Pediatrics ... At the time of the survey there were approximately six hundred members of that surgical section. I cannot remember how many were questioned there, but it was over half and that was reported in a journal called *Pediatrics* in the year 1977 and there it was very clear that a very large proportion of pediatric surgeons in this country, and there was also a little section about pediatricians, were perfectly willing to acquiesce to the request of a family not to treat a child if they didn't want that child, and many of the circumstances that were mentioned in that survey were very simple procedures such as simple intestinal obstruction, not associated with any other anomaly, and as I recall, fourteen per cent of the surgeons questioned said if indeed the parent said they didn't want the child operated upon even though they knew it would be certain death, and it was a simple, easy thing and a normal child would be the result of that procedure, they said they would acquiesce to the family's concern. And in the President's Advisory Commission on Biomedical Ethics . . . there are two other surveys mentioned . . . which I think are also very telling. One was a survey of pediatricians in the West who said that the majority of them would acquiesce to the parents' request not to operate upon the child if they didn't want that child, and in a Massachusetts survey of pediatricians a majority of those who answered the survey said that they would not even suggest an operation in a child who had Down's syndrome, so I think it is widespread.

In a later chapter we will examine in more detail the surveys cited by Koop. The reason for quoting Koop's testimony at this point is that it served as a preliminary to the following series of devastating questions from Judge Gesell:

JUDGE GESELL: So what is it that you consider customary medical care? I mean how would you as a practising physician, how would you understand that?
DR KOOP: It would have to be—the reasons that those regulations don't go into chapter and verse for everything that occurs in a child is because that would result in a textbook.
JUDGE GESELL: They don't go into anything.
DR KOOP: They don't go into anything.
JUDGE GESELL: So what does the regulation mean when it says 'customary medical care'?
DR KOOP: Well, I think that every physician knows what is essentially customary.
JUDGE GESELL: Would you mind telling me?
DR KOOP: Yes. It differs for every case but let's take the ones that you mentioned a moment ago when you talked about a child who is born without an intestine . . . we would consider customary care in that child the provision of a bed, of food by mouth, knowing that it was not going to be nutritious, but not just shutting off the care of that child . . . nor do we

intend to say that this child should be carried on intravenous fluids for the rest of its life.

JUDGE GESELL: How are the number [*sic:* read 'members'?] of your organizations, the pediatric associations to find out what you think is right?

DR KOOP: I think we all essentially agree, sir.

JUDGE GESELL: Is it written down anywhere?

DR KOOP: No, but again, it's customary . . .

JUDGE GESELL: The affidavits seem to indicate that there's some disagreement between physicians as to what is customary care.

Poor Dr Koop. Having argued that the regulations were needed because a very large proportion of paediatricians were ready to go along with the wishes of parents and not operate on a Down's syndrome infant—precisely the result the regulation had been devised to prevent—he was in an impossible situation in trying to maintain that all the regulation demanded was 'customary medical care'.

Dr Koop's difficulties obviously made an impression on Judge Gesell. In his decision declaring the regulation invalid, he said:

this Court is forced to conclude that haste and inexperience have resulted in agency action based on inadequate consideration. This is reinforced by the text of the rule itself. For example, the rule provides that it is a violation of federal law to deny a handicapped infant 'customary medical care'. Yet as all the evidence received by this Court from both parties has made clear, and as even the most cursory investigation by the Secretary [for Health and Human Services] would have revealed, *there is no customary standard of care* for the treatment of severely defective infants. The regulation thus purports to set up an enforcement mechanism without defining the violation and it is virtually without meaning beyond its intrinsic *in terrorem* effect.

One would have thought that Judge Gerhard Gesell had made the point very plainly: in this context, the standard of 'customary medical care' will not work. The end of this tale, however, is still to be told. Following the Court's decision striking down the Interim Final Rule, the Department prepared its new 'proposed rule', intended presumably to meet the objections which had led to the demise of the Interim Final Rule. In the supplementary information to the proposed rule, issued on 5 July 1983, the Department repeats, in more formal and precise language, the results of the surveys mentioned in court by Dr Koop. The Department states, for instance, that according to the survey published in *Pediatrics*, no fewer than 76 per cent of paediatric surgeons said they would acquiesce in parents' decisions to refuse consent for surgery in a Down's syndrome infant with a blockage in the intestine. Other surveys quoted indicated broadly similar results—in each case, a majority of the sample of paediatric surgeons or paediatricians were prepared to go along with a parental request like that of the parents in the Baby Doe case. Despite this conclusive evidence of the absence of any standard of customary care that would lead to the treatment of such infants, however, the new proposed rule would require hospitals receiving federal funds to post the same notice as required by the Interim Final Rule—including the same reference to a standard of 'customary medical care'.

Puzzling as this persistence at first seems, a careful reading of the supplementary information makes it possible to see what the Department has in mind. The standard of 'customary medical care' it wishes to apply to a case like that of Baby Doe—that is, a retarded infant with an unrelated medical problem—is the standard of care customary for infants with similar medical problems, but without the mental handicap. For this reason the Department cites the *Pediatrics* survey as indicating that only 7.9 per cent of paediatric surgeons would acquiesce in parents' decisions to refuse consent for surgery to remove an intestinal blockage if the infant has no other anomaly.

This 7.9 per cent is presumably the figure Dr Koop was trying to recall when he cited a figure of 14 per cent at the hearing. He may not have appreciated that the *higher* this figure is, the *weaker* the case for saying that the decision not to treat Baby Doe was discrimination based on the infant's handicap. Even a figure of 7.9 per cent is high enough to cast some doubt on this claim, for it makes it clear that there is no *universally* accepted standard of 'customary care' for infants with intestinal blockages whose parents do not wish them treated, even when there is no mental handicap. Still, the 7.9 per cent is markedly different from the 76 per cent who would acquiesce where there is both the blockage and the Down's syndrome. Hence if the standard of care that would be taken by all but 7.9 per cent of paediatric surgeons can be regarded as 'customary medical care', the failure to provide this customary care in the case of the mentally handicapped infant suggests the probability of discrimination based on the existence of the mental handicap.

In cases like that of Baby Doe, where the life-threatening medical problem is one that can be found in infants who have no other problems as well as in infants with Down's syndrome, the appeal to a standard of customary care has nothing to do with the distinction between ordinary and extraordinary means. It is, rather, an appeal to a standard of normal treatment, by which a discriminatory denial of treatment may be assessed. To use the standard in this way is, of course, to assume that all human lives are of equal value—it is this assumed equality that makes the 'discrimination' wrong. We have already seen that medical decisions are frequently made which are in conflict with this egalitarian stance—for instance, in the treatment of infants born without brains or without intestines. Thus the very standard of customary medical care to which the Department appeals in a limited range of cases is itself, taken as a whole, an offender against the underlying concept of the equal value of human lives. And we have also seen that the Department itself endorses this departure from the equal value standard in these situations, misconstruing as 'medical decisions' the quality of life judgements on which the decisions not to treat these cases are based.

In any case, where the life-threatening medical problem is found only among those born with severe handicaps which cannot be fully corrected, the appeal to customary medical care will not help to detect 'discrimination' based on quality of life judgements; for then there is no class of normal infants in which a standard of customary care exists. Spina bifida, one of the most common serious birth defects, falls into this category. Infants with this defect are often treated on a selective basis, and the selection is quite openly based on the prospects for an acceptable quality of life. In the next chapter we shall examine the treatment decisions made for infants with spina bifida. As we shall see here there is no standard of 'customary medical care' which is independent of quality of life judgements.

The 'Final' Rule

In order to illustrate the difficulties of defending the view that all human life is of equal value, we have followed the story of the Reagan administration's attempt to formulate its policies on the treatment of severely handicapped new-born infants. For completeness, we shall conclude this chapter by bringing the story up to date.

The Department of Health and Human Services received 16,739 comments on the proposed rule it issued on 5 July 1983. Ninety-seven per cent were in support of the rule, many written in virtually identical terms as a response to appeals by groups like the 'Christian Action Council'. One hundred and forty-one paediatricians or new-born care specialists sent in comments; of these, 72 per cent opposed the rule. The American Academy of Pediatrics also made a lengthy submission, which included documentation of the harm done to hospitals trying to cope with medical and human crises by sudden descents of the 'Baby Doe Squad'. For instance, at Vanderbilt University Hospital, a 'hotline' call led to three investigators and a neonatologist examining, after midnight, each infant in the facility, and diverting the hard-pressed hospital staff from patient care for a total of fifty-four staff-hours. The neonatologist described the hospital's care as 'exemplary'. More dramatic still is a comment quoted from a New Mexico paediatrician:

Because of the fear I had in being 'reported,' I recently spent one agonizing hour trying to resuscitate a newborn who had no larynx, and many other congenital anomalies. The sad part was that both the parents in the delivery room watched this most difficult ordeal. It was obvious to me that this was in no way a viable child but I felt compelled to carry on this way out of fear someone in the hospital would 'turn me in'. I am sure that you who sit in Washington are not faced with such difficult decisions at two o'clock a.m.

On 9 January 1984, the Department issued a new rule, which it optimistically entitled the 'Final Rule'. Comments like that just quoted must have had some effect, because the Final Rule was in some respects a retreat from the heavy-handed intimidation that had characterized previous versions of the rule. This gradual retreat is reflected in the size and positioning of the notice to be posted in hospitals: the notice sent out with the March 1983 Interim Rule measured seventeen inches by fourteen; the July Proposed Rule required the notice to be no smaller than eleven by eight-and-a-half inches; now the notice could be as small as seven by five inches. Moreover the notice did not have to be posted where parents and visitors can see it, but only at nurses' stations where it could be seen by health-care professionals. The wording of the notice had also been toned down: for instance, the reference to violations of state criminal and civil laws was deleted on the grounds that the statement was 'unnecessary' and 'potentially inflammatory'.

The most significant innovation in the new rule was the suggestion that hospitals may wish to set up 'Infant Care Review Committees' which would discuss problem cases, and with which the department would consult, in the first instance, if any alleged violations were reported to it. This suggestion picked up a recommendation of the American Academy of Pediatrics, and was clearly another attempt at conciliation.

That the Department should seek the views of those on the spot before rushing to its own decision is, of course, desirable; but the Department made it clear, beneath its conciliatory language, that it was still the boss. As Dr Koop said during the press conference at which the Final Rule was announced: 'The rules do no more than continue to provide an effective method of enforcing Section 504 in connection with the health care of handicapped infants.'

The new rule itself said that 'the Department does not seek to take over medical decision-making regarding health care for handicapped infants', but then added that the parents and physicians must act within the framework set by law, including the Section 504 prohibition of discrimination. The Department specifically rejected the suggestion that with the review boards in place, the government could refrain from playing a role in enforcing this statute with regard to handicapped infants.

So far as the interpretation of Section 504 is concerned, the new rule contained only minor changes. References to 'customary medical care' were finally dropped. The criterion of 'medically beneficial treatment' now had to bear all the weight of distinguishing cases like anencephaly (which the Department still said need not be treated) from cases of Down's syndrome with an intestinal blockage (which the Department said should be treated). We have seen that this distinction cannot really be a medical judgement, yet the new rule continued to insist that 'present or anticipated physical or mental impairments of an infant' are not a permissible basis for withholding treatment. So far as the provision of all 'medically beneficial treatment' was concerned, the Department indicated that its position 'remains unchanged'.

The American Academy of Pediatrics, presumably believing that the new rule was as good as it was likely to get, was now prepared to accept the situation. The American Medical Association, however, was not. Together with the American Hospital Association, the American College of Obstetricians and Gynecologists, the American Academy of Family Physicians, the Hospital Association of New York State, and the Association of American Medical Colleges, the AMA took the view that the federal government should not be involved in decisions about the medical treatment of severely handicapped new-borns. These organizations challenged the Final Rule in the US District Court for the Southern District of New York, arguing that medical decisions be left in the hands of parents, with the advice of the physician and other members of the medical team. Rather than regulating care, the federal government should, these organizations said, distribute information about new methods of treatment and improve support systems that help parents care for their infants.

On 23 May 1984, the government's Baby Doe regulations were struck down once more, this time by Judge Charles Brieant. Judge Brieant followed an earlier ruling by a higher court, in the so-called 'Baby Jane Doe' case (not to be confused with the original 'Baby Doe' case). In that case the Department of Health and Human Services had filed suit against University Hospital, in Stony Brook, New York, demanding access to the medical records for 'Baby Jane Doe', a disabled infant whose doctors were alleged to be treating her less vigorously than the government's regulations would require. The court had held that Section 504 of the Rehabilitation Act applied only to issues of education, employment, and transportation, and did not apply to medical decision-making. On appeal, this view of the Act was reaffirmed by the US Court of Appeals. Judge Brieant accepted this decision, and held that the Final Rule was 'invalid, unlawful, and without statutory authority'.

The federal government has said it will appeal against this ruling; but supporters of the Baby Doe rules decided to use a different approach. Since the courts had rejected the attempt to base the regulations on Section 504 of the Rehabilitation Act, there was no legal basis for further regulations, and it was necessary to legislate. The vehicle used was a bill to reauthorize a federal programme against child abuse. An amendment was attached to this bill, requiring all states to develop procedures for the purpose of responding to reported cases of the withholding of 'medically indicated treatment' from disabled infants with life-threatening conditions. Any state which did not have such procedures in place within a year of the enactment of the amendment would lose its federal grant for programmes directed at preventing child abuse.

Like the Final Rule, the new legislation relies on the notion of 'medically indicated treatment' in order to give the appearance that it is not making quality of life decisions. The amendment defines 'medically indicated treatment' as all treatment likely to be effective in ameliorating life-threatening conditions, except for the following three situations:

(a) when the infant is 'chronically and irreversibly comatose';
(b) when the provision of treatment would:
    (i) merely prolong dying,
    (ii) not be effective in ameliorating or correcting all of the infant's life-threatening conditions, or
    (iii) otherwise be futile in terms of the survival of the infant;
(c) the provision of such treatment would be virtually futile in terms of the survival of the infant and the treatment itself under such circumstances would be inhumane.

It is, however, absurd to pretend that this is simply a definition of 'medically indicated treatment'. It might be better to describe it as Congress's opinion of what is 'ethically indicated treatment'. The judgement that human life in an irreversible coma is not worth prolonging is, of course, a judgement based on quality of life considerations. Even more transparently, the reference to inhumane treatment in the last clause of the definition allows ethical judgements weighing the suffering of the infant against the doubtful prospects of a life-prolonging treatment.

The amendments to the Child Abuse Prevention and Treatment Act came into effect in October 1984. In several respects they are significantly less rigid than any of the earlier Baby Doe rules: they allow the states to set up their own procedures for dealing with reports of the failure to provide treatment; the penalty for failing to comply with the act does not fall on the specific hospital involved, but on the state as a whole, which loses a federal grant under the child abuse prevention programme; and as we have just seen, they give greater scope for ethical considerations in the decision against providing treatment. Much will depend on how the individual states carry out the tasks allotted to them, but it seems that the effect on the treatment of severely disabled infants will not be nearly as drastic as it would have been if the initial Baby Doe rule had survived intact.

3 DECIDING WHEN LIFE IS WORTH WHILE: THE TREATMENT OF SPINA BIFIDA

The defect

Rembrandt's well-known painting *The Anatomy Lesson* depicts a learned doctor dissecting a corpse in front of an engrossed audience. The doctor is Nicholas Tulp, author of *Observationes Medicae*. This book, published in Amsterdam in 1652, contains the first modern medical description of an infant born with a section of its spinal cord split and exposed, instead of forming a tube and being covered with skin in the normal manner. Tulp called the condition 'spina bifida'—a spine divided in two.

Spina bifida takes several forms. Sometimes the defect is very minor and requires no treatment, or can be easily treated without leaving any noticeable effects. Unfortunately there is also a more severe form, known medically as spina bifida with myelomeningocele (or sometimes, just to add to the confusion of everyone other than doctors, as spina bifida with meningomyelocele). From now on, when we say 'spina bifida' we will be referring only to the more severe forms. In these there is a swelling in the middle of the baby's back, from which the spinal fluid leaks. As a result the child is highly prone to infection; more serious still, however, is the fact that the nerves which run along the spine are damaged. Children with this defect will, if they live, be partly or completely paralysed in the legs. They will be unable to control their bowels or bladder. Often they have a deformed spine. In some 65 per cent of cases they develop hydrocephalus, or 'water on the brain'. This condition, the result of an accumulation of fluid in the cavities of the brain, causes the head to swell and leads to brain damage from the pressure on the neural tissue. Thus many

children born with spina bifida become mentally retarded—
although some are of normal intelligence.

The frequency of spina bifida varies from place to place, and is
much rarer in some ethnic groups than others. It is often said to
occur once in every thousand births, but in Japan it appears to
occur only once in about four thousand births, while in South
Wales, Dublin, and Belfast it has been recorded as often as once
in every 250 births. Happily, the incidence of spina bifida is now
falling in almost all areas. Scientists are puzzled about these
variations, and have put forward several possible explanations,
ranging from genetic factors to soft water, the use of analgesics,
the eating of potatoes, and vitamin and mineral deficiencies.
None of these hypotheses is supported by conclusive evidence and
there may well be more than one factor involved. At present the
most promising hypothesis appears to be that which links spina
bifida with vitamin and iron deficiencies.

The treatment

Until the second half of the twentieth century, almost all babies
born with spina bifida died at birth or within a few weeks
thereafter. In many cases, midwives and family doctors made
sure that the babies did not survive; to save the mother
difficulties, they were often described as 'stillborn'. Even if the
doctors tried to keep these infants alive, infection from the open
wound over the spine was virtually inevitable; and before
antibiotics, there was nothing to be done to combat it. The
general medical attitude was nicely understated in an article by
two doctors published in the *New England Journal of Medicine* in
1943: 'Delay in surgical intervention is the wisest general course
to pursue.' Left to themselves, the babies soon died; and if they
were treated, they still died.

During the 1940s, some surgeons tried operating on infants
born with spina bifida. They were able to close the wound on the
spine. Unfortunately this meant that the cerebro-spinal fluid
which would have leaked out of the wound now accumulated in
the brain, causing hydrocephalus and brain damage. If the
pressure became too great, the child would die. The fluid could
be tapped and drawn off with a syringe, but it was scarcely
feasible to do this continually. Doctors therefore tried inserting a

permanent polythene tube under the skin of the head. This drained the excess fluid into the heart and thus into the bloodstream, where it was dispersed without damage. The tube needed a one-way valve, to stop the blood flowing up into the brain. The problem was that small pieces of tissue in the fluid were constantly blocking the tube and valve, necessitating frequent operations to clear the blockage. This problem was solved by John Holter, a Pennsylvania hydraulics technician who found himself, in 1955, the father of a boy with spina bifida. Holter's son had the tube implanted soon after birth, but within ten days it was blocked and he needed a second operation. When it became blocked again a few days later, Holter decided to see if he could do something about the problem. Working in the evenings and at weekends, he soon came up with a simple valve which he took along to his son's surgeon. Despite understandable initial scepticism, the surgeon decided to try the new device, no doubt because it offered hope where previously there had been none. It soon became obvious that it worked remarkably well, becoming blocked far less frequently than the old system. Holter set himself up in business, manufacturing the 'Holter valve' and selling it to the parents of children with hydrocephalus. Within a few years it was in wide use. Because antibiotics were now also readily available, it suddenly became possible to keep alive, indefinitely, thousands of children who would otherwise have died very soon after birth.

At this point the story switches to Sheffield. Like Derby, where John Pearson died, Sheffield is an industrial city in the north of England. At the time (the 1950s) the area had a high rate of spina bifida. Dr Robert Zachary, of the Department of Child Health at Sheffield University, was one of the first surgeons to operate on spina bifida children, even before Holter invented his valve. After the valve became available Zachary, together with W. J. M. Sharrard, an orthopaedic surgeon, and John Lorber, a paediatrician, became enthusiastic about the need for active treatment of spina bifida. In an influential paper published in 1963, Sharrard and his colleagues stated categorically that spina bifida must be operated on as soon as possible, since otherwise further—and irreparable—nerve damage could result from the drying of the wound. Some years later Dr Anthony Raimondi, Professor of

Neurological Surgery at Chicago's Northwestern University, described the effect of this paper:

From 1962 or 1966 this particular cant was being spread around to all neurosurgeons in the world, and especially Americans who are very sensitive (perhaps we have an inferiority feeling with respect to the language) to what the English say. We adopted this policy instantaneously and repaired every myelomeningocele immediately. It was shown to us that if we did not, the children suffered terribly. At that time, the final conclusion was that immediate closure of the back is a surgical necessity.

John Lorber has described the treatment that followed upon acceptance of this view:

The fully active treatment usually begins with the closure of the wound on the back, removing any abnormal tissues, replacing the spinal cord as far as possible in its proper place in the spinal canal and then covering it with the appropriate layers and finishing it off with a covering of the skin. The next important aspect is to investigate whether the baby has or has not got hydrocephalus. If he has, what is its degree? If the hydrocephalus is serious, the appropriate therapy is surgery using shunt methods incorporating a uni-directional valve or valves to control the intracranial pressure . . . The next step is usually the assessment of kidney function and the assessment of the orthopaedic situation. How much paralysis is there? It can be total from the waist down, it can be trivial, and anything in between. Then, what from the orthopaedic point of view is more important, what are the deformities? Now when there is partial paralysis, which can be of infinite variety and degree, then because the muscles are not in balance they can cause the growth of most bizarre deformities and great complexity, and dislocation of joints, particularly of the hip—this is where a very major part of the orthopaedic surgery comes in. There may be some children who have thirty or forty orthopaedic operations before they leave school.

For twelve years, every infant with spina bifida in Sheffield was treated in this manner; and the insistence of the Sheffield school that this was the only ethical way of treating spina bifida had its effects. To quote Lorber once more:

vast numbers of babies were treated through the 1960s, irrespective of the severity of their neurological handicaps. Doctors felt morally forced to refer all babies for surgery, and many surgeons who did not agree with this policy felt that they had to operate for fear of public criticism or worse. The parents were rarely adequately informed or consulted. They were usually told that their infant *had* to be operated on and they *had* to sign a document signifying their agreement. At that time they had no idea what that operation meant for the future of their child, and for the whole family.

The results soon became manifest. Some years later, John Lorber summed up the outcome of 848 children treated in Sheffield during the period in which every infant was treated as actively as possible. Exactly half of the infants were still alive, aged then between four and fourteen. Of those who had died, three quarters had died during the first year; the other deaths were more evenly distributed during the succeeding years. These later deaths were mostly caused by complications of the drainage tube, or by hydrocephalus, or kidney failure.

Disturbing as these deaths were—particularly when parents lost their child after several years of devoted care—active treatment clearly led to the survival of more children. But was survival enough? Gradually Lorber started to think about the kind of lives the children he had treated were surviving to lead. His records showed him that of the 424 survivors of the period of universal active treatment, only six had no handicap. Seventy-three, or 17 per cent of the survivors, were classified as having a 'moderate' degree of handicap; 345, or over 80 per cent, were severely handicapped. Those in this latter group had at least two, but usually more, of the following conditions: no bowel and bladder control, or a urinary bypass with frequent kidney infections and progressive chronic kidney damage which may lead to renal failure; paralysis to such a degree that they are unable to walk without caliper splints, crutches, or other appliances, and must rely on a wheelchair for part of the day; pressure sores on feet, knees, or buttocks; hydrocephalus which is treated by a drainage tube, which then requires new operations to deal with frequent complications. (Some children had had over forty such operations on their drainage tubes.)

These are the physical problems the survivors of active treatment had to confront. There were also mental disabilities: 144 of the children (approximately a third) were retarded; of these 51 were severely retarded.

The spread of the policy of active treatment began to have

noticeable effects on institutions that dealt with handicapped people. One study of a special school for the handicapped in South Wales showed that from 1958–63, before active treatment became common, fewer than 8 per cent of the children had spina bifida. From 1964–6, the figure was 21 per cent; by 1967 it was 34 per cent. Decisions made by individual doctors were placing a greatly increased burden on the limited resources available for helping people with disabilities. In his book *The Biocrats*, Gerald Leach estimated that if Britain were to provide special schools for every spina bifida saved, it would have to build, *every month*, a new school with places for fifty children, and would have to train ten skilled people to staff the school; moreover it would have to continue to build and staff schools at this rate for fifteen years, for that was how long it would take the population of spina bifida children to stabilize.

The medical cost of the new policy was also considerable. As we have seen, some children had thirty to forty orthopaedic operations, and others may have had—despite the Holter valve—forty operations to deal with complications to the drainage tube. Then there were urinary bypass operations to deal with incontinence, and a host of other forms of treatment needed to make the most of the child's limited possibilities. Writing in the *British Medical Journal* in 1971, Dr Eliot Slater claimed: 'In the first five years of life most survivors spend an average of two years in hospital, mainly in spells of one to two weeks. Admissions are numbered in dozens, and the child is hardly out of hospital before the time is nearing for him to go back again.' John Lorber's figures for hospital stays in Sheffield are considerably less than this suggests, but he states that his hospital had a deliberate policy of early discharge because of the great pressure on beds—hence his patients were hospitalized only for acute conditions and 'spent much less time in hospitals than would have been desirable'. Despite this, figures on 103 surviving children with spina bifida show that they spent a total of 2796 weeks in hospital, an average of more than six months per child. Lorber also estimated the cost of this treatment, and considered that the average cost per child could not be less than £3000 per annum. (This was in 1972, 'pre-inflation' figures.)

As all these consequences of active treatment for all spina

bifida infants became apparent, dissenting voices began to make themselves heard.

The selective treatment debate

Although the active treatment of all spina bifida babies came close to being standard medical practice in the 1960s, there were one or two specialists who refused to follow the trend. Two Liverpool doctors, P. Rickham and T. Mawdsley, reported in 1966 on the fate of 55 infants born with severe forms of spina bifida who had not been referred for treatment: all of them had died within six months of birth. Rickham and Mawdsley defended the non-treatment of these babies, saying that the mere saving of life is not enough, unless the lives are worth saving. Donald Matson, a leading British paediatric surgeon of an earlier generation, wrote in 1968, shortly before his death, that he did not operate on the more severe cases of spina bifida because he saw it as the doctor's and the community's responsibility 'not to prolong such individual, familial and community suffering unnecessarily, and not to carry out multiple procedures and prolonged, expensive, acute hospitalization in an infant whose chance for acceptable growth and development is negligible'. In Melbourne, Australia, the Royal Children's Hospital's Spina Bifida Clinic—one of the largest and most experienced spina bifida units anywhere—developed a policy of selecting only the more hopeful cases for active treatment. In both Oxford and Edinburgh, too, some form of selection was practised.

These pockets of resistance to the trend did not in themselves give rise to much debate among members of the medical profession, let alone among the general public. The Melbourne, Oxford, and Edinburgh groups, for instance, did not publish accounts of their practices during this period. The first real signs of debate among the medical profession came in 1968, when Robert Zachary published an article in *The Lancet*, a leading British medical journal. The title of the article was 'Ethical and Social Aspects of Treatment of Spina Bifida'. Zachary wrote that there are three possible ways of handling infants with spina bifida: to kill them; to encourage them to die, either by not feeding them or by not treating infections and other complications; or to encourage them to live. Outright killing, Zachary wrote, is contrary to a widely accepted ethical principle which has been the basis of medical practice since the time of Hippocrates. Nor was the second alternative any better:

To leave a child without food is to kill it as deliberately and directly as if one was cutting its throat. Even the prescribing of antibiotics for infection, such as pneumonia, must now be considered as ordinary care of patients.

This left only the third alternative. The child must be encouraged to live. The remaining issues were therefore simply the medical questions about which method of management gives the child the best chance to live, and—but in second place—which method of treatment will reduce the handicap to a minimum.

This time Zachary's views did not go unchallenged. One doctor wrote describing the ethical justification offered for the treatment of children with spina bifida as 'shallow and cruel'. To this Zachary replied that he was assuming that spina bifida babies should not be killed; and given this premiss, treatment should be undertaken to reduce the children's handicaps to a minimum. A subsequent letter from Dr Ian Wickes suggested that between treating all spina bifida infants, and killing some of them, there lay a middle way: 'to let Nature take its course'. Dr Wickes added: 'Over the years, without any active intervention on my part, over 90 per cent of the untreated babies I have seen have died before their first birthday.' The policy of universal treatment, Wickes suggested, often was instituted as the easiest way out of a dilemma, rather than as the result of careful thought:

Now that surgical treatment is available for such babies, the easiest way out for the doctor is to transfer the neonates to a unit where all such babies are operated upon without delay. The parents, in their confused and highly disappointed state, will gladly clutch at any offer to help, fervently hoping that the miracle of modern surgery will put the baby right. It will take time before the awful truth dawns upon them and by then it will be too late to step back. Then their only course is to put on a brave face—one that warms the heart of the surgeon in the follow-up clinic. The advent of such a severely handicapped child into a family will transform the lives of all its members—in some cases permanently and completely. That some parents gain fulfilment by dedicating their lives to the care of such children is one of the saving graces of this tragic story, but who can be sure that their lives would have been emptier with a healthy replacement?

Dr Wickes was supported by another correspondent, Dr L. Haas, who referred approvingly to 'The old dictum we were taught as medical students, "Thou shalt not kill; but need'st not strive officiously to keep alive." ' Dr Haas described the care of a severely handicapped survivor as 'an intolerable strain on the family, especially the mother'; and pointed out that 'in the vast majority of cases' the mother 'will forego her chances of having further normal children'. As for the survivors, 'they have to find their place in society as paraplegics with incontinence, subject to repeated urinary infections and bedsores.' For all these reasons, Dr Haas regarded non-interference as 'the kinder course of action' and concluded: 'I personally never see the problem of the untreated survivor . . . Nature if left alone will always correct its own mistakes in these cases.'

Dr Zachary, however, also had his supporters. One group of three doctors pointedly described Dr Wickes' policy of 'letting Nature take its course' as 'highly ambiguous'. With treatment, they said, 'there is a better than even chance that, if he survives, the baby will grow up as a normally intelligent human being'—and they asked if that was not to be preferred to 90 per cent mortality within the first year. A surgeon, Mr Ellison Nash, objected that Dr Wickes was, as a paediatrician, not himself involved in the operative treatment, and was 'denying neonates their right to a surgical opinion'. Mr Nash challenged Dr Wickes to publish the progress of his 10 per cent of untreated survivors, speculating that they would have brain damage which could have been avoided and paralysis more extensive than it need have been. Dr Wickes was, Nash concluded, 'extending the principles of social abortion into the neonatal period'.

Although Zachary's article and the ensuing correspondence had raised many of the key issues in the debate over selective treatment, it appears to have had little effect on the dominance of the practice of treating all infants with spina bifida. The influence of the Sheffield group, with its policy of operating on all infants within 24 hours of birth, remained strong. Zachary was, of course, a leading member of that group; but as recently as 1967 he had been joined by both Sharrard and Lorber in a paper which stated bluntly: 'there is no place for the selection of patients for conservative management rather than operation.' As the sixties ended, however, some members of the Sheffield group admitted to doubts about the policy they had pioneered. They began to discuss the situation. Zachary, a staunch Roman Catholic, remained firm in his support for active treatment; someone was needed to put the opposite point of view. John Lorber was asked to do so—he said later that the role fell upon him 'almost by accident'.

The group met in the living-room of Lorber's solid Sheffield home. They listened to Zachary, who could see no ethical alternative to treatment. Then Lorber presented an analysis of the results of the policy of universal active treatment at Sheffield. They were, he said, disappointing: 'Massive effort has led to much avoidable suffering at an exorbitant cost in manpower and money.' He claimed that initial enthusiasm for the Holter valve had resulted in its being used uncritically. As he was later to write:

We must decide our priorities to ensure that, with all the intensive effort and good will, we shall not do more harm than good. Until quite recently, far too many infants with spina bifida were allowed to die or deteriorate for want of expert care. The pendulum has now swung too far: there are now many with dreadful handicaps who a short time ago would have died.

Lorber urged that the group should concentrate its attention on the soluble problems of the less handicapped children, rather than attempt to keep all children alive irrespective of the problems they would face. The considerable experience of the Sheffield group meant, Lorber said, that it was possible for them to find suitable criteria for selective treatment. If an infant within a few hours of birth had one or more of five 'adverse criteria', the outlook was so uniformly bad that treatment should not be recommended. These 'adverse criteria' related to such matters as the size and location of the opening over the spine, the existence of severe paralysis or spinal deformity, very bad hydrocephalus, and other major defects or brain damage. Lorber claimed that if such infants had not been treated in the past, not a single moderately handicapped surviving child would have been lost; those not treated would all have been infants who had either died despite treatment, or survived with severe handicaps. The consent of the parents would be sought for the course of treatment, or lack of treatment, that was to be followed—but Lorber was convinced that the parents would accept the advice given to them.

What of those infants—and on Lorber's criteria it would be the majority of spina bifida babies—who would not be selected for treatment? Was there not a risk that they would survive anyway, in a much worse condition than if they were treated? Lorber did not think so. He could point to the paper published in 1966 by the two Liverpool doctors, Rickham and Mawdsley: of 55 infants with spina bifida not referred for treatment, all were dead within six months. 'No treatment', Lorber stressed, did not just mean 'no operation'. It meant ordinary feeding, but nothing else: 'no incubators, no oxygen, no tube feeding, and no antibiotic drugs. To deny an infant the potential benefit of an operation and then prolong life by other means is irrational.'

Despite Zachary's insistence that the proposed system of selective treatment was unethical, the group as a whole agreed with Lorber that they should cease treating all infants with spina bifida. In two influential articles, the first appearing in 1971 and the second the following year, Lorber published his analysis of the outcome of 794 cases of spina bifida treated unselectively in Sheffield. The first paper concluded with arguments for the desirability of a more selective approach. The second set out Lorber's criteria for selection.

The change of heart in Sheffield swung the tide of medical opinion against universal active treatment. Soon after Lorber's first article appeared, the *Medical Journal of Australia* published a leading article endorsing similar criteria for non-intervention in spina bifida. The Oxford and Edinburgh groups published reports of their selection of cases for treatment in 1973. In the *British Medical Journal*, the spina bifida clinic at Melbourne's Royal Children's Hospital published details of 295 cases in which selection had been practised between 1961 and 1969. Of these, 79 had not received active treatment, and all but two of this group had died; almost half died in less than a month, 70 per cent within three months, and 90 per cent within six months. The surviving treated children were compared with the published results from Sheffield, and found to have done strikingly better; almost half were in the 'moderately handicapped' category, with normal intelligence and able to get around with, at worst, short splints; by comparison, at Sheffield 85 per cent were in more severely handicapped categories.

The issue of the *British Medical Journal* in which these results were reported also carried two other articles on spina bifida. One came from another leading unit, in Cambridge, and discussed possible criteria for selection. The other article was, once again, by Lorber. In it he described the results of the first eighteen months of selective treatment in Sheffield. Thirty-seven infants with spina bifida had been admitted during this period. In twelve cases, active treatment had been recommended and accepted by the parents. The remaining 25 infants were not treated. Of those treated, one had died, but only one of the remainder was severely handicapped. Of those not treated, 72 per cent had died within three months, and all were dead in less than nine months. On the basis of these results selection was, Lorber said, the 'least bad solution' to an insoluble problem.

In America, too, doctors were prepared for the first time to state publicly that they did not seek to prolong the lives of all infants with spina bifida. In the same year as these Australian and British reports, the leading American medical journal, the *New England Journal of Medicine*, published a study by Drs Raymond Duff and A. G. M. Campbell on 'Moral and Ethical Dilemmas in the Special-Care Nursery'. Duff and Campbell, who worked in the Department of Pediatrics at Yale University, had investigated the causes of death in 299 infants in the Yale–New Haven Hospital special-care nursery, and found 43 of them to be related to decisions to withhold treatment. Of these infants, 7 were spina bifida cases. Duff and Campbell saw both treatment and non-treatment as raising 'unsatisfactory dilemmas', but they clearly did not favour a return to treatment in all cases. Instead they saw a need to break down 'the public and professional silence on a major social taboo' so that the ethical issues could be discussed and, if necessary, the law changed to allow these dilemmas to be worked out.

After the publication of these articles, the debate took a new turn. Notwithstanding the strong disagreement of some surgeons, who continued to operate on all cases of spina bifida referred to them, the principle of selective treatment itself was now widely accepted. It was endorsed by the British Government's Department of Health and Social Security in its publication *Care of the Child with Spina Bifida*. It was also supported by meetings of spina bifida associations, consisting of parents of spina bifida children, social workers, and others connected with people with spina bifida. Hence the focus of controversy rapidly shifted from *whether* selection should be carried out to *how* it should be carried out. In particular, two issues were raised: what should the criteria of selection be? And what should happen to those not selected for treatment? We shall consider these issues in turn.

Who should survive?

It is a measure of Lorber's boldness that he was prepared to spell out, in some detail, when active treatment should be recommended and when it should not. Furthermore, he made no attempt to disguise the recommendation against treatment as the mere refusal to prolong life in a dying patient. 'The main object of selection', he wrote, 'is not to avoid treating those who would die early in spite of treatment, but to avoid treating those who would survive with severe handicaps.' In other words, Lorber was ready to make a prediction, on the first day of life, about the quality of life each spina bifida infant was likely to have; and he was also ready to give his opinion on when that life would not be worthwhile.

Lorber's criteria were designed to ensure that no infants would be denied treatment if they had a chance of surviving with only moderate handicaps. To understand what this means, we must look at how Lorber classified degrees of handicap. His 'moderate physical handicap' category covered children who were incontinent or had a urinary bypass operation, enabling the urine to be collected in a bag outside the body; they were able to walk without calipers, although they may have limped or indeed have had surgical boots; they may have lacked feeling in their legs; they may have had hydrocephalus which either did not need a drainage tube, or was well controlled by means of the tube. Any child who had any one, or any combination, of these problems was classified as moderately handicapped, although as Lorber pointed out, this is 'moderate' only in a spina bifida context: 'the combination of incontinence with partial paraplegic deformities and a well-controlled hydrocephalus may not be considered moderate by the patients or their parents.'

'Severe physical handicaps', in Lorber's classification, covered any child with a handicap more severe than those just described. This included chronic urinary infections; kidney disease; paraplegia requiring the use of calipers, crutches, or wheelchairs; severe spinal deformities; precariously controlled hydrocephalus; blindness, fits, or other less common defects. In addition, Lorber classified those with an IQ of 80 or above as being of normal intelligence, those between 60 and 80 as retarded, and those below 60 as severely retarded.

We need not concern ourselves with the technical aspects of the 'adverse criteria' Lorber suggested paediatricians should use as a basis for recommending against treatment. This is a matter for medical specialists. The important ethical issue is the kind of life that can be predicted for those who are not to be treated. In Lorber's studies of 794 children admitted to the Sheffield unit on the first day of life, none of those with one or more adverse criteria survived without severe physical handicap. Conversely, all of those who did survive with only moderate handicaps had been initially assessed as having no adverse criteria. Lorber drew the obvious conclusion: a decision to withhold treatment from those with adverse criteria would not have reduced the numbers surviving with only moderate physical handicap.

What of mental handicap? Here Lorber could not claim that the results were so clear-cut. Mental handicap could not be predicted at birth with nearly the same degree of reliability as physical handicap. Referring to those with adverse criteria, Lorber said that 'only one-fifth' had an IQ of 80 or over, and 'very few' were over 100. 'The few brighter children', Lorber added, 'all have very severe physical handicaps.'

This inability to separate out all the children with normal intelligence did not deter Lorber. In the absence of reliable methods of predicting mental handicap, he considered predictions of severe physical handicap to be a sufficient basis for selection. This remains the major point of difference between, on the one hand, Lorber and those who use his criteria; and on the other hand, those who are prepared to select among spina bifida infants, but not in the way Lorber recommends.

Lorber has defended his position thus:

> Using our criteria, some children who would have survived with normal intelligence will be excluded from treatment and will die. Nevertheless it is my experience, as it is that of psychologists, social workers, teachers, and parents, that those young people who are severely handicapped by multi-system defects suffer far more if they have normal intelligence than if they are retarded. Only the intelligent realise fully what they have been through, what they have missed and will miss. Only the intelligent will worry about the frustrations of employment, loneliness, lack of opportunity and of normal family life. Only they will worry about their future and who will look after them when their parents are too old or are no longer alive.

In addition to this view of the likely future suffering of the normally intelligent but severely physically handicapped person, Lorber relied on the wishes of the parents. If anything, they were more likely to be opposed to treatment than his own recommendations:

> No parent has ever wished for operation if after full explanation about their baby's condition the advice was against active treatment. The right to a second opinion is always offered: it has never been taken up . . . A few parents disagree with the advice that their infant should be treated. If the infant's condition was near the borderline for selective treatment, no attempt was made to persuade or force the parents against their judgment.

If the infant effectively lacked parents who would make a judgement about its future, that was itself a reason against treatment:

> The worst-affected children are those who were illegitimate and others who were immediately abandoned by their families. They live in institutions, retarded and often permanently bedridden. Their chances in life are so unfavourable that the criteria for active treatment should be even stricter.

One of the most outspoken critics of Lorber's criteria of selection has been Dr John Freeman, a leading Baltimore paediatrician.

Dr Freeman agrees that some form of selection has to be carried out, and he agrees that the parents should take part in the decision; but he does not think that the consent of the parents tells us much:

> the parents who go to Dr. Lorber get Dr. Lorber's side of the story and Dr. Lorber says he offers them the chance to go to the doctor next door, but the parents never make that decision. They go along with what he tells them and 75% of the children don't get treated. I provide an equally reasoned and equally compassionate discussion to the parents and the parents go along with what I want to do and 95% of the children get treated. It concerns me greatly that a given child if born in Sheffield has a 75% chance of being dead: that same child born in Baltimore . . . has a 95% chance of being alive. And yet this is a decision made by the parents on the advice of either Dr. Lorber or myself. That's scary.

Obviously Freeman is right to say that the doctor cannot simply slough off responsibility on to the parents. The information and advice provided by the doctor is all the parents have to go on, and it would take an unusually strong-willed couple to go against medical advice. But as we have seen, Lorber is prepared to defend his criteria and thus to shoulder the responsibility for the advice he gives. Why does Freeman give such different advice?

One reason seems to be a degree of scepticism about the possibility of assessing the quality of another person's life. At a symposium in Montreal in 1976 Freeman shared the platform with Lorber, and said:

> One of the questions to which this symposium should direct its attention is: do we have any right or any ability to assess the quality of life for another? . . . The child growing up with a disability or handicap has a far different perception of his quality of life than an adult who suddenly becomes disabled or handicapped. Do we even have the ability to project ourselves into such a child's situation?

One might, of course, question whether this form of assessment is so difficult. Is it really impossible for someone like Lorber, with his vast experience of people with spina bifida, to say that the lives of the worst affected are so full of pain and disease, and so lacking in the redeeming aspects of human existence, that they are not worth living? But let us put this question aside for the moment, so that we can ask what would follow from this scepticism if it were justified. It does not take us very far. Freeman appears to think that if we cannot know that a baby's life will be miserable, we should do what we can to keep that baby alive. If we are truly ignorant of what a severely handicapped baby's life will be like, however, its quality of life gives us no reason either to treat it or not to treat it. If we cannot assess the life at all, it might be wonderful or it might be awful; we have no way of telling. Therefore the decision would have to be based on other factors. Lorber might then refer to the effect on the family of bringing up a severely handicapped child; or he might appeal to the need to make the most effective possible use of scarce medical resources. These factors might still point to selection on the basis of Lorber's criteria, despite the fact that the child's quality of life has dropped out of consideration. Freeman, of course, might have other reasons for treating more children than Lorber would treat . . . but we do not need to continue this imaginary debate. The point is simply that scepticism about our ability to assess other lives does not, in itself, point either to treatment or to non-treatment.

Freeman has another reason for rejecting Lorber's criteria. Pointing out that the IQs of those Lorber does not treat are similar to the IQs of those he does treat, and that both groups have a similar incidence of incontinence and hydrocephalus, Freeman asks: 'is the increased incidence of life in a wheelchair worse than death? This would appear to be his message. Would any of you rather be dead than in a wheelchair?'

This last question sits badly with Freeman's previous remarks about the general difficulty of making assessments about others, and the differences between a child growing up with a disability and a suddenly disabled adult. But that is not the only ground on which we should reject the question. All of us know that we are beings who have been alive for some time in the past and will, if all goes well, be alive for some time in the future. We have future-orientated goals and purposes. These provide us with reasons—maybe not the only reasons, but important ones—for wishing to continue to live. Confinement to a wheelchair would interfere with our ability to achieve our goals, but it would not—unless we were unusually fixated on, say, running—prevent us fulfilling at least *some* of them. Death, of course, would prevent us accomplishing *any* of our future aims. That is at least part of the explanation why *we* would rather be in a wheelchair than dead. It is clearly a consideration that is irrelevant to the selection of new-born infants, who lack any conception of themselves as beings with a future.

Freeman's question about life in a wheelchair invites a further question: is it correct to pose death as the alternative with which such a life is to be compared? Several comments quoted earlier in this chapter suggest a different comparison. Ian Wickes, in his letter to the *British Medical Journal* criticizing Zachary's article, referred to the parents having 'a healthy replacement'. Dr Haas seemed to have the same idea in mind when, in his letter in the same journal, he wrote that in the majority of cases, if the child with spina bifida survives, the strain on the family will be such that the mother 'will forego her chances of having further normal children'. Eliot Slater, from whose article we quoted in our discussion of the amount of hospitalization required by spina bifida children, has contrasted the 'long, long course of suffering' for the baby and the family, if the severely handicapped child's life is preserved, with the alternative if the baby dies soon:

At this stage the loss to the family in the death of the child is one which can normally be repaired within about a year. Given an abnormal child, parents will very likely limit their further reproduction; if the child is lost, they will have another one, and this time (in all probability) the child will be normal. We should compare the difference in the lot of the family with a disabled child and that of the family with a normal child. Keeping a badly damaged child alive is likely to eliminate the potential existence of a normal one.

John Lorber also takes this into account in assessing the total impact of the severely handicapped child upon the family: 'because severely affected infants were "saved", many more potentially normal lives never started because their parents did not dare to have other children.'

Should we, in the light of these comments, perhaps be comparing life in a wheelchair, not with death, but with the life of one of these normal children whom the mother would have been able to have if the child with spina bifida had died? To some this question will seem bizarre: how can one compare an existing life with a merely potential life, a life that has not even been started? Does anyone really think that we can make up for the death of one child by giving birth to another? Yet to others—and not only doctors—the question (which we shall discuss in greater detail in Chapter 7) makes sense, and the answer is affirmative. For instance, a grandmother wrote to Prospect, a British support-group for the parents of severely disabled children: 'Had the poor little mongol been allowed to die, as he so easily could, my daughter might have had one or two healthy children in his place—giving more life, not less.'

Consider, too, what happens when a defect is diagnosed not immediately after birth, as in the cases we have been discussing, but some months before birth, as often happens with modern techniques for detecting abnormalities during pregnancy. Spina bifida can be diagnosed during pregnancy, by measuring the amount of a substance called alpha-fetoprotein in the amniotic fluid—the fluid surrounding the foetus in the womb. This fluid can be drawn out through a hollow needle, using a technique known as amniocentesis. Amniocentesis is not totally without risk to the foetus, however, and so is only recommended when there is a higher than normal risk that the foetus may be defective—for instance, if the woman has previously given birth to a child with spina bifida. (Such women have a roughly 7 per cent chance that their next child will have a similar defect.) If the test reveals that the pregnant woman is indeed carrying a foetus with spina bifida, she is offered an abortion. In considering this offer, what question should the woman be asking? Should she be asking whether it is better for the foetus to die than to live to become a child in a wheelchair? Or should she be asking whether it would be better for this foetus to die so that she can then become pregnant again, with at least a 90 per cent chance of having a normal child?

In these circumstances, almost all pregnant women decide on an abortion. They make this decision, not only when the defect diagnosed is spina bifida, but also when the defect is a less disabling one, such as haemophilia. It is hard to imagine anyone considering death to be preferable to life with haemophilia; yet women who carry the haemophilia gene are routinely tested during pregnancy and, if the tests are positive, routinely avail themselves of the opportunity to terminate the pregnancy and try again.

We are not, at this stage in our discussion, concerned to say whether these women make the right decisions; we mention their choices only to point out that here, when we are dealing with a foetus rather than an infant, most of us do not ask the questions Dr Freeman asked. We do not ask if we would rather be dead than have the kind of life we can expect that foetus to have; we are much more likely to compare the life-prospects of the foetus with those of the normal child we would hope to conceive after the termination of the existing pregnancy. Why, then, should we not make a similar comparison when deciding whether or not to treat the infant whose problem was not diagnosed until after birth?

Here we are raising a host of complex issues, including such perplexing matters as whether one can ever regard one human being as in some sense a 'replacement' for another. These issues are undoubtedly relevant to the moral decisions about selective treatment with which we are concerned, and we will not, in the end, be able to avoid confronting them; for the moment, however, we will leave them, and the issue of criteria for selection, to one side. Instead we shall switch our attention to the other major debate about how selective treatment should be handled. As it happens, this debate relates to one relatively straightforward difference between abortion and selective treatment, the difference between the fate of the foetus and the fate of the untreated infant.

What happens to the untreated?

When a woman carrying a defective foetus is offered an abortion, she knows that the consequence of her accepting the offer will be the rapid and certain death of the foetus. Whether this death is also painless is controversial—the age at which a foetus is likely to be able to feel pain has been variously placed by different authorities at between nine and thirty-two weeks, and in any case the pain felt would depend on the techniques used to perform the abortion. But with the most commonly used abortion procedures, the foetus dies in a matter of seconds.

The deaths of spina bifida infants not selected for treatment do not occur so quickly. This is something which has particularly concerned Freeman, and his concern may be another factor in the differences between the advice he and Lorber give to parents. At the conference in Montreal he produced a table on how long spina bifida infants selected for non-treatment lived. Results from four different groups of doctors were charted separately. The table showed that while most untreated infants died within three months, between 10 and 20 per cent of the untreated children were still alive at one to two years—'waiting patiently', as Freeman put it. Only Lorber's patients, Freeman noted, died earlier. They were all dead within nine months.

Even the nine months it takes some of Lorber's patients to die is a long time for the family and for the child. The prospect of a child surviving, untreated, for a long time is not a pleasant one. Freeman is well aware of what long-term survival can mean. In an article in *Pediatrics* in 1974, he described one such case:

An 8-year-old white boy was recently brought to the Birth Defects Treatment Center for recommendations about future care. He was the third child of middle class parents and was born and treated elsewhere. At birth he was found to have a large meningomyelocele with a neurologic deficit below T_{12}. [This means he was one of the more severely affected spina bifida infants.] The parents were told that he would die. He was given routine care, did not develop meningitis, and remained at the hospital until 5½ months of age when he was transferred to a state institution for chronic care. At 10 months of age, because of progressive enlargement of his head which made nursing care difficult, he was transferred to another hospital where a ventriculoatrial shunt was placed [i.e., a drainage tube with Holter-type valve] and the back was repaired. The child was returned to the state institution.

By 2½ years he was using two word sentences, but was found to have cortical blindness. Over the next several years he had multiple orthopedic procedures, including replacement of dislocated hips, tendon achilles lengthening, osteotomies and repair of fractures. He was always returned to the institution. At 6 years of age he was found to have severe hydronephrosis [literally, 'water on the kidneys'—a kidney disease] and an ileal loop was performed [an operation to divert the urinary passage so that it emerges from the side of the body, where urine can be collected in a bag].

At 8 years of age he is in a school for the blind and has an IQ of 80. He goes home to his parents on weekends, but they have established little rapport with him. It is difficult for him to sit because of the marked paralytic kyphosis [spinal deformity] which also interferes with the ileal stoma [the opening for the urinary passage] so that a collecting device cannot be kept in place. His hips have redislocated; the hydronephrosis is of moderate degree. The family is receiving psychiatric help to cope with this child when he is at home.

After describing this tragic situation, Freeman adds his own comment:

If the goal of the original non-treatment was the death of the child, the child should be considered a non-treatment failure. If the goal of the original physician had been total care, the child would still have been paraplegic, but possibly with a normal IQ, with vision, without hydronephrosis, and quite possibly with a family which could have developed an emotional relationship to him.

Admittedly, this boy did not receive 'non-treatment' in Lorber's sense of that term. For instance, when his head began to swell with hydrocephalus to such an extent that nursing became difficult, the hydrocephalus was drained to relieve the pressure of fluid building up in the brain. Lorber has said:

It is essential, once the decision not to operate has been reached, that nothing should be done which might prolong the infant's survival . . . The greatest temptation for the surgeon is to operate on the hydro-cephalus if the infant's head is growing rapidly. Such a temptation must be resisted, because progressive hydrocephalus is an important cause of early death. Once an operation is performed a succession of others is bound to follow. The end result is worse than either total treatment from the beginning or no treatment at all.

This is, of course, exactly what happened in the case Freeman described; but while Lorber might consider it inconsistent with 'non-treatment', others do not. For instance Anthony Raimondi, an American paediatrician who selects some spina bifida infants for non-treatment, has offered this version of what the term means:

Non-treatment does not mean that we leave the back open, that we allow the head to attain its ultimate size, that we allow eschars [an area without skin] to develop, and that we allow the child to die of fluid deprivation. Non-treatment means we repair the back, of course, as we would repair any open wound. Sometimes, in non-treatment, we would shunt the child for nursing care, so that the head does not get exorbitant in size and the skin does not break down over the scalp.

Given this definition of 'non-treatment', it is only to be expected that—odd as it may sound—patients not being treated by Raimondi will survive much longer than patients not being treated by Lorber. But what are the limits of non-treatment? In an article written in 1977, long after the split in the Sheffield team, Zachary reminded his readers that in the days before any spina bifida babies were operated on, some of them still survived, their open wounds healing naturally under the protection of a simple dressing. 'How is it then', Zachary asked pointedly, 'that those who write about the value of selection can point to a high mortality, usually 100 per cent, in those that they have selected out?' Zachary answered his own question:

these babies are receiving 60 mg./kg. body weight of chloral hydrate, not once but four times a day. This is eight times the sedative dose of chloral hydrate recommended in the most recent volume of *Nelson's Paediatrics* . . . No wonder these babies are sleepy and demand no feed, and with this regimen most of them will die within a few weeks, many within the first week.

On a BBC programme with Ian Kennedy—who was later to give the Reith Lectures on 'The Unmasking of Medicine'—Lorber was closely questioned on this point. He rejected Zachary's claim that the dosages were excessive, stating that they were within the range of pharmaceutical recommendations, except very, very occasionally, when higher doses were necessary for pain relief. Kennedy then asked Lorber if it was not the case that he wanted those babies not selected for treatment to die. Lorber replied: 'The principal objective of selective treatment for those who are not treated [is] that their life should not be prolonged, which is a different matter from saying that their life should be shortened.' Kennedy pressed on, referring to reports by other doctors that Lorber's untreated patients all do die, whereas theirs do not. Lorber said that the longest survivor of his untreated patients lived about two and a half years, which was what one might expect, given that the most severely affected babies with spina bifida were being selected for non-treatment rather than the whole spina bifida population. Kennedy then concluded this section of the discussion by remarking:

Clearly, all is not well. For example, chloral hydrate isn't listed in Martindale, the standard work on drugs, as an analgesic, yet Dr. Lorber justifies his use of it as being to ease pain. Sedatives, of course, relieve pain because the baby will sleep, but, unlike analgesics, they will by inducing sleep also cause the baby not to demand food.

John Freeman was interviewed on the same programme and said of Lorber that 'many physicians will accept his criteria and his statements that these children die quickly [but these physicians] don't know the tricks and therefore they care for a child and wait for it to die quickly and a good percentage of the children don't die and certainly don't die quickly.' Kennedy pressed Freeman on what he meant by 'tricks'. Freeman said that the choice of word may have been bad, but then added: 'the fact that sedation and analgesics are used, the fact that children are fed on demand in England is quite different than what is done in the United States.'

We can now make an educated guess about why Lorber and Freeman give such different advice to the parents of spina bifida babies. Their differing assessments of the worth of life in a wheelchair may be part of the story, but we doubt that it is the whole story. We suspect that the other element is the much greater confidence Lorber can have—given the English practice of using sedation—that the untreated babies will all die within a reasonably short period of time. In the United States, where the use of sedatives and demand feeding would be an unusual and perhaps—for the doctor—risky procedure, Freeman can have no such confidence. He is well aware of the risk that an untreated child will survive to be like the eight-year-old boy he has described. This must be a powerful factor in leading Freeman to advise treatment in cases where it is not clear that, without treatment, the child will die soon. Similarly, the fact that Freeman is unable to assure parents that their child will die if untreated must put immense pressure on them to give their consent to active treatment.

We speculate that it is the risk of legal proceedings, and not any ethical objections, that constrains Freeman against adopting Lorber's method of managing the untreated infants. The basis for this speculation is that Freeman has himself argued forcefully for legal changes to allow doctors to take more direct steps to end the lives of babies who are being allowed to die. In an article entitled 'Is There a Right to Die—Quickly?' he wrote:

Having seen children with unoperated meningomyeloceles [severe spina bifida] lie around the ward for weeks or months untreated, waiting to die, one cannot help but feel that the highest form of medical ethic would have been to end the pain and suffering, rather than wishing that the patient would go away.

It is time that society and medicine stopped perpetuating the fiction that withholding treatment is ethically different from terminating life. It is time that society began to discuss mechanisms by which we can alleviate the pain and suffering for those individuals whom we cannot help.

Is Freeman right to reject the belief that not treating someone is ethically different from ending that person's life? If he is, many spina bifida infants could be saved from a slow, lingering death; and doctors and parents would not have to make the agonizing choice between active treatment, with possible lifelong misery, and non-treatment with the possibility of long-term survival in an even worse state. The choice would then be much more like that faced by the couple who discover during pregnancy that their child has spina bifida. As in that situation now, if the parents did not think the child should live, they would be in a position to choose swift and certain death.

These are large issues, with ramifications that go well beyond spina bifida. They obviously affect, for instance, the management of Down's syndrome infants as well. If Freeman is right, then whatever we think of the decision not to treat Baby Doe, once that decision had been made there was no ethical justification for allowing the baby to starve to death over six days. But if it is permitted to take direct steps to end life, then it is not only Down's syndrome babies with life-threatening defects such as intestinal blockages whose lives are put in question. The existence of this defect is relevant only because it makes it possible to ensure that the baby dies by doing no more than withholding treatment; if a lethal injection is allowed in this case, why not in the case of a Down's syndrome baby with no other defect? Clearly we need to take a close look at the distinction between withholding treatment and killing.

4 KILLING AND LETTING DIE

The issue

One of the first widely publicized cases of an abnormal infant deliberately being allowed to die is 'The Johns Hopkins Case', so named after the Johns Hopkins Hospital in Baltimore, where the events took place. In many respects the case is similar to that of Baby Doe: the infant had Down's syndrome and a blockage in its digestive system. The blockage could have been removed by surgery, but the mother, who was a nurse, refused to consent to the operation. The father accepted this decision, taking the view that his wife was more knowledgeable about such cases than he was. The baby was therefore left untreated. It could not digest food taken through its mouth, and no attempt was made to feed it by any other method. In contrast to the Baby Doe case, neither the doctors nor the hospital made any attempt to take the parents' decision before a court. A further contrast with the Baby Doe case is that the baby took much longer to die: fifteen days.

A dramatized version of these events was made into a film entitled *Who Should Survive?*, produced by the Joseph P. Kennedy Foundation in Washington, DC. At Monash University, we show the film to students taking an undergraduate philosophy course on 'Contemporary Moral Issues'. The film shows how, after the parents have made their decision, the baby is placed in a side room with a sign on its cot: NOTHING BY MOUTH. Nurses are shown rocking a crying baby, trying to comfort it. The film discusses how difficult it was for the nursing staff to be unable to do anything but watch the baby wither away from dehydration and hunger. The film also shows the doctor talking on the phone to the baby's father, who called daily to find out 'how things were going'. To this the doctor can say nothing, except that everything is happening as one would expect, just a little slowly.

Not surprisingly, students find the film disturbing. Most of them believe that what they have seen should not have happened. Less predictably, however, of this large majority who think that these events should not have taken place, by no means all disagree with the parents' decision to refuse permission for the operation. What many of them find objectionable is not the decision that a Down's syndrome baby should not be kept alive; it is to the manner in which that decision was implemented that they object. They are horrified that death should have been a fifteen-day ordeal for the nurses, the doctors, the family, and most important, for the baby. 'If the doctors were not going to challenge the refusal of permission to operate,' a student will often ask, 'why couldn't they do something to end the baby's suffering sooner?'

That is the question we shall examine in this chapter. As in the Johns Hopkins case, the Baby Doe case, and the case of spina bifida infants who have been judged too severely affected to warrant treatment, the question arises only after the crucial decision not to provide life-prolonging treatment has been made. We make no assumption, at this stage, about *when* we are justified in making this crucial decision. In particular, we have said nothing about whether it is a defensible decision in the case of Down's syndrome infants with digestive system blockages. Yet since almost everyone—even, as we saw in Chapter 2, President Reagan's Surgeon General, Dr C. Everett Koop—believes that it is *sometimes* right not to attempt to prolong life, the question arises for almost every doctor treating newborn infants: given that the baby's life will not be prolonged, would it not be kinder—and ethically preferable—to kill it?

In asking this question we are, of course, aware that any doctor administering a lethal injection to an infant would risk a murder charge. This may also be true, however, of a doctor who deliberately allows an infant to die—most legal systems recognize that there can be murder by omission as well as murder by action. The law is, however, too complex for us to discuss here. Nor do we need to discuss it, for we are not asking what any individual doctor, working within a particular legal system, should do. We are asking a more fundamental question: when other things are equal, is there a morally significant difference between allowing a baby to die, and killing that baby? In asking this question we do not need to take account of the law. It is, if anything, the other way round: if we were to discuss what the law in this area ought to be, then we would need to ask whether there is a morally significant difference between killing and allowing to die. The moral issue comes first; only when it has been answered can we assess the law and see if it should be reformed.

The medical mainstream

The feasibility and desirability of treatment of a grossly handicapped infant, especially in the neonatal period, is one of the most difficult decisions in paediatrics . . . For centuries the mainstream of medical opinion has abhorred the extremes and has trod the middle path. This was expressed in classical form by the nineteenth-century English poet Arthur Clough (1819–61):

> Thou shalt not kill; but need'st not strive
> Officiously to keep alive.

So wrote G. Keys Smith and E. Durham Smith in their 1973 article in the *British Medical Journal*, reporting on selective treatment for spina bifida at the Royal Children's Hospital in Melbourne. The lines they quote from Clough are often quoted by doctors discussing the difference between killing a patient and allowing that patient to die. In the last chapter we saw that they were referred to with approval by Haas in his contribution to the debate triggered off in *The Lancet* by Zachary's article on the treatment of spina bifida: 'The old dictum we were taught as medical students' is how Haas described them, and this is probably how most doctors think of Clough's couplet. Ironically, it is the very opposite of how Clough himself thought of his most quoted lines. They come from a poem called 'The Latest Decalogue'. Here are the opening lines:

> Thou shalt have one god only; who
> Would be at the expense of two?
> No graven images may be
> Worshipped, except the currency.

As these lines make clear, the poem is a bitingly satirical attack on those who profess to respect the Ten Commandments, but in fact betray their spirit at every point. For Clough the idea that it is all right to allow people to die, as long as one does not actually kill them, is just this sort of betrayal of the spirit of the commandment.

For anyone with an inclination for historical detective work, it would be fascinating to find out just how Clough's satirical lines were transformed into an 'old dictum' taught to medical students, and even into the 'classical form' of the mainstream of medical opinion. We must, however, confine ourselves to more urgent tasks: to show that the author of these oft-quoted lines did not share the views of those who now quote them, is not to refute the view in support of which they are being quoted. Clough, it may now be said, was simply unable to see the valid point behind the attitude he was satirizing. Certainly the attitude is now widely held, especially amongst doctors. In our survey of nearly 200 obstetricians and paediatricians in Victoria, all but two agreed that in some circumstances it was proper to decide against using all available means to keep an infant alive; yet only 31 per cent of obstetricians and 40 per cent of paediatricians were prepared to accept that active euthanasia could ever be justified. In other words 99 per cent of doctors were ready to allow an infant to die, but of these more than 60 per cent were not ready to kill it.

An American survey in 1975 of 457 paediatricians and paediatric surgeons produced even stronger support for the distinction. In this survey, referred to by Dr C. Everett Koop in his testimony before Judge Gerhard Gesell, the doctors were asked to imagine that the parents of a Down's syndrome baby with a blockage had refused consent to surgery, and that they—the doctors—had decided to accept this decision. Would they then stop all supportive treatment, such as tube feedings? Would they terminate the infant's life by an injection of drugs such as morphine? A large majority of the doctors replied that they would stop all supportive treatment, but only six doctors said that they were prepared to give a lethal injection. Admittedly, these results have to be treated with caution. More than a third of those who sent back the questionnaires did not answer this question; it is possible that they were reluctant to put on paper their readiness to break the law. Moreover, a few who said that they were not prepared to kill nevertheless added comments describing this course as 'most humane but illegal' or 'what I would prefer to do but it is illegal under present laws'. These comments make it clear that the doctors were indicating what they would actually do in the present situation, not what they thought ought to be done in an ideal situation. Nevertheless, the survey suggests that in America, as in Australia, most doctors distinguish between allowing to die and killing.

Medical associations support doctors in these views. The American Medical Association, as we have seen, condemns mercy killing as 'contrary to that for which the medical profession stands', but under certain circumstances accepts 'the cessation of the employment of extraordinary means to prolong the life of the body'—in other words, allowing the patient to die. The Australian Medical Association, in a submission to the Law Reform Commission of Western Australia in 1982, has said: 'Surely when it is deemed to be in the best interests of the child that its life should not be prolonged, the ability to refuse to prolong its life should exist.' The submission then went on to admit that on moral or philosophical lines it was extremely difficult to draw a line between actively killing and passively allowing someone to die; nevertheless, the submission said, 'doctors felt the distinction very strongly'.

In the final section of the last chapter, we saw some of the consequences of these attitudes for those spina bifida infants who are not selected for treatment. One consequence already noted is that many babies take a long time to die. Another consequence is that the final outcome—life or death—is often determined not by any rational assessment of the severity of the infant's handicap, but by chance factors, such as whether the infant happens to contract an infection in its first few days of life. This chance element is especially apparent when Down's syndrome infants with simple intestinal blockages are allowed to die, while those without such blockages live. The blockage has nothing to do with the severity of the mental handicap. It ought therefore to be quite irrelevant to the question of whether an infant born with that particular handicap should live or die. Yet because it allows parents the option of refusing consent to an operation, it can be the determining factor in this life or death choice. The accidental presence of the blockage means that parents can choose to let the infant die, whereas if the baby did not need surgery they would not be able to choose to kill it.

An even more striking illustration of the role played by 'accident' comes from the treatment of Andrew Stinson, an extremely premature and marginally viable baby born to Peggy Stinson, a Pennsylvania teacher, in December 1977. Despite a firm statement by Peggy and her husband that they wanted 'no heroics', Andrew was kept alive for nearly six months. Long before the end of that period, it was clear that if he survived at all he would be seriously damaged. Andrew needed a respirator to keep him breathing, but the doctors would not take him off it—to do so they regarded as wrong, presumably because it involved a deliberate human act. As Peggy Stinson put it in her journal:

I shouldn't say they 'took him off'—they couldn't do that, since that would be immoral and illegal. They had to hope for an appropriate accident; once Andrew became accidentally detached from the respirator and had breathed for a couple of minutes, they could declare him 'off' and *omit* to put him back on while they wait for his inadequate breathing to kill him. This is the moral, legal, and 'dignified' way.

Had Andrew not become accidentally detached, he might have gone on being kept alive indefinitely; but such accidental detachings occur routinely. Normally this triggers an alarm, and the re-attachment is equally routine—unless the decision has been made that it is better for the baby to die.

It is striking how far some doctors will go to ensure that infants they are 'allowing to die' actually do die—while still refusing to advocate active euthanasia. Here is a statement from Herbert Eckstein, a London paediatric surgeon, referring to a spina bifida baby that is not to be treated:

It is in my opinion quite impossible to kill off such a baby, but if surgical treatment is withheld then it is only reasonable to withhold other forms of treatment such as antibiotics, oxygen, and tube feeding . . . In our experience to date all children with myelomeningocele who were refused surgical treatment have died within a month and if a baby is not to be treated then the surgeons and nursing staff should do nothing to prolong life.

John Lorber takes a similar stance. As we have seen, he has stressed that once the decision not to operate has been reached, 'nothing should be done which might prolong the infant's survival'. Lorber makes no secret of the fact that the object of non-treatment is 'not to avoid treating those who would die early in spite of treatment, but to avoid treating those who would survive with severe|handicaps'. In the light of this statement, it is obvious that non-treatment has failed in its object if the patient survives. To say the same thing in positive terms: the object of non-treatment is that the patient should die. Moreover Lorber acknowledges, as any humane person would: 'It is painful to see such infants gradually fading away over a number of weeks or months, when everybody hopes for a speedy end.' Indeed, we have already seen that some doctors think Lorber's use of the sedative chloral hydrate goes a long way towards ensuring that everybody's hopes are fulfilled. Nevertheless Lorber says: 'I strongly disagree with active euthanasia.' We must now examine the reasons why Lorber, Eckstein, and so many other doctors hold this view.

'Letting nature take its course'

Apart from the celebrated 'old dictum' of Arthur Clough, the most oft-recurring refrain in this debate is that allowing patients to die is different from killing because the doctor who allows a patient to die is merely 'letting Nature take its course'. We saw Dr Ian Wickes, in his contribution to the debate over Zachary's *Lancet* article, suggest that 'to let Nature take its course' is a middle way between treating all spina bifida infants and killing some of them. In the same debate Dr Haas was thinking along similar lines when he said that 'Nature if left alone will always correct its own mistakes in these cases.' John Lorber has said that selective non-treatment is 'another name for letting nature take its course.' Dr Vincent Collins, writing in the *Journal of the American Medical Association* on 'Limits of Medical Responsibility in Prolonging Life', offered this characterization of the distinction between killing and allowing to die:

In [euthanasia] one directly causes life to end, whereas by discontinuing therapy one permits death to occur by omitting an act and permitting nature to take its course . . . When one permits death by not continuing therapy, the harm that is done is done by nature acting.

In his book *The Patient as a Person*, the Protestant theologian Paul Ramsey puts it this way:

In omission no human agent causes the patient's death, directly or indirectly. He dies his own death from causes that it is no longer merciful or reasonable to fight by possible medical intervention.

The thrust of all these comments is that if we kill, we are responsible for the resulting death; if, however, a doctor allows a patient to die, it is nature that is responsible. This is a slightly odd suggestion for medical practitioners to make, since medicine is largely an attempt to prevent nature taking its course. Nevertheless, the suggestion needs closer scrutiny. First we need to distinguish two possible interpretations. Is the suggestion that when death results from an omission the doctor is not *causally* responsible for the death? Or is it that the doctor is not *morally* responsible for the death? To be sure that we have covered the point of the appeal to nature, we must deal with both these possibilities.

The first possibility is that when we allow someone to die, we are not causally responsible for the death. Suppose we are dealing with a severe case of spina bifida, one that we have decided not to treat. The baby develops an infection. We have antibiotics at hand which we know could cure the infection, but because this baby is not being treated, we do not give antibiotics. As we expected, the infection worsens and the baby dies. Can we say that because the baby died of an infection, we did not cause the baby's death? Is this simply 'death from natural causes'?

This approach relies on an intuitive sense of 'cause' which further thought shows is indefensible for two reasons. First, it is unable to tell us which omissions merely permit nature to act, and which go beyond this; for presumably those who take this approach will not describe *all* deaths resulting from omissions in this way. They would not want to say that Dr Leonard Arthur was merely permitting nature to take its course when he wrote 'Parents do not wish baby to survive. Nursing care only' on the medical record of John Pearson—who was, remember, a Down's syndrome baby with no other apparent abnormalities. Obviously, if starving to death were merely allowing nature to take its course, there would be an easy way for the parents of any unwanted infant to ensure that it died without their having caused its death. On the other hand, if death by starvation were not death by 'natural causes', would those who take his approach want to invoke 'natural causes' in a case of death by an infection that is as preventable as starvation?

The second objection to the view we are considering is that there is no satisfactory account of what it is to 'cause' something, according to which deaths by omission are caused by 'nature' rather than by the person who omitted to act. As the Oxford legal philosophers H. L. A. Hart and A. M. Honoré have pointed out in their influential book *Causation and the Law*, we often regard a human omission as the cause of something which, from a different perspective, may seem very much an act of nature:

the cause of a great famine in India may be identified by the Indian peasant as the drought, but the World Food Authority may identify the Indian Government's failure to build up reserves as the cause and the drought as a mere condition.

Here we can see the philosophical naivety of the idea that nature, rather than a deliberate human omission, causes the death of the untreated baby who develops an infection. John Stuart Mill pointed out long ago that the cause of an event is 'philosophically speaking . . . the sum total of the conditions positive and negative taken together'. By 'conditions positive and negative' he means both those that had to exist, and those that had to *not* exist, for the event to occur. Thus the cause of a guest being burnt to death in a hotel fire might be that there was an electrical short circuit *and* that there was inflammable material nearby *and* that there was no sprinkler system *and* that the fire alarm had not been serviced for three years and so did not go off . . . The list could be extended indefinitely, because there would have been no deaths if the hotel had been empty, or if it had never been built in the first place, and so on. There is really no such thing as 'the cause' in the sense of one condition or event which has some objective claim to being the single determining factor. It is only against a background of our particular interest in questions such as how an event could have been prevented that we sometimes single out 'the cause' of an event. In the example just given we are unlikely to refer to the existence of the hotel or the presence of the guest as the cause of the death, since we take hotels and their guests for granted as part of the background. What about the electrical short circuit? Electrical engineers might well single this out as the cause of the death; they might, for instance, use this fire as a case study in electrical hazards, and on this basis suggest improvements in electrical design and safety which would eliminate such occurrences. A public inquiry into the death, on the other hand, would be more likely to focus on who is to blame. From this perspective, the short circuit may not be seen as the cause of the death, since we know that such things do happen from time to time, given the prevailing standards of electrical safety. The inquiry would probably conclude that the death was the result of the management's negligent disregard of standard precautions against fire.

This example shows how the notion of a single event being 'the cause' swiftly breaks down, once we give our attention to a particular consequence and the different reasons why we might be interested in it. Suppose that we are interested in why a baby died. We may be told that the baby contracted pneumonia and died of 'natural causes'. But if we know that many other babies in the same hospital also contracted pneumonia and did not die from it, this answer should not satisfy us. We are interested in why *this* baby died, and a condition which also applies to many other babies who did not die cannot answer our inquiry. So we press the point, and are told that the other babies were given antibiotics which enabled them to overcome the pneumonia; this baby, on the other hand, was a Down's syndrome child, had been rejected by its parents, and so was not given antibiotics. Now we know what differentiates this baby with pneumonia from the other babies with pneumonia: this one was not given antibiotics. Since antibiotics could have cured the pneumonia, the doctor's omission is the causal factor that made the difference between this baby living or dying. Hence we can appropriately describe the doctor's failure to treat the pneumonia as the cause of death.

So it cannot be said that when a doctor refrains from treating a patient, the patient's death is caused by 'nature' rather than by the doctor. Both the illness and the omission are part of 'the sum total of the conditions positive and negative taken together' which is the full causal account of the death. We can properly single out any one of a number of these conditions as *the* cause, depending on our particular interests in the matter.

Let us try the other possible interpretation of the remarks by Vincent Collins, Paul Ramsey, and the other writers we quoted earlier: could it be that when death comes as a result of an omission rather than an action, no one is *morally* responsible for the death, because it is only 'nature taking its course'?

This is even less plausible than the previous claim, especially in the medical setting, where the doctor has a clear moral responsibility for the care of the patient. Of course, we are not morally responsible for all our omissions. If I am standing on the beach while someone drowns in the surf fifty metres away, I will not be morally responsible for the death if, concentrating on a game of beach cricket, I fail to notice the person signalling for help. Even if I did notice the signal, but was unable to help because I cannot swim a stroke and there was no one else who could be summoned in time, I will not be responsible. If, however, I noticed the signal and could easily have carried out the rescue, but refrained from doing so because I didn't wish to interrupt my sunbathing, I bear considerable moral responsibility for the death. If I happen also to be a lifeguard and was on duty at the time, my moral responsibility for refraining from rescuing the drowning person is greater still. Moral responsibility arises only when we have some control over our actions in a situation, and it is strengthened when we have a specific duty that is relevant to what is happening.

When John Lorber and Herbert Eckstein leave infants to die of pneumonia without giving antibiotics, they are not like the person who did not notice that there was someone drowning nearby. They are well aware of the condition of the infants and its likely lethal nature. Nor are they like the person who notices the victim but is unable to help. They have at their disposal powerful drugs which in almost all cases will effect a cure. They are not even like the ordinary sunbather; they are more like the lifeguard—not, of course, in respect of their motives, but in respect of the degree of moral responsibility they bear. Just as lifeguards have a well-recognized duty towards swimmers, so doctors have a well-recognized duty towards their patients. Doctors who deliberately leave a baby to die when they have the awareness, the ability, and the opportunity to save the baby's life, are just as morally responsible for the death as they would be if they had brought it about by a deliberate, positive action. This does not mean, of course, that it is necessarily wrong for doctors to leave a baby to die: it means only that the responsibility for doing so cannot be evaded by saying that the harm is done by 'nature acting'. The responsibility for the baby's death is the doctor's, and it is one which must be squarely faced.

The doctrine of double effect

At this point we briefly mention another view, sometimes confused with the distinction between killing and letting die: the 'doctrine of double effect'. This doctrine is regarded as important by Roman Catholic theologians and moralists, and a considerable literature has been built up around it. We shall not probe the intricacies of this doctrine. We refer to it only in order to show that, whatever its merits, it is not relevant to the decisions made by doctors like Lorber and Eckstein.

The doctrine of double effect relies on a distinction between what we directly intend to do, and what we merely foresee will result from our act. Thus, in a classic application of the doctrine, Roman Catholic theologians have permitted doctors to remove a cancerous womb from a pregnant woman. The doctor foresees, of course, that the foetus will die as a result of the operation. Nevertheless the doctor does not directly intend the death of the foetus. The direct intention is to save the woman's life. If there were a way of doing this which allowed the foetus to live, the doctor would take that way. Unfortunately there is not. Hence the death of the foetus is an unwanted side-effect of a laudable intention, and the doctor is not regarded as killing the foetus.

It is easy to see that this doctrine will give rise to some very fine distinctions, especially when it is coupled—as it is in Roman Catholic moral theology—with the view that the end does not justify the means. For instance, a case which seems very similar to the one just described is that in which the head of the foetus has, during delivery, become lodged in the vaginal passage. If all attempts to dislodge it are unavailing—not likely nowadays, but it did happen when medical techniques were less sophisticated—

the only way to save the life of the woman is to insert an instrument which will crush the skull of the foetus. The outcome is then the same as in the case of the cancerous womb. The foetus dies, but the woman lives. Despite the similarity of results, Roman Catholic theologians did not, and still would not, permit doctors to perform this operation. To carry it out, they said, the doctors had to form the direct intention to crush the skull of the foetus, which is of course equivalent to killing it. Even though the motive of the action was the same as in the previous case, the death of the foetus was here not an unwanted side-effect, but the directly intended means to the desired end. As such, it was the direct killing of an innocent human being and absolutely prohibited.

The difficulty of seeing much moral significance in the distinction between these two cases has led many people to reject the doctrine of double effect—and we would, if it were necessary for us to take a stand on the question, reject it for this and other reasons. For our present purposes, however, it is only necesary for us to point out that when, say, John Lorber selects a patient for non-treatment, he does directly intend the death of that patient. To quote him again: 'The main object of selection is . . . to avoid treating those who would survive with handicaps.' Recall, too, Lorber's instruction that the temptation to operate on the hydrocephalus must be resisted 'because progressive hydro-cephalus is an important cause of early death'. Clearly Lorber does intend the death of those patients he selects for non-treatment—otherwise selection would not reduce the number who survive with handicaps, and might even—as Freeman's case of the surviving untreated boy suggests—increase the handicaps these patients will have. There is no sense in which these deaths are mere 'unwanted side-effects' of a course of action pursued for some other, more vital goal.

As we can see from Lorber's statements, the fact that a death occurs as a result of an omission rather than as the result of an action has nothing to do with the doctor's intention. One can intend to cause a death by an omission, just as one can intend to cause a death by an action. Whatever its merits, the doctrine of double effect is quite separate from the claim that we are not responsible for the results of our omissions.

The Lorber–Harris debate

We have used John Lorber as a standard example of a doctor who selects some severely handicapped infants for an early death. We have done this not because we believe his practice is unusual, but because he has written so explicitly about what he is doing. We have also mentioned that he is opposed to active euthanasia. Since we have quoted so frequently from his writings, it is only fitting to give his reasons for this opposition.

Lorber raised the question of active euthanasia in his 1975 Milroy Lecture on 'Ethical Problems in the Management of Myelomeningocele and Hydrocephalus'. His objections are worth quoting at length:

It may . . . be inconsistent or hypocritical to oppose active euthanasia, yet support non-treatment, or what is often called passive euthanasia. However, active euthanasia may brutalize the persons who carry it out. It would be wrong for a doctor to order his junior or his nurses to carry out such a task if he cannot bring himself to do it.

I strongly disagree with active euthanasia, especially for babies and children, who cannot possibly ask for it or give their considered consent. It would be impossible to formulate legislation, however humane are the intentions, that could not be abused by the unscrupulous. There have been plenty of horrific examples of this in the past, especially in Hitler's Germany. Few just or compassionate persons would wish to give such a dangerous legal power to any individual or group of people.

Yet for some severely handicapped spina bifida babies or others who are equally severely handicapped it would be the most humane way to deal with a desperate situation. It is painful to see such infants gradually fading away over a number of weeks or months, when everybody hopes for a speedy end. It is this consideration of lingering death that still compels some doctors to treat, reluctantly, all babies, in spite of the suffering such a policy will entail.

Nevertheless, no treatment is not necessarily equivalent to passive euthanasia. No treatment with normal nursing care is a safeguard against wrong diagnosis and against deliberate misdiagnosis for an evil purpose. If an infant's condition is not as grave as was thought, he will live, and he can then be given optimal care if he has any handicaps.

John Harris, an English philosopher whose work has focused on moral responsibility has published a detailed critique of this passage in the *Journal of Medical Ethics*. He finds four separate arguments in it, and deals with them in turn. Lorber then replies to Harris, in the same journal. This debate gives us an unusual opportunity to see how a practising physician handles a philosopher's critique of his published views on an ethical issue. We shall follow the sequence of arguments set out by Harris, and consider Lorber's reply to each point.

The argument from brutalization

Lorber opens his objections to active euthanasia by asserting that active euthanasia may brutalize those who carry it out. Lorber cites no evidence of this, and as Harris points out, evidence would be hard to find. So we are balancing a mere speculative possibility against the real and known pain and distress of patients, family, and medical staff. Anyway, why assume that the more humane approach is the more brutalizing? 'In the absence of any evidence,' Harris says, 'it is plausible to suppose that the responsibility of bringing about a slow and distressing death would be more rather than less brutalizing than would a quick and merciful killing.' Harris might have added that there is plenty of testimony on the harrowing effects of these slow deaths. Writing about the Johns Hopkins case with which we began this chapter, Dr Anthony Shaw has said: 'The baby's lingering death (15 days) severely demoralized the nursing and house staffs. In addition, it prolonged the agony for the parents, who called daily to find out if the baby was still alive.'

In his reply to Harris, Lorber remains unconvinced:

it would be wrong to assume . . . that active euthanasia would be less traumatic, either to parents or to professional staff who may be expected to carry this out. The killing may be quick and painless, but the aftermath of thoughts and guilt complexes in the parents and persons involved is likely to be much worse than caring for the baby in a humane way until it dies. There is no question of self-deception or hypocrisy here. Furthermore, though many parents do express a wish, when their infant is very handicapped, that the doctor should put an end to the life painlessly, this is illegal and I would strongly disagree with any suggestion that we ought to carry out an illegal act however logical it may seem to be to some.

Lorber's reference to the law is indicative of the different perspectives of philosopher and practitioner. Harris is not, as we understand him, advising doctors to flout the law. He would like to see the law changed and he is urging doctors to cease supporting a law which prevents these tragic situations being resolved in the most humane possible manner. It is important to keep these issues separate. The first and more fundamental issue is: what should the law be in this matter? This is the question Harris is discussing. The second issue is: given a law which prohibits active euthanasia, what should doctors do? Harris does not discuss this issue, which would lead us into quite different topics, into political philosophy and the obligation to obey the law. We shall not go into these topics either.

So let us consider the other aspects of Lorber's reply. It may indeed be the case that given the moral attitudes which are widely held in our society, some people would experience greater guilt if they actively killed an infant than if they allowed that infant to die. But is it true that there is no self-deception involved here? The supposition that there would be greater guilt after active killing only makes sense if the people involved believe that deliberately allowing an infant to die is somehow not morally equivalent to killing it. Perhaps they believe that it is only 'letting nature take its course'; perhaps they think there is a command-ment against killing, but no commandment to 'strive to keep alive'. Once people come to see that there is no basis for the moral distinction between killing and deliberately withholding treat-ment so that a severely handicapped infant will die, the psychological burden of guilt and remorse will surely swing the other way: it will be consoling to know that in tragic circum-stances one did the very best for all concerned by ensuring that death took place swiftly and painlessly.

Finally, we wonder if Lorber's admission that many parents do ask for active euthanasia does not undercut his assertion that the guilt complexes in the parents are likely to be worse if active euthanasia is performed. Might not the parents be the best judges of their own feelings in this matter?

Lorber adds a separate claim to this argument: 'It would be wrong for a doctor to order his junior or his nurses to carry out such a task if he cannot bring himself to do it.' With this claim Harris has no argument, but he points out that the whole issue is what, in conscience, people ought to do. The implication is that if, on reflection, we can see that active euthanasia is preferable to passive euthanasia, then doctors ought to be able to bring themselves to do it.

Lorber's comment on this follows on immediately from the last passage quoted, in which he pointed out that active euthanasia is illegal. He then said: 'Even if it were legal I should certainly never do it.' Since this statement is made without further explanation, it is presumably to be taken as a personal psychological report. As such, it explains why Lorber stresses the objection to ordering others to do what one cannot bring oneself to do; but it has no bearing on what other doctors, without the same feelings against active euthanasia, might quite properly do. The 1975 survey of American paediatric surgeons and paediatricians revealed that if it were legal at least some doctors would have preferred to carry out active euthanasia, rather than leave a baby to die.

The argument from lack of consent

Lorber said that he strongly disagreed with active euthanasia, 'especially for babies and children, who cannot possibly ask for it or give their considered consent'. This is, however, a peculiar objection for Lorber to make, for it applies equally to selective non-treatment for babies and children. As Harris says: 'selective non-treatment is intended to result in death and it does, and those who die cannot possibly ask for it or give their considered consent'.

This looks a conclusive reply. In his rejoinder Lorber admits, as he must, that 'one cannot get the consent of the baby to non-action' but he adds that equally 'one cannot get their consent for all the major operations and procedures which have been carried out on them'. This is true too, of course, and it would be a valid reply to someone who was arguing that because infants cannot give their consent, one must keep them alive no matter how severe their handicaps will be. It is not, however, a relevant response to Harris, who is arguing that if we are going to allow infants to die by deliberately not treating them, active euthanasia would be preferable. Obviously the consent of the parents is all one could have in either case—and Lorber has admitted that many parents do ask for active euthanasia for their infant. So if active euthanasia were legal, the consent of many parents would be readily forthcoming.

The 'last door' argument

Lorber had said that 'no treatment with normal nursing care' is a safeguard because 'If an infant's condition is not as grave as was thought, he will live and he can then be given optimal care if he has any handicaps.' Harris calls this 'the last door argument' —meaning that a lethal injection would close the last door on the infant's chances, whereas 'no treatment' leaves the door open. It is an argument often made against active euthanasia, for adults as well as for children.

As Harris points out, in the case of the children Lorber selects for non-treatment, the alleged safeguard is a very chancy business: 'If a child selected for non-treatment contracts an infection and dies because it is not given antibiotics, or if it requires resuscitation which is not given and it dies, there will be no opportunity to discover whether the diagnosis was wrong or not.' This is correct. Normal infants can contract infections. Before antibiotics were available, many of them died. Death from this cause is no indication of future handicap. The same can be said of many other causes from which these untreated infants die: while in the rare case of an untreated infant surviving—a very rare case among Lorber's patients—it may be possible to say that a diagnosis was wrong, in most cases of untreated infants dying it will not be possible to say that the diagnosis was right. Moreover, if infants do survive, there will also be some whose condition is every bit as grave as it was thought to be, and now even graver because of non-treatment. In the case of a child dying from an infection without being given antibiotics, the withholding of the drugs was effectively closing the last door on that infant's chance of survival. A lethal injection would have done no more.

Lorber does not respond to this criticism.

The slippery slope argument

Finally we come to Lorber's assertion that no matter how humane our intentions may be, we will find it impossible to formulate legislation that is not open to abuse. Lorber refers to Hitler's Germany as an instance of what can happen when 'such a dangerous legal power' is put in the hands of any individual or group of people. Here Lorber is advancing a 'slippery slope' argument. Once we take the first step on to the slope, so these arguments run, we shall be unable to avoid sliding all the way down the abyss; therefore no matter how innocent that first step may seem, we had better not take it.

Harris makes two points in reply. The first is a point he has made more than once: that what Lorber says of active euthanasia applies equally to Lorber's own practices. Lorber and others already have, Harris reminds us, the power to adopt a course of action that will bring about the deaths of their patients. As Harris says, 'The power is awesome but it is already exercised,' and he adds that if we fear it may be abused, the best safeguard is to bring these life and death decisions out in the open, where there can be the widest possible public debate and scrutiny. To ensure this, Harris suggests, we should legalize non-voluntary euthanasia, restricting it to patients who are clearly incapable of consenting and where death is clearly in the best interests of the patient. We could then build into the legislation whatever safeguards we wished—presumably Harris has in mind procedures like a requirement for a second opinion from a senior physician, or the approval of a hospital ethics committee, or of some other tribunal.

The only reply Lorber makes to this point is that he cannot conceive of any legislation which could draw up a list of criteria as to who should be killed for the sake of mercy and who should carry out such an act. But while it may be politically difficult to get such legislation at present, we can see no ultimate barrier to drawing it up. If there are doctors prepared to consign an infant to death from, say, hydrocephalus, we cannot see why there should not be doctors willing to give a lethal injection. As for the criteria determining who should be killed, there is no reason why legislation would have to spell this out in detail; it could be left to the doctor, acting with the agreement of the parents and in consultation with another senior physician; or it could be left to some other committee or tribunal. It is hard to see why this would be worse than the present informal system of letting infants die. This system effectively gives to one doctor acting alone the power to make the life-or-death decision.

Harris's second point against the slippery slope argument is a brisk rejection of the claim that there is any analogy between Nazism and what he is proposing. Lorber does not respond to this rejection, so perhaps he accepts that the analogy is far-fetched. Nevertheless we see a need for a more thorough discussion, because people persist in raising the spectre of Nazism whenever active euthanasia is mentioned. They frequently cite Dr Leo Alexander, a psychiatrist who worked with the United States Counsel for War Crimes in Nuremberg from 1946–7. In 'Medical Science under Dictatorship', an article published in the *New England Journal of Medicine* in 1949, Alexander asserts that the path to genocide began with the Nazi euthanasia programme which Hitler ordered on 1 September 1939, the day the Second World War began. The gist of Alexander's article, so far as euthanasia is concerned, is to be found in this oft-quoted passage:

Whatever proportions these crimes finally assumed, it became evident to all who investigated them that they had started from small beginnings. The beginnings at first were merely a subtle shift in emphasis in the basic attitudes of the physicians. It started with the acceptance of the attitude, basic in the euthanasia movement, that there is such a thing as a life not worthy to be lived. This attitude in its early stages concerned itself merely with the severely and chronically sick. Gradually the sphere of those to be included in this category was enlarged to encompass the socially unproductive, the ideologically unwanted, the racially unwanted, and finally all non-Germans. But it is important to realize that the infinitely small wedged-in lever from which this entire trend of mind received its impetus was the attitude toward the nonrehabilitable sick.

This passage has evidently persuaded many people that we must resist the idea that there is 'such a thing as a life not worthy to be lived', and that hence we must resist all steps towards euthanasia. Here two important points need to be made. The first we have already argued for, in Chapter 2: everybody accepts that some lives are not worth living. Obviously those who select some spina bifida infants for non-treatment, with the object of reducing the number of infants who survive with severe handicaps, are in no position to deny that they judge some lives as not worth living. It is not, however, only John Lorber and his colleagues who make such judgements. Even C. Everett Koop makes them, for he does

not advocate prolonging the life of an infant born without a brain
or without an intestine. Unless we are prepared to prolong such
lives, we must admit that we judge some lives to be not worth
living. As we saw, appeals to such doctrines as the distinction
between ordinary and extraordinary means also rely on quality of
life judgements, albeit in a camouflaged form. So if the judgement
that some lives are not worth living were enough to put us on the
slippery slope towards Nazism, we would already be well down
that slope; on the other hand the fact that such judgements are so
inescapable, and must have been made in every society, should
be sufficient grounds for doubting Alexander's claim that they
have anything to do with the uniquely abhorrent Nazi policies.

Our second point is more specifically addressed to the accuracy
of Alexander's understanding of Nazism. In 1976 the Hastings
Center, the leading American centre for bioethics research, held a
conference on 'The Proper Use of the Nazi Analogy in Ethical
Debate'. At that meeting Professor Lucy Dawidowicz, an
eminent historian and author of *The War Against the Jews, 1933–45*,
pointed out that we can easily slip into error when we take terms
used by the Nazis and translate them literally, without regard for
the way the Nazis used them. As Dawidowicz says of terms like
'euthanasia':

when we apply these terms to the Nazi experience, we should see them in
quotation marks, for they do not have our meaning. These terms and the
programs they stood for were integral aspects of Nazi racism. Nazi
racism derived from a theory about the ultimate value of the purity of the
Volk, a word meaning 'people' or 'nation' which in Nazi usage took on a
quasi-mystical sense.

Dawidowicz then considers a Nazi term of obvious relevance to
Alexander's contention:

Those persons or groups of persons that were considered harmful to
racial health, that is, racial purity, were characterized by the racial
ideologists as 'valueless' life, which was slated for destruction. The
German term was *Vernichtung lebensunwerten Lebens*, literally, 'the destruction of life unworthy of life,' generally translated as 'valueless' life. The
'valuelessness' of such life was measured in terms of the health of the
Volk, itself an abstract concept, not a physical reality. This health had no
bearing on individual health, on family health, even on public health, or
the health of society.

In the light of these comments, it is easy to see that Alexander has badly misunderstood the Nazi terminology. The misunderstanding vitiates his attempt to use the historical experience of Nazism as an argument against euthanasia as we now understand the term. When the Nazis talked of 'a life not worthy to be lived' they meant that the life was unworthy because it did not contribute to the health of that mysterious racial entity, the *Volk*. Since our society does not believe in any such entity, there is no real prospect that allowing active euthanasia of severely handicapped new-born infants would lead to Nazi-style atrocities.

Having dealt with the Nazi analogy, let us return to the slippery slope argument in itself, rather than to its specific application in the claim that euthanasia will lead to Nazi-like atrocities. Perhaps the best answer to such arguments was given by Sam Gorovitz, an American philosopher, when testifying before a United States Ethics Advisory Board inquiring into the ethics of research on *in vitro* fertilization (the 'test-tube baby' technique). A previous witness had suggested that accepting this technique might put us on a slippery slope, with a society like the one portrayed in 'Brave New World' at the end of it. Speaking as an experienced skier, Gorovitz pointed out that we frequently make judgements about which slippery slopes we can handle and which we cannot: 'It is a question of control, and in part, of judgment.' Another American, Clifford Grobstein, developed this point in his book on new reproductive techniques, *From Chance to Purpose*. Grobstein draws attention to the crucial role played by our purposes. As long as our purposes are clearly spelt out, and we know how far we are willing to go, there is no reason to fear slippery slopes. Any new proposal that lies outside our original purposes will have to be considered afresh, and at that point we can always refuse to take the further step.

Beyond 'letting die'

In this chapter we have examined several ways in which philosophers, theologians, and doctors have attempted to find moral significance in the distinction between killing and letting die. Some appealed to philosophical doctrines about responsibility and intention, others made pragmatic objections about the finality of killing and its liability to abuse. None of the philosophical doctrines succeeded in showing the distinction to be morally significant. On the pragmatic issues Lorber struggled hard, but in vain, to defend an essentially indefensible position against Harris's criticisms. We therefore conclude that, at least in the medical cases we have been considering, killing an infant is not worse than letting that infant die. Often it will be better, because the swifter death will cause less suffering.

For many of our readers, we suspect, this conclusion will have been plain all along, and the present chapter a philosophically laboured defence of the obvious. These readers will agree with John Freeman who, as we saw at the end of the previous chapter, said that society and medicine should stop 'perpetuating the fiction' that killing and letting die are ethically different. We agree that this view is a fiction, but we have considered it necessary to deal with it at length because it is a fiction that is widely believed, and believed with deep conviction. To give up the fiction is to give up the belief in the sanctity of human life; and this is something that few people are prepared to do.

The thrust of this book so far is that no one really believes that all human life is of equal value, but many people pay lip-service to this belief and adopt disguises which make it difficult to recognize that they are not in fact acting in accordance with what they say. Other people are open in their rejection of the view that all human life is of equal worth, but still are not prepared to admit that it would be right to take the quickest means to end a life that is not worth living. They too are trying to draw a veil over the extent to which their policies and practices are incompatible with the traditional Judaeo-Christian doctrine of the sanctity of human life. Thus all our argument to this stage has been a kind of philosophical undressing. The point has now been reached at which we can gaze on our practices in their naked truth. Many people find nudity shocking, however, and this instance, we can safely predict, will prove no exception. We must therefore ask ourselves: do we dare openly to confront the traditional views about the sanctity of human life that are so deeply embedded in the moral consciousness of our society? Or should we hastily cover ourselves up again with our inadequate, but comforting, fig leaves?

In the next two chapters we shall see whether the traditional views are as solidly based as they appear to be. If not, the fact that our arguments have led us into confrontation with these views is no reason for refusing to follow these arguments where they lead.

5 INFANTICIDE: A BROADER PERSPECTIVE

Dare we openly challenge the belief that all human life is sacrosanct?

Perhaps our society can get away with doctors quietly allowing severely handicapped infants to die in the relative seclusion of a hospital ward; but the public rejection of the sanctity of human life might be quite another thing. Is this belief not fundamental to any civilized society? Will not its rejection lead inevitably to a diminution of respect for others, and so to an increase in brutality, war, and murder?

In this chapter we shall show that the doctrine of the sanctity of human life, as understood in the Western tradition since Christianity prevailed, is not in any sense a fundamental tenet of a civilized society. There have been innumerable human societies which have not shared the Western belief in the sanctity of all human life—and many of these societies have as strong a claim to the label 'civilized' as our own.

The Western belief in the sanctity of life covers a wide range: it prohibits the intentional termination of the life of any innocent human being. Accordingly it cannot accept the mercy killing of the sick and dying at any age. Admittedly, the doctrine contains terms that cry out for further definition: 'intentional', 'termination', 'innocent', 'human', and 'life' all contain a degree of vagueness or ambiguity. We have already touched on some of the problems involved in defining an 'intentional' act, and in deciding whether 'allowing to die' is equivalent to killing. But these are not the only aspects of the doctrine that raise difficult questions. In wartime, are those who feed and clothe the soldiers 'innocent'? Is the unborn foetus really 'human life'? Fortunately we have no need to discuss these further questions. Babies are undoubtedly innocent and undoubtedly human. The prohibition of infanticide, therefore, is as clear an application of the sanctity of life doctrine as any. That the life of a new-born baby is as much deserving of protection as the life of any adult—maybe, because of its youth and innocence, *more* deserving of protection—is basic to the Western attitude to human life.

Acceptance of infanticide, in any culture, is enough to show that that culture does not share the Western belief in the sanctity of human life. Since this book is about the treatment—or non-treatment—of infants, we naturally focus on infanticide. By looking at how some non-Western cultures regard infanticide, and then at the development of the Western tradition, we shall achieve three objectives: we shall see how other cultures would handle the problems discussed in this book; we shall obtain a broader, less culturally-bound perspective on these problems; and we shall gain a better grasp of the historical framework within which these issues continue to be discussed. What follows is, therefore, a digression from the direct discussion of the issues raised in the preceding chapters: but it is a digression from which we shall return better equipped to confront the central issue those chapters have raised.

The Netsilik Eskimo

The Netsilik Eskimo live in Canada's remote Northwest Territories, often well inside the Arctic Circle. At the beginning of this century, Knud Rasmussen carried out a detailed survey of infanticide among the Netsilik people living at Malerualik, on King William Island. He reports having gone into every tent and spoken with every woman in the community. He found that out of a total of 96 births, there had been 38 cases of infanticide. All the infants killed had been females. Assuming that an equal number of males and females had been born, this means that out of 48 female births, only 10, or approximately 20 per cent had been permitted to live.

Several different techniques were used to put these new-born infants to death. In winter, the child was often placed in the igloo entrance. Her cries carried to other, perhaps less fertile, families the news that there was a baby available for adoption. If none wanted her, she soon froze to death. Suffocation was also practised, usually by holding a furry skin over the infant's face. During summer, a small grave was sometimes dug and the infant placed inside it, and left there until it died.

The decision to kill a child could be made by the mother, the father, the grandfather, or the widowed grandmother. Frequently, the father made the decision. The anthropologist Geert van Steenhoven recounts the following case: Ogpingalik, a famous bowman, poet, and shaman from Pelly Bay, was the father of 20 children, 10 boys and 10 girls. Of the girls, nine were put to death following Ogpingalik's orders.

When the tenth child was born . . . Ogpingalik was busy in the sapotit, i.e. in the weir, where the arctic char are speared. For these Eskimos this is one of their most exciting activities . . . The catch was very good at the moment when the news of the birth reached Ogpingalik. He finished his spearing, then returned to his tent where he allowed [the infant] to live.

The decision whether an infant should live or die was not, however, always made so casually. Rasmussen reports a conversation with an older woman, during which the woman told him:

If my daughter Quertiliq had a girl child I would strangle it at once. If I did not, I think I would be a bad mother.

The woman apparently felt that she would be a bad mother because letting a female infant live would prevent her own daughter from having a son in the near future, a son who would one day be a hunter and provide the family with food. If a woman has to suckle a female infant for two to three years, she will not be able to have a son during this period and might endanger her own and her family's survival.

This need to limit the burden on scarce food resources appears to be the main reason for the Netsilik practice of infanticide. In a harsh environment, the family or larger group relied heavily on adult males to provide the means for survival. Women gathered plant food during the summer, but over the long arctic winters the male hunters were the sole providers of food. Moreover hunting was dangerous and many men were killed during their long hunting trips. This led to a second reason for female infanticide: without it, there would have been considerably more female adults than males. Hence the community relied on female infanticide, both to balance the sex ratio among adults, and to ensure that there were enough hunters to provide food over the winter.

The !Kung of the Kalahari

If we switch to the Kalahari Desert—an environment almost as extreme, if in a very different way, as arctic Canada—we find infanticide practised regularly among !Kung Bushmen. (The '!' before 'Kung' is used to indicate a kind of glottal click not reproducible in normal English letters.) These people live near the border that divides Namibia from Botswana. Until recently the !Kung lived in complete independence, wholly by hunting and gathering—they had no agriculture, no herds, no dogs, no beasts of burden, and were virtually untouched by white influence.

Among the !Kung, sex roles were clearly defined as far as the provision of food was concerned: the men hunted for meat and the women had the task of gathering vegetable foods and firewood for themselves, their families, and their dependants. Both the meagreness of the resources of food and water and their nomadic life-style put pressure on the !Kung to keep their population in balance with the environment and to have their children well-spaced. While fertility was naturally low, two other factors kept the size of !Kung families small: infant mortality and occasional infanticide.

!Kung women had no knowledge of abortion methods and contraception was not practised. However, infanticide was performed by !Kung women when they regarded it as necessary: when infants were born defective; when mothers gave birth to twins (one of each pair of twins was killed); when one birth followed another too soon and the baby would drink the milk still needed for an older child; and when the woman felt she was too old to produce milk for another baby. From an evolutionary standpoint, this practice helped the mother to function among a nomadic people where life-style and long nursing periods placed high demands on women. Some anthropologists thus believe that during our pre-agricultural period, the Paleolithic (which comprises almost 99 per cent of human history), infanticide was universal and may have been as high as 50 per cent of live births during some of that time.

One anthropologist, Richard B. Lee, has studied the activities of !Kung women in some detail. He reports that these women, on each day of food gathering, walked from two to twelve miles, carrying 15–33 pounds of vegetable foods on their homeward trip. When the group moved from one area to another to find new hunting and gathering grounds, the woman carried all her family's belongings, weighing some 11–22 pounds. Lee concludes that an adult woman walked about 1,500 miles a year and for a large part of this distance, she carried substantial burdens of food, water, firewood, and other goods. This is not all. The !Kung woman often carried another major burden: one or even two children. !Kung women generally nursed their children until they were about four years old and carried them constantly until they were about two. At three, a child was still carried most of the time, and by that age, a !Kung child weighed more than 30 pounds. Richard Lee estimates that a child, by the time it was four years old, had been carried by its mother for some 4,900 miles—and by that time she may have had another child.

Thus it is not surprising that !Kung women believed that it was necessary to space their children 3 or 4 years apart. If a woman gave birth whilst she was still nursing and carrying an older child, she might have decided to kill the new-born infant. To give birth, a woman went into the bushes, away from the encampment. She would either go alone or be accompanied by her mother. If she decided not to keep the baby, it was buried with the afterbirth and reported back to the community as still-born.

When speaking of the necessity to kill some infants, the !Kung explained it in terms of their being unable to provide adequately for all children. They want children, they explained to the anthropologist Lorna Marshall, all the children they can possibly have; but, they said, they cannot feed babies that are born too close together. They insisted that Bushmen children must have strong legs and that it is mother's milk that makes them strong. Since the !Kung did not have milk from cows or goats and no cereals to feed an infant, two infants could not be kept alive by the mother's milk. If fed on the adult diet of tough meat, roots, and nuts, neither child would thrive and both might die. Hence, the newly arrived infant was killed to safeguard the life of the older sibling—a child already accepted into the community and loved and cherished by its parents. If asked why she practised infanticide, a !Kung woman might thus have the same reason we already encountered in our discussion of the Netsilik: she might have replied that she felt she would be a bad mother if she did not. Given that the !Kung are often regarded as a model of what life was like for the ancestors of all of us, this may have been the attitude of mothers for most of the period of human existence.

The Tikopia of Polynesia

Our first two examples have been hunter-gatherer groups, living in harsh conditions. Let us now consider the people of the small Polynesian island of Tikopia. The Tikopia, as they are known, live in what many of us would consider a tropical island paradise. The climate is warm, the soil fertile, crops grow abundantly, and the ocean provides a supply of fish. Until the introduction of Western influence, the Tikopia lived in a well-functioning social system and in a state of equilibrium with their food resources. Their principal means of population control were infanticide, suicidal sea voyages by young men, celibacy, and war.

In his book *We, the Tikopia*, the distinguished anthropologist Raymond Firth gives a comprehensive account of life on Tikopia. Firth visited the island in the 1920s, at a time when the people were only just beginning to be affected by foreign cultures.

Land was the most important resource for the Tikopians since it was the main source of food. In order to prevent the land from being divided into smaller and smaller holdings, it was customary for the eldest son to inherit the land. The younger male members of the family were often expected to remain single. To this effect the head of the house might have issued an injunction to them not to marry on the grounds that the children of their elder brother would require all available food resources. Deference to family interests was strong, and the choice to remain single was quite often voluntary.

Among married couples, coitus interruptus was practised to limit family size. Whilst abortion techniques were known and sometimes employed by unmarried girls, married women preferred infanticide. If an unwanted child was born, Firth reports, its face was turned down at birth and it was allowed to smother. The decision whether to kill a child or not rested with the father, and his decision was typically motivated by a comparison between potential food supplies and family size. Thus the incidence of infanticide varied considerably from family to family.

According to Firth, the population of Tikopia was, until the arrival of Christian missionaries, in a state of equilibrium with available food resources. As a result of contact with European religious morality, traditional checks on population were no longer working to the same extent as before. Already in the 1920s, Firth reports that because of the attitudes of missionaries to extra-marital sex, young men were encouraged to get married rather than to stay single, because staying single did not, for the Tikopians, mean that they had to abstain from sex. Young men, unfamiliar with the notion that they had 'sinned' when they engaged in extra-marital intercourse, were forced by mission teachers to marry the girl or woman in question. Once married, sexual relations were more likely to result in pregnancy and, since abortion and infanticide were regarded no more favourably by the missionaries than extra-marital sex, the result, Firth says, would be to upset the former equilibrium between resources and population.

This observation led Firth to adopt an attitude sharply critical of Christian morality in general, and of the sanctity of life doctrine in particular:

but for the moral preconceptions of the interpreters of the Christian religion the old checks would act in a perfectly satisfactory manner. A celibacy in which chastity was not enforced, and a discreet infanticide, would serve to maintain the population in equilibrium, and would accord with the feelings of the people themselves . . . It might be thought that the so-called sanctity of human life is not an end in itself, but the means to an end, to the preservation of society. And just as in a civilized community in time of war, civil disturbance or action against crime, life is taken to preserve life, so in Tikopia infants just born might be allowed to have their faces turned down, and to be debarred from the world which they have merely glimpsed, in order that the economic equilibrium might be preserved, and the society maintain its balanced existence.

The forebodings that Firth had, as early as 1929, were well-founded. In 1952–3, two hurricanes struck the island, and a terrible famine followed. While the hurricanes can scarcely be blamed on Christian missionaries, and famines caused by natural disaster had occurred in the past, the severity of this famine was probably the result of the overcrowding of the small island which followed upon the breakdown of traditional methods of population control.

Japan

Some may dismiss the Netsilik, the !Kung, and the Tikopia as primitive, uncivilized people, whose experiences are of no relevance to our own. We do not take that view; nevertheless, it is interesting to look at the practice of infanticide in Japan during the eighteenth century and the first half of the nineteenth century, until the opening to the West began to have its effect. No one familiar with Japanese art and culture could consider Japan in that period as a 'primitive' or 'uncivilized' nation.

In some respects the situation of the Japanese was similar, though on an incomparably larger scale, to that of the people of Tikopia. Arable land was in strictly limited supply. Until the eighteenth century, villagers had an average of five to six children. This meant that by 1750 there was no spare arable land to be brought into production; malnutrition and famine were common. Thus the need to limit family size was great. Contraception appears not to have been used. The noble and samurai classes favoured abortion, for which they had both chemical and mechanical techniques; but for the peasants who made up 90 per cent of the population, abortion was too expensive or too risky. They used infanticide, and used it so widely that most families soon had no more than three children. Infanticide also allowed the Japanese families to ensure that the male line continued, which was important because family descent was through males. The ideal Japanese peasant family consisted of two sons and one daughter, the second son being a kind of insurance against something happening to the first and the daughter being exchanged for the wife of the first son.

So accepted a practice was infanticide that a number of common euphemisms were used to describe it—*mabiki*, for example, which means 'thinning', as the peasants would do with their rice seedlings. If the birth was attended by a midwife, she would not assume that the baby was to live: she would ask if it was 'to be left' or 'to be returned'. The unwanted infants were traditionally buried near a shrine or in the household yard.

Estimates of the percentage of infants killed vary. One historical source asserts that in Kyushu, one of the main islands of Japan, two out of every five infants were killed. Another historical source has it that 30,000 children were killed every year among the 100,000 households in Chiba Prefecture. These claims have often been said to be exaggerated, but a recent demographic study by Mildred Dickeman has concluded that they are believable, and that overall the infanticide rate in this period was in the region of 10–25 per cent of live births.

This large-scale destruction of human life was not limited to the very poor who were genuinely unable to rear their children. In a detailed study of Nakahara, a small village about one hundred kilometres from Kyoto, Thomas Smith and Robert Eng have looked closely at infanticide during the period 1717–1830. Their findings:

Infanticide seems to have been widely practised there by what might be thought to be the most respectable and stable part of the population: married couples who, at a time when divorce and early death were common, lived together through the wives' fecund years, a term completed by only 59 per cent of first-married couples. Also, infanticide seems to have been practised by large holders as well as small, and by all holders as often in good as in bad crop years.

The apparent objectives of infanticide, Smith and Eng conclude, were limitation of family size, an equilibrium of some sort between family size and farm size, achieving a desired distribution of the children's sexes, and possibly spacing the children in a way convenient to the mother. Yet the authors remain puzzled by the gulf between what they have found, and what Western preconceptions of normal human practices had led them to expect:

We could understand infanticide if it had been a function of poverty—a form of self-preservation—as we believed at the beginning, but it was not wholly, or perhaps even mainly, that. In important degree it seems to have been a kind of family planning with long-range objectives. One is bound to wonder about the nature of the objectives of planning, and how they were symbolized and phrased so that infanticide could become (apparently) a normal, even conventional, form of behaviour.

Perhaps one clue to the differences between Japanese attitudes and our own is that, as I. Taeuber has written in *The Population of Japan*:

In Japan, family limitation was not only consistent with, but occurred in the service of, the ancestor-oriented family system. It was not a fundamental deviation from the family values of the great Eastern cultures.

Another crucial factor, of course, is the simple fact that Japan remained, until the middle of the nineteenth century, virtually untouched by Christianity.

Unlike almost every other non-Western culture, the Japanese kept Christian missionaries out and avoided becoming anyone's colony. Thus although the industrial revolution reduced or eliminated the need for infanticide, the practice was never suppressed by outside forces. As a result, Dickeman suggests, 'Japan retains an understanding of the necessity for often painful acceptance of survival imperatives lost by most modern nations . . . That heritage surely played some role in one of the most dramatic national reductions in population increase in modern history.'

Homo infanticida?

We have looked only at four societies in which infanticide was openly practised. It would be easy, if tedious, to extend this list. Most cross-cultural studies of non-Western societies have found that the majority accepted infanticide in at least some circumstances. For instance, a sample compiled by C. Ford to analyse human reproduction and birth control found that of 64 societies, only 19 expressly forbade infanticide. A later study by J. W. Whiting examines 88 societies; infanticide was practised in 71 of them. Another investigation turned up information about infanticide in ethnographers' reports for 393 societies, of which 302 were said to practise infanticide at least occasionally. Moreover the investigators were inclined to believe that this *underestimated* the prevalence of infanticide, since many societies which claimed not to allow the practice had considerably more male than female children. The most plausible explanation of this is that infanticide does exist in these societies, but the people who spoke to the anthropologists denied it because they were aware of Western disapproval.

We see no value, however, in piling up cases. The four societies we have discussed are enough to show that infanticide is compatible with a stable, well-organized human society. This does not mean, of course, that it is morally right. Slavery has also been practised in stable, well-organized human societies. One cannot validly argue from the fact that something is widespread to the judgement that it is good. On the other hand, we can reject the assertion that infanticide, because it breaches the doctrine that all human life is sacred, will necessarily have disastrous consequences in other areas of human life. There is no evidence suggesting that the lives of anyone except infants were more at risk among the Netsilik, the !Kung, the Tikopia, or the eighteenth-century Japanese, than they are among citizens of the United States of America, where infanticide evokes popular moral abhorrence and is legally murder. The murder rate in Japan is less than one seventh of that in the United States— despite the centuries in which one might have expected the widespread acceptance of infanticide in Japan to have had a corrupting effect on public respect for human life.

Even if people who accept infanticide do not murder adults more frequently than those who do not, perhaps they lack tender feelings towards their children? The anthropological literature suggests otherwise. In most societies where infanticide was practised, children were very much cherished and were the objects of tender, loving care. As Laila Williamson points out, most 'primitive' peoples loved and wanted children, and they were more indulgent with them than are many parents in Western societies, who spank and punish their children in various ways. The !Kung, for example, had a naturally low fertility rate which may have frustrated the desire of some parents to have children. The cause of low fertility, the !Kung explained, is the stinginess of their god, who loves children and tries to keep them all to himself in heaven, rather than let them come down to earth to bring happiness and joy to their parents. !Kung mothers were prepared to kill their infants if they regarded this as necessary; once accepted into the community, however, a child became the object of gentleness, love, and affection. Lorna Marshall gives the following account:

!Kung babies are carried most of the time by their mothers, tied in soft leather slings against their mother's side, where they can easily reach their mother's breast. They nurse at will. !Kung women have excellent lactation. All the babies are plump. The babies wear no clothes and are in skin-to-skin contact with their mothers ... They sleep in their mothers' arms at night. When they are not in their mothers' arms or tied to their sides, they are in someone else's arms, or if they are set down to play, they clamber over their elders as they lie chatting and resting, or play within arm's reach. The babies are constantly in the presence of people who are gentle and affectionate with them and who are watchful. The babies have no special toys, but are allowed to play with any of the adults' possessions that come into their hands and mouths, except knives and hunting equipment. These items are hung carefully in the bushes, out of the reach of children.

The !Kung never seem to tire of their babies. They dandle them, kiss them, dance with them, and sing to them ... Altogether, the babies appear to be as serene and contented as well-fed young puppies.

Other communities who practised infanticide were similarly affectionate to their children. Of the Netsilik Eskimo it is said that they were 'extremely devoted to their children . . . Children of all ages [are] an endless source of joy to their parents, despite the sacrifices that their rearing entails ... Relations between grandparents and grandchildren are marked by ceaseless fondling and joking.'

From our own cultural perspective, it may be difficult to understand how parents who are warm, affectionate, and protective toward their children are, at the same time, able to put some new-born infants to death—yet to the people concerned these two attitudes did not appear irreconcilable and inconsistent.

One possible explanation links this with a delaying of the moment at which the child is accepted into the family or community. Among the Netsilik, for example, infanticide was permissible only up to the time at which the infant was given a name. Once the infant had been named, it became a full member of the community and could not be killed. In this respect the Netsilik are typical of many societies which allow infanticide. In ancient Athens, unwanted new-bron infants could be exposed to the elements, but only until the Amphidromia, a family ceremony in which the child was carried around the hearth, receiving religious consecration and its name. Once this ceremony had been performed, exposure was not permitted. All this tallies with the conclusion reached by Ford in his cross-cultural study:

infanticide is most readily condoned if it occurs before the infant is named and has been accepted as a *bona fide* member of its society. It seems that the primary and fundamental restriction in most societies is the taboo on murder, i.e. killing a member of the ingroup. The less eligible a child is for membership in the group, the less seriously the act of killing the child is viewed.

Other scientists have seen infanticide as something very deeply ingrained in human nature. Some animals are known to kill their offspring when food is scarce or conditions bad—Zuckerman's famous study of baboons in the dreadfully crowded conditions of the London Zoo showed this, for instance—but human infanticide is, of course, much more deliberate. This has led J. V. Neel, a geneticist, to make a shocking suggestion:

man is to my knowledge the only [mammal] who regularly and without 'external' provocation purposely and knowingly commits infanticide . . . There have been many attempts to define that point at which our primate ancestors crossed the threshold to 'true' man. Most definitions involve tool-making or speech. I suggest that an equally sound definition is the point at which parental care evolved to the level of permitting rapid population increase, with the concomitant recognition of the necessity to limit natural fecundity.

Since infanticide is much easier to carry out and requires a considerably less sophisticated understanding of human reproduction than abstinence, contraception, or abortion, Neel is suggesting that we first became truly human when we began deliberately killing our children.

We do not endorse Neel's suggestion, but it is no more far-fetched than the idea that belief in the sanctity of all innocent human life is a prerequisite for any civilized society.

A deviant tradition

The preceding pages have shown that we live in an unusual society. We reject infanticide. We reject it not only for population limitation and sex selection, but even for children born with major handicaps. That, at least, is our 'official' morality.

Why do we take a view so different from that of the majority of human societies? No doubt many historical factors are involved; but there are distinctive features in the Judaeo-Christian tradition which have clearly played a major role.

In classical Greece and Rome, infanticide was common practice. In his *Republic*, Plato supported infanticide and argued that in an ideal society the quality of the citizens would be maintained by ensuring that defective infants, along with the offspring of inferior citizens, were 'quietly got rid of'. Aristotle, too, was concerned with population questions. In his *Politics* he argued for a law that no deformed child should be allowed to live. These recommendations by the two greatest ancient philosophers would not have seemed anything out of the ordinary to their contemporaries. The celebrated legislative code said to have been drawn up for Athens by Solon, the founder of Athenian democracy, required that deformed infants be put to death. Spartan law, said to have been formulated by the legendary Lycurgus, contained a similar provision. Indeed, infanticide was such an ordinary and natural event that it was an accepted topic for humour in the comedies of the time.

The Greek practice of infanticide—which chiefly took the form of exposure—was continued by the Romans. According to myth, Rome itself was founded by two exposed infants, Romulus and Remus, who are said to have been suckled and raised by a wolf. In Rome, custom or law enjoined the destruction of deformed infants and, according the law of the Twelve Tables mentioned by Cicero, 'monstrous abortions' were not allowed to live. Even the Stoic moralist, Seneca, renowned for his humanitarianism, stated quite unapologetically that 'unnatural progeny we destroy; we drown even children who at birth are weakly and abnormal'. Seneca held that it was an act of reason to separate what is useless from what is sound, and Pliny the Elder defended infanticide on the grounds that the population must be regulated.

All this changed very dramatically with the coming of Christianity. Before we describe this change, however, we must first trace the roots of the Christian attitude in the Hebrew tradition. Here the first thing we notice is the emphasis on fertility. Genesis tells us that God created Adam and Eve and blessed them, and then gave them his first command: 'Be fruitful and increase, fill the earth and subdue it.' The command was repeated to Noah after the flood and later God again told Jacob to be fruitful and found a nation.

All this must have counted against infanticide, at least for population limitation. The early Hebrews may have occasionally sacrificed their children for religious purposes—Abraham, of course, was about to do so until told by God to sacrifice a ram instead. (His reward for having been willing to give up his only son was a characteristic one: God said 'I will greatly multiply your descendants until they are as numerous as the stars in the sky and the grains of sand on the sea-shore.') After this incident it seems that human sacrifices to the Hebrew God ceased; but we still read in Leviticus, in a series of laws clearly aimed at keeping the Hebrew people from lapsing into the ways of the other peoples with whom they mingled: 'You shall not surrender any of your children to Molech and thus profane the name of your God.' Even at a much later period, infanticide was not totally unknown, for we find Isaiah declaiming against those who are 'sacrificing children in the gorges, under the rocky clefts'. Still, with the possible exception of early sacrifices, the Jewish people never seem to have accepted infanticide in any open form. For this they stood out among their neighbours. The Roman historian Tacitus, for instance, thinks it worthy of remark that the Jews 'take thought to increase their numbers: for they regard it as a crime to kill any [unwanted] child'.

Despite the clear prohibition on infanticide, Jewish law recognizes one curious qualification which must have mitigated the severity of the consequences of the prohibition. The killing of a new-born child is punishable as murder only if the child has been carried to term and delivered after a full nine months' pregnancy. Otherwise the child is not considered definitely viable until it has lived for thirty days after birth. It would, of course, have been impossible to prove that a pregnancy had lasted nine months—the rabbis refer to a nine-month separation between the parents as evidence, but this must have been rare indeed. The killer of a child whose viability is in doubt is not liable to be tried before a human court, although the offender is still said to be answerable before 'the heavenly tribunal'. Normal mourning regulations are also not observed in these cases. Even after the thirty-day period has expired, the exemption will be allowed if it can be shown that the child definitely was born in the eighth month of pregnancy or, significantly, if it was delivered in maimed state. (We cannot help wondering if this rule did not serve as a device for permitting the destruction of deformed infants without seeming to violate the general ethical prohibition on taking human life, in much the same way as the distinctions between killing and allowing to die, and between ordinary and extra-ordinary means serve today.)

When Christianity emerged from its Hebrew roots it took with it the Jewish prohibition on infanticide, strengthened and given greater weight by some doctrines of its own. The classic account of the moral transformation Christianity worked on the ancient world is W. E. H. Lecky's celebrated *History of European Morals from Augustus to Charlemagne*. Though written more than a century ago, Lecky's words are difficult to improve upon:

The first aspect in which Christianity presented itself to the world was as a declaration of the fraternity of men in Christ. Considered as immortal beings, destined for the extremes of happiness or of misery, and united to one another by a special community of redemption, the first and most manifest duty of the Christian man was to look upon his fellow men as sacred beings and from this notion grew up the eminently Christian idea of the sanctity of human life . . . it was one of the most important services of Christianity that besides quickening greatly our benevolent affections it definitely and dogmatically asserted the sinfulness of all destruction of human life as a matter of amusement or of simple convenience, and thereby formed a new standard higher than any which then existed in the world . . . This minute and scrupulous care for human life and human virtue in the humblest form, in the slave, the gladiator, the savage, or the infant, was indeed wholly foreign to the genius of Paganism. It was produced by the Christian doctrine of the inestimable value of each immortal soul.

Although it is true that even before the rise of Christianity some philosophical and religious schools, other than Judaism, expressed a strong respect for human life, it is generally agreed that such views were only held by a minority. The Hippocratic oath, for example, which scholars assign to the fourth century BC, already strongly disapproves of abortion, euthanasia, and suicide —independently of Judaeo-Christian influence. However, writers in the field hold that this oath represented only a small segment of Greek opinion and was not generally accepted until Christianity had completed its domination of the ancient world. In AD 318 the first Christian Emperor, Constantine, issued a decree declaring that the slaying of a son or daughter by a father was a crime; by the end of the fourth century subsequent Emperors had turned infanticide into an offence punishable by death.

Why was Christian opposition to infanticide so firm? Primarily, no doubt, because Christians simply took over the Jewish view that to kill any human being, from the moment of birth, is murder. Yet the Christians went beyond the Jewish view, rejecting the 'thirty days after birth' limitation on earthly prosecution of the culprit. There were several Christian doctrines which may have contributed to this more stringent attitude. Christian teachings tell us that human life is in God's hands. As the Protestant theologian Paul Ramsey puts it, 'we are stewards and not owners of our lives'. Ramsey is echoing an idea with a long history: it can be found in very similar terms in Thomas Aquinas, and also in John Locke. From this view it follows that only God has the right to take the life of an innocent human being; parents who dispose of their infants are usurping God's rights.

Lecky gives greater weight to another Christian doctrine, that of 'the inestimable value of each immortal soul'. Whereas to the pagans, he says, the painless extinction of a new-born infant was not to be compared with the death of an adult, to the Christian theologian 'infant life possessed a fearful significance' because the infant was destined to live forever in heaven or hell. Nor was this all. Lecky points out that the Christian doctrine of original sin as taught by the Church Fathers meant that the infants bear responsibility for Adam's fall, and are doomed eternally to hell, unless saved by baptism:

That which appealed so powerfully to the compassion of the early and mediaeval Christians, in the fate of the murdered infants, was not that they died, but that they commonly died unbaptized.

Glanville Williams, a noted legal scholar, accepted Lecky's view in his book, *The Sanctity of Life and the Criminal Law*. It was, said Williams, 'the horror of bringing about the death of an unbaptized child' that lay behind Christian opposition to both abortion and infanticide. On the other hand John Noonan, a Roman Catholic professor of law, has described this statement as 'baseless' and said flatly that the Christian position did not originate with any narrow theological or philosophical concept. According to Noonan, the Christian position is based simply on 'the humanity of a being'.

We are not persuaded by Noonan's attempt to dismiss the significance of the special theological doctrines referred to by Lecky and Williams. For one thing, it is necessary to ask why the early Christians considered 'the humanity of a being' so significant. Perhaps it seems obvious to us that the fact that a being is human is reason enough for holding that it must not be killed, but this did not seem obvious to the Greeks or Romans. Why did the Christians differ so markedly in this respect from their contemporaries? We know that Christians, unlike pagans, believed that every human being has an immortal soul. We also know that they believed that human lives are God's property. It would be surprising if these beliefs had nothing at all to do with the distinctive Christian attitude to infanticide.

As for the further Christian doctrine about the fate of unbaptized infants, there is ample evidence that this view was widely held. As Fulgentius, a Christian saint of the sixth century, wrote:

It is to be believed beyond doubt, that not only men who are come to the use of reason, but infants, whether they die in their mother's womb, or after they are born, without baptism in the name of the Father, Son, and Holy Ghost, are punished with everlasting punishment in eternal fire, because though they have no actual sin of their own, yet they carry along with them the condemnation of original sin from their first conception and birth.

Augustine, perhaps the most influential of the Church Fathers, also believed that unbaptized children would go into eternal fire. Some medieval laws refer with special condemnation to the killing of an unbaptized child. The charter of the first known foundling hospital, set up in Milan in 789, included a reference suggesting that the founder was motivated by the desire to prevent the deaths of unbaptized infants. Even today, the Catholic view has not changed greatly. The *New Catholic Encyclopedia*, published in 1967, has this to say on the topic:

Fate of Unbaptized Infants. Many theories have been offered concerning the fate of infants who die without Baptism. The most common opinion until now has been that, since Baptism is necesary for salvation, unbaptized infants who die cannot enjoy supernatural happiness.

The *Encyclopedia* then discusses the theory that such infants go into limbo, rather than to hell, and refers to a statement made by Pope Pius XII in 1951, when addressing a gathering of midwives, to the effect that 'as things are at present, no other way besides Baptism is seen of imparting the life of Christ to little children'.

Thus the evidence bears out the claim made by Lecky and endorsed by Williams. The view of infanticide which came to be part of the accepted Western moral tradition is different from the views held by most other human societies, including those that existed in Europe until the coming of Christianity. These differences correspond to religious doctrines characteristic of the Judaeo-Christian tradition: the injunction to be fruitful and multiply; the belief that human life is in God's hands and is only His to take; the belief that every human being has an immortal soul; and the belief that unbaptized infants go to hell or, at best, into limbo. Precisely what role each of these doctrines played it is difficult to say. It would probably be a mistake to place too much weight on the peculiar idea that a benevolent God could condemn unbaptized infants to eternal hellfire. After all, as Lecky himself said, the Christian influence changed Roman attitudes to slaves, gladiators, and savages, as well as to infants (though later slaves and 'savages' under the tender mercies of Christians in both North and South America might well have wondered about this). Christian theologians objected, and still object, to suicide and voluntary euthanasia, as well as to infanticide—and here too they differ from the Romans and from people of many other cultures. Hence it seems that beliefs about human immortality and especially God's dominion over our lives were more fundamental than special fears about the fate of unbaptized infants. True, Christianity ushered in a degree of hostility to infanticide that is, so far as we have been able to discover, unique among all human cultures; but it did so on the basis of a much broader attitude to human life in general. This attitude we have referred to as the doctrine of the sanctity of human life.

For more than fifteen hundred years, Christian teachings dominated Western moral thinking. Those who rejected it were systematically persecuted. During this long era of totalitarian enforcement, Christian moral views gained an almost unshakeable grip on our moral thinking. The idea that all human life has a special sanctity has become an ingrained part of our moral consciousness. It is therefore not easy for us to detach ourselves from the intellectual legacy of these centuries; yet this is what we must do if we are to face the crucial moral issue raised by the treatment of severely handicapped infants. Christianity has ceased to be the only accepted basis of our moral beliefs and laws. In a pluralist society which accepts the separation of Church and State, laws cannot be defended by showing that they are in accordance with the beliefs of one particular religion. But can the idea of the sanctity of human life stand independently of the religious tradition from which it sprang?

6 WHAT'S WRONG WITH THE SANCTITY OF LIFE DOCTRINE?

About this chapter

In this chapter we argue that the sanctity of life principle cannot rationally be defended. If we are right about this, the principle cannot be used as a ground for objecting to euthanasia for severely handicapped new-borns—or at least, it cannot be used by those who wish to persuade all reasonable people independently of their religious beliefs. It may still be possible to defend the principle within the framework of some religions—but that will not impress those who do not happen to adhere to those particular religions.

Because this chapter puts up philosophical arguments against the sanctity of life principle, it is more abstract than the other chapters in this book. This is unavoidable if we are to show by rigorous argument that the sanctity of life principle is unsound. Perhaps what we have said in earlier chapters will have already persuaded some of our readers of this conclusion; but we have a more ambitious aim than the persuasion of those already sympathetic to our views on these questions. The argument we shall present is so clear-cut that henceforth the onus will be on those who invoke the sanctity of life principle to show where our refutation goes wrong. If they cannot do so, they will not be justified in appealing to the sanctity of life principle, for they will be appealing to a principle that has been shown to be philosophically unsound.

Sanctity of life or sanctity of human life?

People opposed to abortion or euthanasia often say that they believe in the sanctity of life. They almost never mean what they say. They do not mean, as their words seem to imply, that *all* life is sacred. If they did they would, presumably, make at least as much fuss about the daily slaughter of pigs, cattle, and chickens as they do about the much smaller number of foetuses killed by abortions. Yet most of those who say they believe in the sanctity of life are not vegetarians. Even if they were, to cut a living lettuce would still be contrary to a belief in 'the sanctity of life', taken literally. When people talk of their belief in the sanctity of life, it is the sanctity of *human* life that they really have in mind.

So in this chapter we shall discuss the view that all human life is sacred. People who hold this belief may differ in the way they state it. Many make exceptions for killing those who are not 'innocent', so as to allow capital punishment, or killing in wartime. Other differences relate to the way in which the principle is stated: some, as we saw in Chapter 2, claim that all human life is of infinite value; others make their claim not in terms of the concept of value, but in terms of an absolute prohibition on taking innocent human life. These differences are of interest to philosophers, but we need not discuss them here. All sanctity of life supporters agree upon the central claim: the killing of a human being is of unique moral significance.

Let us spell out one implication of this key claim. In saying that the killing of a human being is of unique moral significance, proponents of the sanctity of life principle are saying that to take the life of a human being—any human being—is in itself, and further consequences apart, far more momentous than taking the life of some other kind of being, for instance a chicken, pig, or cow. The principle of the sanctity of human life is a principle which serves to separate humans from non-human animals, and mark out human life for special attention. By comparison with the taking of human life, to take the life of a non-human animal is of relatively minor significance. The difference between killing a human and a non-human animal, according to this view, is not one of degree but of kind.

What could justify a sharp distinction in moral significance between taking human life and taking animal life? Only some relevant difference between the two groups. Many possible relevant differences might be suggested. Joseph Fletcher, a Protestant theologian, has listed some 'indicators of humanhood'.

His list includes self-awareness, self-control, a sense of the future, a sense of the past, the capacity to relate to others, concern for others, communication, and curiosity. Other writers have emphasized rationality, the use of language, and autonomy. For our purposes it is not necessary to discuss which of these characteristics serve best to distinguish our own species from others. Many of them are related to others—one could not, for instance, have a sense of the past and future without at least some minimal degree of self-awareness and some capacity for rational thought. Taken as a cluster, these characteristics have undeniable moral significance. It is entirely reasonable to suggest that it is much more serious to take the life of a being possessing all or most of these characteristics than it would be to take the life of a being possessing none of them.

Various grounds could be offered for saying that these characteristics are relevant to the seriousness of killing. Some people regard it as self-evident that the life of a rational, autonomous being is of greater value than the life of a being lacking these characteristics. Others focus especially on the capacity for self-awareness, and on the sense of the future. A self-aware being with a sense of the future can have hopes and desires about what might or might not happen to it in the future. To kill it is to prevent the fulfilment of these hopes and desires. This is a wrong which we cannot possibly do to a being that does not even understand that it exists as a separate being, with a past and a future.

Michael Tooley, an American philosopher now living in Australia, has developed this argument more systematically than anyone else. Tooley argues that only 'continuing selves' have a right to life. To be a continuing self it is not enough to have merely momentary desires or interests. Instead one must, at some time, be able to see oneself as existing over time. Thus only beings with a degree of self-awareness and a sense of the future can have a right to life.

For the moment we shall merely note that there are reasons for holding that the characteristics mentioned are relevant to the significance of taking life. Further discussion of these views we shall put off until later, because we must return to the issue of the distinction between taking human life and taking animal life.

The crucial mistake

We have seen that the doctrine of the sanctity of life is really a doctrine about the sanctity of human life. We must now look at a crucial ambiguity in the term 'human'. When Joseph Fletcher called his list of characteristics 'indicators of humanhood', he meant that these characteristics were distinctive of human beings—the kind of things that mark out humans from all other animals. This is the sense given by the *Oxford English Dictionary* when it says that 'human' means 'having or showing the qualities or attributes proper to or distinctive of man'. It is the sense we have in mind when we say that an infant born without a brain is more like a vegetable than like a human being. There is, however, another sense of the term 'human' in which the infant born without a brain is, undeniably, a human being. This is the sense of 'human' which means, in effect, 'member of the species *homo sapiens*'. In every cell of their bodies, the most grossly deformed infants born of human parents still possess the human genetic code. They are obviously not members of any other species. Therefore in the strict biological sense of the term they are human beings.

We have already seen that the first of these two senses of the term 'human' does refer to characteristics which are relevant to the moral significance of taking life; but what of the second sense, which draws the distinction between humans and others in terms of species membership alone? This distinction cannot be relevant to the moral significance of taking life. To claim that it is relevant is to make precisely the kind of claim made by the crude white racist who asserts that the killing of a black is less morally significant than the killing of a member of his own race. Like race or sex, species is not in itself a morally relevant characteristic.

Species might be indirectly morally relevant if it were a reliable indication of the possession of other, directly relevant capacities, such as those listed by Joseph Fletcher. But a moment's thought shows that this is not the case. We saw in Chapter 2 that there are some infants who are human in the biological sense, but do not and never will possess any of Fletcher's 'indicators of humanhood'. Anencephalics—infants born with most of their brain missing—are in this category; so are infants who have suffered massive brain haemorrhages. Thus there are some who are humans in the sense of being members of the species *Homo sapiens* but not in the morally significant sense of having the distinctively human characteristics we have mentioned.

Is the converse also true? Are there some beings who possess the distinctive characteristics but are not members of the species *Homo sapiens*? This is more controversial. Certainly chimpanzees and gorillas show some degree of self-awareness. Washoe, the first chimpanzee to be taught sign language, was asked, as she was looking into a mirror, 'Who is that?' She made the signs for: 'Me, Washoe'. There is also good evidence that chimpanzees plan for the future. Jane Goodall, observing wild chimpanzees in Uganda, has given an account of how a lower-ranking chimpanzee who noticed a banana in a tree did not move directly towards the fruit, but instead went elsewhere until a higher-ranking chimpanzee had left the area; only then, some fifteen minutes later, did the first chimpanzee return and take the fruit.

Just as some members of the species *Homo sapiens* do not possess the characteristics usually regarded as distinctive of our species, so there are some beings who are not members of our species who do appear to possess, at least to some degree, these characteristics. If we were simply to compare the characteristics of different individuals, irrespective of species, it is clear that we would have to go much further down the evolutionary scale before we reached a point at which non-human animals had capacities as limited as the most severely retarded humans. Not just chimpanzees, but also the animals we commonly kill for food—pigs, cows, and chickens—would compare favourably with anencephalic infants, or those who have suffered massive brain haemorrhages.

Many people consider any such comparison of humans and animals to be offensive, but the facts cannot be denied and we gain nothing by pretending otherwise. Pigs, cows, and chickens have a greater capacity to relate to others, better ability to communicate, and far more curiosity, than the most severely retarded humans. Obviously there are gradations between the normal members of different species. Equally obviously, there are gradings within species, and especially within the human species. There is no clear-cut distinction between humans and other animals in respect of capacities like self-awareness, a sense of the past and future, or rationality. Instead there is an overlap: the best-endowed non-human animals rank well above those members of our species whose capacities are most limited.

Since the boundary of our species does not run in tandem with the possession of the morally significant capacities, the species boundary cannot be used as the basis for important moral distinctions. If we are prepared to give less weight to the killing of a being simply because it is not a member of our own species, despite its having capacities equal or superior to those of a member of our own species, how can we object to racists discriminating against those who are not of their own race, although these others have capacities equal or superior to those of members of that race?

Now we can see what is wrong with the traditional principle of the sanctity of human life. Those who hold this principle invariably take 'human' in the strictly biological sense. They include within the scope of the principle all members of the species *Homo sapiens* and no members of any other species. The principle is 'speciesist'; it is indefensible for the same reason that racism or sexism are indefensible. Those who hold the principle are giving great weight to something which is morally irrelevant —the species to which the being belongs. The traditional principle of the sanctity of human life elevates a morally insignificant characteristic into something of the utmost importance.

What went wrong?

Why is so central a part of our ethics based on a morally irrelevant distinction? One might be tempted to say that it is simply an instinct for any creature to regard the lives of members of its own species as far more valuable than the lives of any other species. To say that this is instinctive—we might have said 'natural'—would not be to justify it. The preference for those whose skin colour and facial features are like our own may also be instinctive or 'natural', but this does not mean that racism is justifiable. In any case, we saw in the previous chapter that belief in the sanctity of human life is very far from being a universal human trait. There are other societies which do not attribute great significance to the killing of an infant. Unlike Western thought, Eastern ways of thinking place humans and non-human animals on a similar level. The first precept of Buddhist ethics, for instance, is simply 'to avoid taking life'. Jains, too, treat all forms of animal life with respect, and go to considerable trouble to avoid harming even insects. Although both Buddhists and Jains will normally consider the killing of a human being to be much more serious than the killing of a non-human animal, the difference is one of degree rather than of kind, and human life is not inherently more sacred than animal life.

The preceding chapter explained the roots of the distinctively Judaeo-Christian doctrine of the sanctity of human life. In traditional Christian theology, membership of the species *Homo sapiens* is a reliable indication of three other morally relevant characteristics: having an immortal soul, being made in the image of God, and being a creature over whom God has retained His dominion. For those who believe that all and only members of the species *Homo sapiens* have an immortal soul, species membership is no arbitrary line, but a mark of an eternal being who will live forever in heaven or hell (or maybe in limbo). One might, of course, ask why Christians believe that God should have given immortal souls to all members of the species *Homo sapiens* (even to those on whom, in His wisdom, He did not bestow a brain); but the answer would be unlikely to satisfy non-believers.

A similar point can be made about the belief that all humans are made in the image of God, or that only God has the right to take the life of a human being, whereas He has given us dominion over the other animals and allows us to kill them as we see fit. If you believe this, and believe that by 'human being' God meant 'member of the species *Homo sapiens*', species membership serves to indicate those Godlike creatures whom you may not kill without 'playing God' and thus presumably incurring His displeasure. Again, however, an inquiring sceptic would wonder why an anencephalic infant more closely resembles God than, say, a pig. The question may seem blasphemous, but it is meant only to draw attention to the fact that God has no physical body. So when Genesis tells us that we are made in the image of God, it cannot mean that we resemble God in our physique or our facial features. If the resemblance is rather in our intellect, our reason, or our moral sense, however, many non-human animals would seem to be more like God than the anencephalic infant.

So far as the alleged usurpation of God's rights over human life is concerned, the sceptic would want to know why God should have chosen to reserve His rights over life for all members of our species, but not for any members of other species. Here, too, we are unlikely to get an answer that will persuade those who do not already accept the tenets of Judaeo-Christian religion.

Now we can see why Western thought has ended up with a fundamental ethical principle which is impossible to defend in rational, non-religious terms. The principle of the sanctity of human life is a legacy of the days when religion was the accepted source of all ethical wisdom. Within the framework of Judaeo-Christian religious belief, it makes some sense (although even within that framework an inquiring mind will soon come up with questions that have no answers). Now that religion is no longer accepted as the source of moral authority in public life, however, the principle has been removed from the framework in which it developed. We are just discovering that without this framework it cannot stand up.

Ethics without religion

In the preceding sections of this chapter we have suggested that the traditional principle of the sanctity of human life is the outcome of some seventeen centuries of Christian domination of Western thought and cannot rationally be defended. From previous occasions on which we have outlined this position, we know that different readers will react in widely differing ways. Some people have always regarded the traditional sanctity of life principle as a religious doctrine, and have seen its gradual erosion and replacement as merely a matter of time. For these readers, what we have been saying will at best be a more rigorous articulation of what they have long sensed; at worst it will be a tiresome labouring of the obvious. For a different group of readers, however, our views will be a shocking attack on the Judaeo-Christian ethic, which for them is the core not only of their world-view, but of any ethical position at all. For this latter group, to reject the religious view of the world is to reject the foundations of all morality.

The present section is addressed to those who believe that without religion there can be no basis for ethics. For many people the possibility of ethics without religion needs no defence, since they make ethical choices daily without any reference to religion. Philosophers and even moral theologians generally agree that ethics does not need religion. Yet others cling to the belief that the two are linked. When one of us wrote a brief article on 'Sanctity of Life or Quality of Life' for the American medical journal *Pediatrics*, the editor received dozens of letters from paediatricians protesting against the rejection of the religious underpinnings of the sanctity of life doctrine. One doctor wrote that the rejection of the traditional Judaeo-Christian heritage would make 'morality a matter of subjective taste'. Another said the article implied that 'man as a moral agent is dead' and went on to ask: 'How can [Peter Singer] explain mankind's perception of moral qualities or his capacity to love, apart from believing we are made in the image of God?' Because we want our position to be rigorously convincing to the widest possible audience, we shall answer these objections.

It is sometimes thought that ethics cannot do without religion because the very meaning of the word 'good' is 'what God wills'. This thought is an old one, discussed by Plato more than two thousand years ago. Plato rejected it because he could see that if the gods approve of an action, it must be because the action is good—in which case it cannot be the approval of the gods that makes the action good. To take any other view is to make divine approval entirely arbitrary: if the gods had happened to approve of torture and disapprove of helping our neighbours, then torture would be good and helping our neighbours would be bad.

Some modern theists have tried to get out of the dilemma set by Plato. They have said that God is necessarily good, and so could not possibly approve of torture. This defence does not work, because if 'good' means 'what God wills', what can it mean to say that 'God is good'? That God is willed by God? But surely this tautology is not what theists want to say when they say that God is good.

Plato's argument proves that words like 'good' and 'bad', 'right' and 'wrong' must have a meaning that is independent of beliefs about what God or the gods approve. The next question is how we find out which acts are good and which are not. At this point attempts to base ethics on religion become appeals to the need for an authority. 'Without the scriptures . . .' people say, or 'Without God's revelation . . .', or even 'Without the authority of the Church . . .' there can be no ethics. But it is notorious that appeals to the scriptures solve nothing. If Christians took the words of Jesus, as presented in the gospels, in their most literal and obvious sense, they would all give up their riches, since otherwise they are as unlikely to go to heaven as a camel is to pass through the eye of a needle; and none of them would retaliate when struck upon the cheek. Now maybe these words were not meant to be taken in their most literal and obvious sense. We shall not try to instruct Christians in the interpretation of scripture; we merely point out that once the possibility of a non-literal interpretation is allowed, we must all use our own judgement. The authority and objectivity of scripture as a source of moral knowledge has disappeared.

The same point applies to religious revelation: those who claim to have received it are not in agreement about its content. Even the authority of that once monolithic structure, the Roman Catholic Church, has broken down, and many people who consider themselves good Catholics disagree with the teachings of the Church on matters like contraception. There is even an American organization, 'Catholics for a Free Choice', which dissents from the usual Roman Catholic view on abortion. If we broaden our gaze to consider not just one Christian denomination, but Christianity as a whole, the diversity of ethical teaching is immense. And what if we widen the view still further, so that we take in not just Christians, but all religious believers? Can anyone then think that religion as such is a source of moral knowledge?

As this last question suggests, religious believers are not likely to claim that religion in the widest sense is a source of moral knowledge; they will rather argue that their own religion is a source of moral knowledge because it is the only true religion. Clearly we cannot assess that kind of claim here. We content ourselves with pointing out that nowadays religious belief normally rests on faith, rather than reason (a development that arose, as Bertrand Russell noted in his *History of Western Philosophy*, after the traditional scholastic arguments for the existence of God had been generally agreed to be invalid). Since we are concerned only with what is rationally defensible, objections based on religious faith are not a challenge to our position. We shall say more shortly about the proper role in a pluralist society of ethical positions based on religious faith.

There is still one question that troubles many who are not religious at all. If we grant that religion provides no satisfactory basis for ethics, on what *is* ethics to be based? Is it perhaps, after all, 'a matter of subjective taste'?

This question has occupied moral philosophers for a long time. While philosophers continue to disagree about the ultimate foundations of ethics, there is increasing agreement that reason and argument have a role to play in ethics. Even if no ethical judgement can, in the end, be shown to be objectively true, some ethical positions can be conclusively refuted. Consistency is a minimal requirement for all rational thought. An ethical position which fails to be consistent must be rejected.

To say that something is a matter of 'subjective taste' is to say that it is pointless to argue about it. If someone doesn't like avocado, there isn't much scope for rational debate; when people disagree about ethics, however, there is plenty of scope for rational debate, as the preceding pages have shown. In that sense, ethics without religion will not become a matter of subjective taste. (For those interested in further probing of the role of reason in ethics, one of us has written elsewhere on this topic, and there is a wealth of other literature available.)

Finally, so far as this discussion of ethics and religion is concerned, what is the proper role of religion in a pluralist, democratic society? The separation of Church and State is now a widely accepted principle, written into the constitution of many democratic societies. Even where, as in Britain, Church and State are not formally separated—the Queen is also the Head of the Church of England—no one would seriously propose that the State should prevent people from holding other religious beliefs, or from holding no religious beliefs at all.

The separation of Church and State implies not only that the State does not insist on some particular form of religious worship, but also that the State does not require that its citizens follow the ethical precepts of some particular form of religion. In many cases this is so obvious that it does not need to be said. Can one imagine an American or British government attempting to outlaw sexual intercourse outside marriage because many religions hold it to be sinful? Can one imagine these governments prohibiting divorce, or the use of contraceptives? The fact that such proposals, if made, would not be taken seriously is testimony to the importance we place on the idea that the State should not enforce religious beliefs or the ethical doctrines that flow from them. We accept this view even if, as in the case of sex outside marriage, the ethical doctrine is quite widely shared among different Christian denominations and some non-Christian religions as well.

We have argued that the traditional doctrine of the sanctity of human life is rationally indefensible, and that its widespread acceptance stems from religious teachings. The principle of the separation of Church and State therefore implies that the State should not enforce the traditional sanctity of life doctrine. Religious believers should be quite free to follow the teachings of their religion on such matters as sex outside marriage or the use of contraception, and to urge others to follow these teachings; no religious believers, however, should expect the State to compel others who do not share their beliefs to act in accordance with religiously motivated views.

In place of the traditional view

We have rejected the traditional principle of the sanctity of human life because the principle gives immense significance to something—biological species—which really has no intrinsic moral significance at all. A more defensible view about the wrongness of killing would need to select a characteristic or set of characteristics which does have moral significance in relation to killing.

Let us begin with the simplest possible characteristics, and move to the more complex ones only if the simpler ones prove unsatisfactory. Since it is logically impossible to kill something that has never been alive, the simplest possible characteristic is life itself. Is it wrong to kill any living thing? A few sensitive people may worry about the ethics of weeding one's garden, but it is hard to see how killing a dandelion can be seriously wrong. The dandelion, we presume, has no conscious experiences. Hence there is no sense in which it suffers, or is missing out on anything, when it dies. To take the life of something that is not even conscious is not, other things being equal, seriously wrong. (We add the 'other things being equal' clause here because it might, for instance, be very seriously wrong to cut down a beautiful old tree, or to kill the last remaining specimens of a rare orchid. The wrong here is not done to the tree or the orchid, but to those who can appreciate them.)

Does consciousness make the difference? It certainly makes *some* difference. Once a being is conscious, there are certain things we ought not to do to it. We ought not to cause it to suffer, or at least not without a sufficient reason. It is also true that to kill a conscious being is to prevent it from having any future experiences. If these experiences might have been pleasurable ones, this may be enough ground to say that it would have been better not to kill. Of course, if the future experiences of the conscious being were likely to consist of unredeemed suffering, that would be a reason for killing.

All this tallies quite well with the way in which we commonly react to killings. Idly plucking plants as we lie in the meadow on a summer's day is not a habit we deplore; idly shooting sparrows from the same meadow would, for many of us, not be acceptable. To put a sick and dying bird out of its misery, on the other hand, is quite proper.

Still, while we may object to killing sparrows as an idle whim, we do not treat the killing of such beings as a matter of great moral significance. We kill animals for food, although we could be well nourished without doing so. Although we do often treat the lives of non-human animals far too lightly, it would be a mistake to equate the killing of a sparrow with the killing of a normal, mature human being. So we still need to press on, and find another characteristic, or set of characteristics, which serves to distinguish the sparrow from such a human being.

We have already looked at some characteristics which are far stronger candidates for this role than species membership: Joseph Fletcher's 'indicators of humanhood', which are, we may recall: self-awareness, self-control, a sense of the future, a sense of the past, the capacity to relate to others, concern for others, communication, and curiosity. There were also three other characteristics emphasized by other writers: rationality, the use of language, and autonomy. We noted earlier that some of these characteristics imply each other, in that one could not have a sense of the past and future without at least some degree of self-awareness and some capacity for rational thought. We also noted some plausible grounds on which it can be held that it is much worse to kill a being with self-awareness and a sense of the future than to kill a being utterly incapable of entertaining any hopes or desires about what might or might not happen to it in the future. We saw that Michael Tooley has suggested that the ability to see oneself as existing over time is a necessary condition for the possession of a right to life.

To invoke the language of 'rights', as Tooley does, is not always conducive to clarity of thought. Too often there is a tendency to treat rights as somehow 'innate' or 'natural' or 'self-evident' and to use claims about rights to block off any further discussion. We often make better progress in understanding moral arguments by dropping the terminology of rights, and dealing directly with the underlying moral considerations by which the claims about rights are supported. So, in the case of Tooley's argument, it might be safer not to talk of being a 'continuing self' as a necessary condition for a right to life, but simply to say that to kill a continuing self is to do something of much greater moral significance than to kill a being who is unable to see itself as existing over time. The philosophical simplicity thus obtained is, however, achieved at the cost of a good deal of clumsiness in expression; and since the language of rights is now so widely used in debates about the treatment of severely handicapped infants we shall make use of it ourselves—always bearing in mind that the expression is no more than a convenient shorthand for the moral considerations on which the right is based.

With this proviso, Tooley's argument is basically sound. Its underlying principle is that the wrongness of an action is related to the extent to which the action prevents some interests, desires or preferences from being fulfilled. This basic principle explains both why it is wrong, other things being equal, to inflict pain, and why it is wrong, other things being equal, to kill a being with a desire to go on living. Any being capable of feeling pain can have a desire that the pain stop, but only a being capable of understanding that it has a prospect of future existence can have a desire to go on living, and only a continuing self can have an interest in continued life.

Tooley suggests that we reserve the term 'person' for those beings who are capable of understanding that they are continuing selves. In this he follows the seventeenth-century British philosopher John Locke, who defined a 'person' as

A thinking intelligent being that has reason and reflection and can consider itself as itself, the same thinking thing, in different times and places.

This definition makes 'person' close to what Fletcher would call 'human', except that it singles out self-awareness and the sense of the past and future as the core of the concept. It is clear that on Locke's and Tooley's definition, 'person' is not identical with 'member of the species *Homo sapiens*'. Neither human foetuses, nor human infants, nor humans with very severe retardation or brain damage would be persons. On the other hand chimpanzees might be, and so might some other non-human animals as well. Thus the notion of a person, as employed by Tooley, reflects no arbitrary, species-based boundary, but characteristics of obvious relevance to the wrongness of killing.

Some will find Tooley's position more shocking than anything we have said so far. In Tooley's view, after all, an infant does not have to be severely handicapped for it to lack a right to life. *No* infant is born with self-awareness or a sense of the future. If Tooley is right, no new-born infant has a right to life. Just when normal human infants acquire some minimal degree of self-awareness is difficult to say—almost certainly not in the first month of life, perhaps not in the first three months, but quite probably within the first year. Whichever way we decide this difficult factual question, infants will be deemed not to have a right to life at birth, nor for some time afterwards.

But what of potential? A normal new-born infant has good prospects of a worthwhile, happy, and fulfilling life, a life with many of the experiences which we think of as making our own lives rewarding and satisfying. Does not this potential distinguish the normal infant from the severely handicapped infant, and give the former, at least, a right to life?

Tooley argues that a right to life cannot be based on potential. His argument is based on a rejection of the moral significance of the distinction between acts and omissions—a distinction we also rejected in Chapter 4. The relevance of the distinction here is as follows: if one holds that it is wrong to kill a new-born infant (or foetus) because that infant (or foetus) will eventually become a person with a worthwhile life, then why is it not also wrong to omit to do an act which would have the consequence that a person with a worthwhile life comes into existence? In other words, if it is wrong to kill, why is it not also wrong to abstain from sexual intercourse that would lead to procreation? Both the omission and the killing have the same consequence: there will not be a person who might otherwise have had a worthwhile life. If the killing does not violate an actual right to life, and is said to be wrong only because of the person who will now not exist, why is it worse than abstinence? We could only regard it as worse if an act was worse than an omission with the same consequences. But this is the mistake we rejected in Chapter 4.

Admittedly, when we refrain from reproducing, there is no being whose life has already begun. Intuitively, this makes a difference. We must recall, however, that when we kill a new-born infant there is no *person* whose life has begun. When I think of myself as the person I now am, I realize that I did not come into existence until some time after my birth. At birth I had no sense of the future, and no experiences which I can now remember as 'mine'. It is the beginning of the life of the person, rather than of the physical organism, that is crucial so far as the right to life is concerned.

Rejecting the distinction between acts and omissions leads us to see that so far as the prevention of the existence of a future person is concerned, killing and not reproducing are similar. Most people hold that there is no moral obligation to reproduce. The world has enough people, and too many future persons are being created already. Even Roman Catholics who oppose the use of artificial methods of birth control do not disapprove of refraining from sexual intercourse during a woman's fertile periods.

All this would suggest that we should give no weight to the potential of the new-born infant. That is the conclusion we must reach if we think that there is no value in bringing extra new people into the world. There is, however, another possible view. We might hold that, other things being equal, it *is* good to bring more people into the world. We might say that the reason we do not object to people refraining from reproducing, is that other things are usually not equal. For one thing, there is the global problem of overpopulation; but let us put this issue aside, and assume we are considering bringing people into the world in a situation in which there is no population problem. There would then still be strong personal reasons which a woman might have for not wishing to go through pregnancy and childbirth. Because we respect a woman's right to control her reproduction, we would leave that decision entirely to her. Once an infant is born, however, as long as there are people willing to adopt it and look after it, reasons of this kind will not apply. Hence some reasons which justify refraining from reproducing will not justify killing a new-born infant, as long as others are prepared to take responsibility for the infant's care.

This means that rejecting the distinction between acts and omissions does not, after all, necessarily lead to the conclusion that *no* weight can be given to the potential of the new-born infant. We can agree that a decision to kill a new-born infant is no more—and no less—the prevention of the existence of an additional person than is a decision not to produce. We can add, however, that women will often have strong reasons against reproducing, much stronger reasons than anyone is likely to have in favour of killing an infant for whom others are willing to care. Unless we are prepared to hold that people ought to reproduce whenever possible, we cannot give *overriding* value to the creation of additional life; but we can give *some* value to it, so that it counts as an important factor in decisions about killing new-born infants. The value of creating additional life would then still be a factor in decisions about reproducing, but it would be much less significant, because it would often be outweighed by reasons which point in the opposite direction.

Whether there is value in bringing additional people into the world is an extremely complex philosophical issue—too complex to deal with in this book. We will, however, touch on it again in the next chapter and draw out some further implications. What we have shown so far is that the potential of an infant can be a reason against killing it. Obviously the greater the infant's potential for a happy and worthwhile life, the stronger this reason is. Thus there may still be good reason to protect the lives of new-born infants even if, strictly speaking, they do not have a right to life. This is a modification of Tooley's position which makes it less shocking than it at first appeared.

There are other reasons why the view we are taking is less radical than it may seem to be. A second reason is that most babies are, fortunately, much wanted and loved by their parents. Anyone who killed a wanted baby would therefore do a terrible wrong to the baby's parents, irrespective of whether the baby has a right to life.

A third reason is that even if a baby were not wanted by its parents, there might well be someone else, or another couple, who very much wants to cherish that child and bring it up as their own. So once again, independently of the rights or interests of the infant itself, to kill the baby would be to harm the person or couple wanting to adopt the child.

A fourth reason is that to say that an infant has no right to life is not to say that it has no rights at all. People sometimes mistakenly assume this to be the case, reasoning that if we are dead we cannot have a right to anything. This may be so, but it does not refute the view that, as long as we are alive, we may have some rights without having a right to life. Consider how differently we think about someone who tortures stray cats, and someone who humanely kills them.

For Tooley, we can have rights only if we are capable of having the requisite desires or interests. If new-born infants are not continuing selves, they cannot have a right to continued life; but it is plausible to suppose that new-born infants can feel pain and prefer not to be in pain; that they can feel cold, and desire not to be cold; that they can feel hungry, and desire not to be hungry. It is therefore plausible to suppose that new-born infants have rights to have their pain relieved, and to be kept warm and fed. These rights are not absolute but they indicate what we ought not to do to infants except for overriding reasons.

These four reasons serve to limit the cases in which killing an infant would be defensible. The fifth reason why our position is less radical than it appears is different. This fifth reason does not restrict the cases in which killing an infant would be defensible: it points out how close we already are to the kind of killing which we are suggesting might be permitted. Recall the now-standard procedure, described in Chapter 3, of finding out during pregnancy whether the foetus is abnormal and allowing—even recommending—an abortion if the test should prove positive. This is not a case of sacrificing the foetus to save the life or health of the pregnant woman. It is, quite straightforwardly, a decision to end at an early stage a life which does not have the usual prospects for a full human existence. The difference between this decision and infanticide is that abortion kills the unseen foetus in the womb, while infanticide kills the new-born infant. In neither case, however, has the life of the *person* begun.

Quite often a defect which would have warranted abortion during pregnancy is not discovered until birth. Has the situation then changed so critically that it is now horrific to contemplate ending a life which three months previously could have been ended with little controversy?

Consider the situation in which Peggy Stinson found herself in December 1976. She was 24 weeks pregnant, but the pregnancy was going seriously wrong. The placenta was in the wrong position and threatening to detach altogether, causing a major haemorrhage that would put her life at risk as well as that of the baby. There was also a possibility of the baby's surviving, but with serious damage. Weighing up these difficulties on 15 December, Peggy and her husband Robert contemplated terminating the pregnancy. This would have reduced the risk to Peggy, and also ensured that they would not end up with a damaged baby. After the abortion, Peggy could have started on another pregnancy, with a high probability that it would develop normally. At 24 weeks, an abortion is legal in the United States; it would remain possible for Peggy to have an abortion for another two weeks.

In a single day, everything changed. On 16 December Peggy went into premature labour. The baby was born alive, but on the margins of viability. The Stinsons emphasized that they did not want any heroic measures taken. Nevertheless they gradually lost control of their child. Doctors threatened to take out court orders if the parents did not consent to treatment. The baby developed all sorts of complications. He was put on a respirator nonetheless. At one point there appeared to be a very real prospect that the hospital would hand over to the reluctant parents a living but grossly impaired child. This led Peggy to some ethical reflections. As she wrote in her diary:

A woman can terminate a perfectly healthy pregnancy by abortion at 24½ weeks and that is legal. Nature can terminate a problem pregnancy by miscarriage at 24½ weeks and the baby must be saved at all cost; anything less is illegal and immoral. That's what they say at Pediatric Hospital, anyway.

Peggy Stinson was quite right to point out the oddity of this situation. After all, the mere location of the foetus or infant, whether inside or outside the womb, cannot make a crucial difference to its moral status. If the foetus at 24½ weeks does not have a right to life, why should we attribute such a right to the new-born baby at the same gestational age?

Opponents of abortion stress the similarities between the foetus and the infant, and urge that since the latter is clearly a human being, with the same right to life as any other human being, so the foetus should also be recognized as a human being with the same right to life as any other. We are not impressed, however, by the fact that both the infant and the foetus are clearly human beings. This is only true in the sense that they are members of the species *Homo sapiens*. Neither ranks as 'human' if judged against Fletcher's 'indicators of humanhood'. Neither is a person, as Locke and Tooley define the term. The new-born infant should therefore be regarded as we now regard the foetus, rather than the other way around.

In accepting abortion, as so many Western nations have now done, we have already taken a major step away from the traditional principle of the sanctity of human life. We have, however, come to place great weight on a boundary line—the moment of birth—that, while clear and precise, is not really crucial from the point of view of the moral status of the foetus or infant. The move to a less precise, but more significant boundary—the point at which there is self-awareness and a sense of the future—is therefore not as big a step as one might at first think.

There is one further point about the dividing line we are proposing. It is sometimes said that if we start to kill severely handicapped infants we will end up threatening disabled adults as well. To allow infanticide before the onset of self-awareness, however, cannot threaten anyone who is in a position to worry about it. Anyone able to understand what it is to live or die must already be a person and has the same right to life as all the rest of us. Disability which does not rule out self-awareness and a sense of the future is totally irrelevant to the possession of the right to life.

Unlike many other forms of homicide, infanticide carried out by parents or with their consent poses no threat to anyone in the community who is capable of grasping what is happening. This fact goes a long way towards accounting for the equanimity with which many other cultures have accepted it. Nor is it only in other cultures that this point has been recognized. Jeremy Bentham, the founder of the reforming school of Utilitarians, criticized the severity with which infanticide was punished in his day, and remarked that the crime is 'of a nature not to give the slightest inquietude to the most timid imagination'. Infanticide threatens none of us, for once we are aware of it, we are not infants.

But doesn't Tooley's view of rights have implications which threaten us all? Wouldn't we still have to worry about the prospect that at some stage, by accident or infirmity, we might lose our ability to be self-aware, and our sense of the future? Would we not then also lose, according to the proposed theory of rights, our right to life? This fear is based on a misunderstanding of the theory of rights. Once a being with a sense of the future exists, that being can have an interest in her or his future existence. This interest should be respected. Obviously no plausible theory could condone the random killing of people while they are asleep. On Tooley's view the interests we have before we go to sleep are enough to give us a continuing right to life during the period of unconsciousness.

Tooley's theory of rights is bound to be controversial,

notwithstanding the reasons why its impact may not be quite so radical as one might at first think. There may be other alternatives which are also worth discussing. That there is a need for some alternative view, however, should be clear. Without the religious framework in which it developed, the traditional principle lacks philosophically sound foundations. Something needs to be put in its place. In this chapter we have suggested a coherent and defensible alternative. It is one thing to have a defensible philosophical theory, however, and another thing to decide what to do in practice. In our final chapters we shall bring the discussion back to the practical choices that confront parents and doctors.

7 IN WHOSE INTERESTS?

If all human infants had an absolute right to life, there would be no point in considering where the true interests of the severely disabled infant lie; nor would the interests of the parents and other members of the family, or of the community as a whole, be relevant. It would be morally obligatory, in every case, to do everything possible to keep the infant alive. But we have now concluded that new-born infants do not have a right to life. This conclusion opens the door to a host of other questions. As we have seen, to deny that infants have a right to life is not to deny the importance of such factors as their potential for a worthwhile life, and the feelings of their parents, or of other couples who may be interested in adopting them. We must now try to sort out some of these factors so that we can make the right decisions.

The interests of the child

The obvious place to begin is with the child. We might ask: is it always in the interests of the child to do everything possible to keep it alive? But this question presupposes that a new-born infant can have an interest in its future existence. As we have seen, there are good reasons for rejecting this presupposition. A new-born infant is not a continuing self. Although it may develop into a person, it cannot strictly be said to have an interest in surviving to become a person, because it lacks psychological continuity with the person it may become. We should therefore rephrase the question: is it always in the interests of the person the child may become to do everything possible to keep the child alive?

 In America and some other countries legal actions have recently been brought against doctors, diagnostic laboratories, and governments to obtain compensation for the 'wrongful life' of a defective child. Shauna Tamar Curlender, for example, was born with Tay–Sachs disease and, through her parents, sued the diagnostic laboratories. The claim was based on the fact that the laboratories had been negligent in not advising the parents that they were carriers of the disease and thus ran the risk of giving birth to a defective child. Had the parents known that they were carriers, Shauna would presumably never have existed. Since the suit was taken out in the name of the child, rather than the parents, the claim only makes sense on the assumption that it would have been better for the child if she had never been born.

One can argue about the details of particular cases. Down's syndrome is especially problematic, because it is often possible for a Down's syndrome infant to live a reasonably happy, if simple, sort of life. An English judge of the Court of Appeal was swayed by this consideration in the case of a baby known to the public only as Alexandra. Alexandra was born in July 1981, in the London borough of Hammersmith. Like Baby Doe, she was a Down's syndrome infant with a life-threatening blockage which needed surgical removal. The parents refused consent for surgery. The Director of Hammersmith Social Services took the issue to court, where it was decided to make the child a ward of the court and to authorize the operation.

Following the court order, the infant was taken to a London hospital for surgery—where the surgeon refused to operate when he learned that the parents had refused consent. Another court hearing was called and this time the parents' decision was upheld. The case was finally decided on appeal. Lord Justice Templeman held that surgery should be performed, on the grounds that the life of a Down's syndrome infant is not 'demonstrably awful'. The decision implied that if the infant had had some other defect, with a 'demonstrably awful' life in store, surgery would not have been ordered.

It may be true that the life of a Down's syndrome infant with no other complications can be reasonably satisfactory, but the situation can be very different if there are complications. In the first chapter we quoted from a letter by John and Susan West about their son Brian, a Down's syndrome baby with no connection between the back of the mouth and the stomach. The Wests refused consent for an operation, but the doctors obtained a court order and operated anyway. In their letter, published in the *Los Angeles Times* in May 1982, the Wests wrote of the 'pain, suffering and misery' their baby had been through during his eighteen months on earth. Brian West died at a little over two years of age, and his father wrote another description of his son's life. Brian went through multiple surgical procedures and numerous periods in hospital. After reconstructive surgery was performed soon after Brian's first birthday, John West recounts:

Whenever we visited him during this time, he was screaming in pain. He was tied spread-eagle in his hospital crib for six weeks to keep him from pulling at his surgical wounds. I don't think he ever recovered from this. When the wounds healed, he never showed the same level of alertness or interest in toys as he did before the surgery. He had recurring episodes of pain as gastric juices backed up into his esophagus (it lacked the valve which is normally present to prevent this). He continued to have numerous bouts with pneumonia.

Brian West had been born in October 1980. Despite the repeated and extremely painful surgery, it was September 1982 before oral feeding could be attempted for the first time: 'They got a little food down, but most was regurgitated.' In November 1982 Brian went into hospital because of breathing problems. He became unconscious and was placed on a respirator. When taken off the respirator, Brian was found to have suffered brain damage and to be blind. He spent five weeks in intensive care.

Whenever he was awake, he was agitated and writhing in his bed . . . The doctors told us they had no idea whether he was in pain or not, but one look at him made your whole body cringe . . . On December 21, 1982, thank God, he died. We loved Brian and we always wanted the best for him.

Considering Brian's life from his point of view—disregarding entirely what his parents went through, and the cost of his medical care—it would have been better if he had died shortly after birth. Extended periods of his life were 'demonstrably awful', so awful that whatever better moments he may have had in his short existence cannot have compensated for them. Those who obtained the court order to save Brian's life did Brian no good: on the contrary, they did him great harm.

Looking back over Brian's life now that it is over, this judgement seems undeniable; but could one argue that at the

time when the court order was granted, it was in the interests of
the person Brian might have become to have the surgery carried
out? After all, it was not then apparent how bad the outcome
would be. John West writes that several doctors have since said
that the operation to reconstruct Brian's oesophagus was
'experimental' in that its success was very uncertain. Still, it *might*
have succeeded. Was the risk worthwhile?

In taking any risk, we weigh the possible benefits against the
possible costs, and try to assess the probability of each. Here the
fact that Brian had Down's syndrome is relevant in two ways.
First, John West has pointed out that it is relevant to the
probability of a successful outcome. Down's syndrome is associated with poor muscle tone and an increased susceptibility to
infections of the upper respiratory tract. The former may make
swallowing in the reconstructed oesophagus more difficult;
the latter causes additional complications. In addition, John
West has suggested, the reduced mental capacities of a Down's
syndrome child could cause a problem when the child has to
learn how to eat with the new oesophagus. But quite apart from
these medical factors, Down's syndrome is surely relevant to the
decision to operate because it means a reduced potential for a life
with the unique features which are commonly and reasonably
regarded as giving special value to human lives. Even allowing
for the more optimistic assessments of the potential of Down's
syndrome children, this potential cannot be said to be equal to
that of a normal child. The possible benefits of successful surgery
in the case of a Down's syndrome child are therefore, in terms of
these widely accepted values, less than the possible benefits of
similar surgery in a normal child. It might be justifiable to run
some risk of the kind of misery Brian experienced, if there were a
fair chance of a reasonably normal life; the same risk might not be
justifiable if the best that could be hoped for was the reduced
potential of the life of someone with Down's syndrome. Judging
only from the point of view of the child, Down's syndrome can be
a factor against surgery when the success of the surgery is
uncertain and there is a risk of misery if it fails.

There are other defects which make it much easier to say that
continued life cannot be in anyone's interests. Lesch–Nyhan
syndrome would be one. This disease is characterized by

profound mental retardation and corollaries of brain damage, such as stiff limbs with peculiar movements, and self-mutilation. To keep such a child alive is to do it terrible harm.

In the case of infants it is, of course, impossible to ask them how they feel about their lives. When infants have been treated, and have survived without mental retardation, we can seek their point of view afterwards. The evidence we have is anecdotal rather than systematic. No one seems to have followed up spina bifida infants and asked those survivors capable of understanding the question whether they are glad they were kept alive. Some have come forward and offered the answer themselves. In reply to an article in the *Journal of Medical Ethics* which proposed law reform so that infants could be allowed to die, Mrs Alison Davies wrote:

In reference to your items on the bill drafted by Mr. and Mrs. Brahams permitting doctors to withhold treatment from newborn handicapped babies, I would like to make the following points.

I am 28 years old, and suffer from a severe physical disability which is irreversible, as defined by the bill. I was born with myelomeningocele spina bifida. Mr. and Mrs. Brahams suggest several criteria for predicting the potential quality of life of people like me, and I note that I fail to fulfil most of them.

I have suffered considerable and prolonged pain from time to time, and have undergone over 20 operations, thus far, some of them essential to save my life. Even now my health is at best uncertain. I am doubly incontinent and confined to a wheelchair and thus, according to the bill, I should have 'no worthwhile quality of life'.

However, because I was fortunately born in rather more tolerant times, I was given the chance to defy the odds and live, which is now being denied to handicapped newborns. Even so, my parents were encouraged to leave me in the hospital and 'go home and have another' and I owe my life to the fact that they refused to accept the advice of the experts.

Despite my disability I went to an ordinary school and then to university, where I gained an honours degree in sociology. I now work full-time defending the right to life of handicapped people. I have been married eight years to an able-bodied man, and over the years we have travelled widely in Europe, the Soviet Union and the United States. This year we plan to visit the Far East.

Who could say I have 'no worthwhile quality of life'? I am sure though that no doctor could have predicted when I was 28 days old (and incidentally had received no operation at all) that despite my physical problems I would lead such a full and happy life. I do not doubt that they were 'acting in good faith' when they advised my parents to abandon me, but that does not mean that their advice was correct.

Not all spina bifida survivors, however, take this view. John Lorber relates:

I asked a group of young adult spina bifida subjects whether they would wish to have a child of their own treated if it was born with severe spina bifida; none would.

It must be very difficult, psychologically, to judge your own life as not having been worth living; and the difficulty will be compounded if you know that your parents have made tremendous sacrifices to keep you alive. This makes all the more remarkable a letter received by the American CBS television network after they had screened a programme which featured John and Susan West:

You posed the question to his parents, 'What would Brian say?' I would like to answer that question for Brian—I feel I have that right since I was also once a very young child at death's door, undergoing excruciatingly painful medical treatment in order to save my life. I was also 'tied down'; I also screamed for mercy for 'them' (Doctors *and* my parents) to stop what they were doing—I screamed so long and so hard the medical staff took to *taping my mouth shut* to cut off the screams (which of course then merely reverberated inside my head) . . . Ask me now: 'was it worth going through—do you appreciate what they did?'
NO.
My answer for Brian is 'Thank you Mom and Dad for wanting to let me die in my own way, at my own time, with my dignity still intact.'
Death is not so terrible.

So there is testimony from both sides—from survivors who under present policies might not have been kept alive, and are glad they are alive, and from survivors who have been kept alive and do not think it was worth it. When the defect is severe mental retardation, no first-hand evidence is possible. We can only reach an estimate based on observation and imagination. As John Freeman pointed out (see p. 63), any such estimate involves the very difficult task of putting ourselves in the position of someone with mental capacities quite different from our own. That *we* would not like to live the kind of life lived by a retarded person is no indication that the retarded person finds life unpleasant. But this scepticism is also not a positive reason for saying that such people are enjoying their lives. It is only a reason for caution. Perhaps we can say that it is in the best interests of a child with Lesch-Nyhan's disease to die rapidly, for the child will suffer considerably and cannot become a person with an interest in continued life. There are, however, many other cases where the criterion of the best interests of the child, or of the person the child will become, gives no clear-cut guidance.

Is uncertainty an argument for keeping alive? If we think of Brian West's life, we will not rush to that conclusion. For another example, look at what happened to Andrew Stinson, the extremely premature child of Peggy and Robert Stinson. Despite his parents' request that 'no heroics' should be used on such a marginally viable baby, all the technology of modern neonatal intensive care was used to keep Andrew alive. During that time he suffered from periodic fits and many other distressing complications. There was a grave risk that he had suffered brain damage. At one point Andrew's doctor told the Stinsons that it must 'hurt like hell' every time Andrew drew a breath. Andrew died at five months. Would any chance, no matter how slight, that Andrew might survive sufficiently intact to lead a worth-while life have been enough to justify putting him through this ordeal? His parents did not think so. Sometimes the cost is so great that it is not right to risk it, despite the possibility of some good coming from it.

The interests of the family

It is often said that the survival of a handicapped child is also the creation of a handicapped family. In some cases that judgement can be too severe; but in others it is the simple truth.

The British National Children's Bureau Information Service has published the following summary of a study of the problems faced by families of handicapped infants in the Bristol area:

Recent studies give an insight into the formidable day-to-day task faced by many families with a severely mentally or physically handicapped

child. Two-thirds of school-age severely handicapped Bristol children
were dependent on their families for at least one aspect of self-care, such
as dressing or toiletting. Forty per cent were incontinent, a problem
involving much extra work. A third needed attention at least once a
night. A third could never be safely left unattended. Forty per cent
interfered with their mother's housework. Fifty-five per cent of mothers
had problems taking the child out, sometimes because of physical
difficulty in getting the child on and off a bus, sometimes because of
behaviour problems. Nearly half of the mothers felt their social activities
were restricted by the child. Most of the problems were more common
where the child was mentally rather than physically handicapped.

The main burden of care falls on the mother. Forty-two per cent of the
Bristol mothers received no help looking after the child at home, and
eighty-two per cent little with housework. The principal relief is provided
by school or day care, few children being excluded from these services
today. Otherwise the father is the chief source of help, but most are
necessarily unavailable when some help is needed and few provide a high
level of assistance in child care tasks or with housework. A few siblings
help substantially but relatives, friends and neighbours give much less
help, and this is mainly confined to baby-sitting or shopping. Practical
help with child-care or domestic tasks from social service departments is
virtually nonexistent.

Charles Hannam, himself the father of a Down's syndrome
child, interviewed several couples with children like his own so
that their experiences could serve as a guide to other parents with
Down's syndrome children. The outcome was a highly successful
book, *Parents and Mentally Handicapped Children.* Down's syndrome
is often considered a mild form of mental retardation. Unlike,
say, spina bifida it involves no serious physical handicap.
Nevertheless some passages from Hannam's book make manifest
the strain of looking after such children. The families all talk
about tiredness, which Hannam describes as

not just the tiredness after a hard day's work, but a sense of total
exhaustion and depression that comes of an accumulation of bad nights,
irritation and 'just coping'. Not enough energy is left for going out in the
evenings and getting away.

One father with a demanding business life said:

by the end of the week sometimes I am pretty weary mentally, and I feel
sometimes Monday morning that the weekend has been a dead loss from

my own selfish angle. That's because relationships in the house have been strained, perhaps because of a broken night's sleep, perhaps because he has been naughty.

Another couple said that they could only go out in the evenings once every couple of months. Hannam asked what stopped them from going out. The mother replied:

Really, it is getting someone to babysit. Most of our friends rely on youngsters, schoolchildren, and we don't honestly feel we can leave him.

The father added:

It isn't only that you see, he gets—he did go through a phase where he persistently had his bowels open in the evening, or worse, he would start to half change himself and the bed would be in a mess and I loathe the idea of neighbours having to clean up after him because I don't like having to do it myself, now he is eight, and so I didn't ask . . . but quite honestly we haven't had anyone to babysit at all, have we?

Hannam sums up the chapter by pointing out that the main burden falls on the mothers:

For the mothers there is no escape unless outsiders come and help or the child can go to a residential unit occasionally . . . Unless there is a babysitter, such 'normal' activities as shopping, hair-cutting for the other children and changing library books become so unpleasant a hazard that they are dropped as far as possible when the handicapped child is at home. The family's activities are geared to the handicapped child's capabilities. There is no choice about this and everyone else has to go to the wall.

Another series of interviews with parents of Down's syndrome children has been carried out by Dr Billie Shepperdson of University College, Swansea. Her report is especially valuable because she raised directly the issue of euthanasia. Of the 77 parents asked, 37 (48 per cent) were prepared to accept the idea that not all handicapped children should be kept alive at all costs. Some of these objected to active killing but were prepared to allow a child to die, whereas others objected to the cruelty of a lingering death. So far as the impact on families is concerned, it is significant that the strongest support for euthanasia came from the mothers of older children. One mother said:

If I knew as I know now I'd have euthanasiaed (*sic*) her. It's cruel for me and cruel for her. There's no life for me while she's here and none for her.

During the first series of interviews, conducted in 1972, another mother said:

Oh if I could have got away with it I would have neglected him because I was so fed up and tired more than anything, so if I could have got away with it I would have neglected him. I'm sorry I didn't in a way. You've got to be honest—they are a tie for the rest of your life . . . there's not going to be any freedom at all.

A follow-up interview in 1981 revealed that this woman had not altered her opinion. Another mother indicated that at birth she was keen for her Down's syndrome child to live, but her feelings had changed as a result of her experiences:

It's all right for those who've never had one to say keep them alive. On the surface things don't look any different but in reality it's a continual strain. You don't show it outside.

These pro-euthanasia comments were matched by an equal number who opposed the practice, and some of these made it plain that they considered the whole experience to have been worthwhile: 'We'd have missed a lot,' one mother said, while another who had wanted her Down's syndrome child to die in infancy said: 'Now she is my life.' The only statistically significant factor associated with the differences in attitude to euthanasia was social class: 68 per cent of those in the higher social classes favoured euthanasia for handicapped children in general, as against 48 per cent of all parents. The difference between the classes was even more marked when the question focused specifically on euthanasia for Down's syndrome children: 56 per cent of those in the upper two social classes were in favour, as against only 33 per cent of the whole group.

In addition to studies of the attitudes of parents, there have been some studies of objectively measurable features of the lives of families with handicapped children. One disturbing difference is that these families have a higher rate of marital break-up. A study of the families of children with spina bifida in South Wales found that the quality of the marital relationship deteriorated over the years and the divorce rate was twice that of a control group. Another study of 60 families, half with a Down's syndrome child and the other half a control group with normal children, also found significantly more unhappy marriages in the families with the Down's syndrome child. In nine of these families there were frequent episodes of open disruption in the marital relationships, or else there was open antagonism, constant nagging, or a complete absence of affection. These marriages were rated as 'poor'. None of the control group had marriages which rated worse than 'moderate'. Although good marriages did not appear to be harmed by the presence of the retarded child, weaker marriages which might otherwise have remained at a tolerable level were more likely to deteriorate.

It is not only the parents who may be under strain because of the presence of a severely handicapped child. Sisters and brothers are also affected, in part because their parents have to give so much of their time and attention to the disabled member of the family, and in part because they—especially if they are sisters— are likely to be asked to do a good deal of babysitting. In a study carried out in the Oxford region, 174 siblings of Down's syndrome children were compared with the next child on the school list. Using well-tried rating scales, the sisters of the Down's syndrome children were much more likely than other girls in their class to have emotional or behavioural problems. Brothers, however, were no more disturbed than other boys in their class.

Stephen Kew, who spent four years as a research psychologist with the Invalid Children's Aid Association in Britain, has made a special study of the siblings of handicapped children. He found that the degree of disturbance among siblings was related to the severity of the handicap. Of those families which had a child with a very severe mental handicap or functional disability, approximately 60 per cent had a sibling rated as disturbed and between 10 per cent and 15 per cent had a sibling rated as seriously disturbed. Where the handicaps were slight, approximately 50 per cent of families had a disturbed sibling and 8 per cent had a seriously disturbed one. Stephen Kew summed up the problems of siblings as follows:

because of the presence of a handicapped child, siblings are often expected to behave in ways that are not appropriate to their ages or abilities. I have looked at some of those circumstances surrounding handicaps of different kinds that are conducive to a slower development by siblings in certain aspects of their growth than they might otherwise expect. We have seen that many children miss out on important aspects of childhood because they are either expected to be perfect children in compensation for their handicapped brothers and sisters or else they are expected to act like adults taking on a child-minding role towards these siblings.

We have seen that as a result of all this children can be backward in their development of speech and language and in other educational spheres. I have suggested also that those children who are not allowed to have a normal brother or sister relationship in terms of their play and general interaction, are likely to suffer socially. Many children are not allowed to fight, play, make a noise, express their anger, or indeed their joy, whenever their handicapped sibling is near in case they upset or harm him in some way. It is most unlikely that children can grow up in such a restrictive atmosphere without their peer relationships, their social attitudes and to some extent their own personalities being affected. When a child is retarded, older siblings tend to be held back in their development and younger siblings lack that spur to develop which a normal sibling would provide.

These statistics need to be supplemented by an insight into what all this can mean on a personal level. We know of no more graphic portrayal of the conflict between the interests of the child and the interests of the family than an article written by an anonymous Melbourne woman whose sister, Barbara, had been born with brain damage caused by rubella. The woman was prompted to write by some glib references to 'the rights of the child' on a talkback radio programme about handicapped infants being allowed to die. So she described her life with Barbara, who did not walk until she was four, was not toilet-trained until she was seven, was constantly demanding, had frequent fits, and slept only two hours a day. As a result her parents had violent quarrels in which one of them would threaten to leave, the neighbours' children ceased to call, and Barbara's brother, who had been slow at school, fell back 'to idiot level'.

And through it all Barbara continued to move like a demented destroyer, hyped up by the constant adrenalin that drowned all calm and logic, unmoved by my father kicking and bellowing at my brother, lashing out at him constantly with the strap, she babbled on and on, shaking you and demanding a response, rocking in her chair and making wild noises, or moving about shifting things and throwing tantrums at every frustration. And never sleeping.

The author of this article wrote that each night on the way home from school she would vomit, so terrified was she of what the time at home would bring. Her article was headed 'The cost of one child's rights' and it ended like this:

I feel my rights as a child and those of every member of my family were overwhelmed by Barbara's rights and that the decision was not made by those who suffered the consequences. I could not endure giving birth to a malformed child, and rather than fight for what I consider to be my rights regarding whether it lived or not, I have never had children.

There are, of course, many handicapped children who are less destructive of family harmony than Barbara. For some families the opportunity to care for a less able or less gifted family member is a positive experience. Cliff Cunningham, who teaches psychology at the University of Manchester and is the author of *Down's Syndrome: An Introduction for Parents*, claims that between 50 and 75 per cent of parents who have had a baby with Down's syndrome report that, once over the initial shock, they found the experience rewarding and strengthening, while fewer than 20 per cent 'see the whole thing as a burden' and never get much joy or reward from the child. No source is given for this estimate, and the nature of the book suggests it may be an optimistic one, but it is certainly true that some can find virtue in what is, for others, a bleak necessity. We are inclined to believe, however, that the experiences of Charles Hannam are more likely to represent a median point between the extremes of lives that are totally wrecked and lives that are rewarded and strengthened. Hannam, from whose interviews with Down's syndrome families we have quoted, is an advocate of the rights of the handicapped. He has spent a lot of time on committees of organizations for parents of handicapped children. His book was published in conjunction with Mind, a British charity concerned with the needs of the mentally handicapped. He was far better informed about Down's syndrome than most parents. His son David, a Down's syndrome child able to speak a few words and understand more, was less severely handicapped than many other children. Yet when David was sixteen, Charles Hannam felt that this was what he wanted to say to him:

I am so sorry, David, I don't want you. I have tried to be good but I haven't done very much for you. I have stayed away from home whenever I knew you would be about, I have looked after you because of Pam, not to help you. I try to sit as far away from you as possible at the dinner table, I snap at you when the sugar goes all over the place. You do all the things I hate so deeply in myself, my own ugliness, my clumsy movements. I want to be a jolly and humorous sort of man and you make me feel hateful, surgically cold and detached. I have thought about murdering you and you are my child . . . I have felt that you were my own special little albatross, hanging around my neck forever.

Shortly afterwards, the Hannams put David in an institution.

The child or the family?

When a handicapped child can experience some pleasure or fulfilment and can lead a life that is not dominated by pain or suffering, prolonging life would seem to be in the best interests of the future person. It may not, however, be in the best interests of the parents or siblings. Which should we choose: the family or the child?

Those who raise this dilemma usually come down in favour of the child, as long as the life of the child is a tolerable one. The most comprehensive recent study of the topic is by the United States President's Commission for the Study of Ethical Problems in Medicine and Biomedical and Behavioral Research. In its report, *Deciding to Forego Life-Sustaining Treatment*, the Commission applies the test of 'the best interests of the infant' in deciding when handicapped infants should be treated. The Commission rejects therapies that are futile or clearly not of net benefit to the infant, but says:

Within constraints of equity and availability, infants should receive all therapies that are clearly beneficial to them. For example, an otherwise healthy Down Syndrome child whose life is threatened by a surgically correctable complication should receive the surgery because he or she would clearly benefit from it.

The Commission is quite explicit about the rejection of family interests:

This is a very strict standard in that it excludes consideration of the negative effects of an impaired child's life on other persons, including parents, siblings, and society. Although abiding by this standard may be difficult in specific cases, it is all too easy to undervalue the lives of handicapped infants; the Commission finds it imperative to counteract this by treating them no less vigorously than their healthy peers or than older children with similar handicaps would be treated.

(We believe that the Commission is in error in assuming that it is wrong to treat handicapped infants less vigorously than older children with similar handicaps. The older children will—unless profoundly retarded—have developed a sense of self-awareness and of the future. They will have an interest in the future of a kind beyond the capacity of any new-born infant. So, as we argued in the preceding chapter, to allow these older children to die for lack of beneficial treatment would be contrary to their interests and hence would do them a wrong which cannot be done to new-born infants. This is not the point at issue now, however, so let us put it aside.)

It is a pity that the Commission did not say a little more about why the interests of the parents and any existing siblings should be disregarded altogether, rather than weighed in the balance together with the alleged interests of the child. After all, there are all kinds of handicaps. In some cases, the balance may come down in favour of life rather than death, but not by anything like the clear-cut margin that would apply when the prospect is for a normal life. The Commission appears to be saying that as long as we have decided that, on balance, continued life is beneficial to the infant, then regardless of how small the margin by which that final decision is reached, the interests of the parents and the siblings count for nothing. The life of Barbara, the rubella-damaged child whose effect on her family we cited earlier, might well have been held to be of benefit to Barbara by some such marginal amount. (We must subtract the frequent fits and tantrums from the pleasures which—let us assume—Barbara could sometimes experience.) If we could have foreseen the effect Barbara was to have on her family, would it have been right to disregard it? Barbara's sister might well wonder why Barbara's supposed interests count, but her own do not.

There is, however, a more fundamental objection to the 'best interests of the infant' criterion invoked by the President's Commission and by many others who have discussed this topic. It is an objection which undercuts the whole dilemma of the 'interests of the child versus interests of the family'. Putting the choice in these terms overlooks someone, or a possible someone, whose interests have been altogether neglected. This is because that possible someone suffers from the most disabling handicap of them all: non-existence. If this sounds mad, read on.

The value of the life of the 'next child'

One of the more firmly established findings about families with a disabled child is that they are less likely than other families to have further children. In one study, out of 160 mothers who could have had more children, 101 decided not to and in 90 of these cases the decision appeared to be directly related to the presence of a retarded child. This confirms the impressions of many of the doctors cited in Chapter 3: Eliot Slater, for instance, was quoted there as saying that parents with an abnormal child will very likely limit their future reproduction, but if the child dies they will have another one which will in all probability be normal. 'Keeping a badly damaged child alive', Slater wrote, 'is likely to eliminate the potential existence of a normal one.' Similar sentiments were voiced by Lorber, Wickes, and Haas; and also by the grandmother who wrote to the parents' support group, Prospect, saying: 'Had the poor little mongol been allowed to die . . . my daughter might have had one or two healthy children in his place—giving more life, not less.'

In the journal Peggy Stinson kept during the long dying of her son Andrew she showed that, like most mothers in her situation, she was concerned about what Andrew's long-term survival in a damaged state might do to her plans to have another child. On 17 February, when Andrew was two months old, she wrote:

I keep thinking about the other baby—the one that won't be born. The IICU (Infant Intensive Care Unit) is choosing between lives. It may already be too late for the next baby. If Andrew's life is strung out much longer, will we have the money, the emotional resources, the nerve to try again?

Unlike many other parents, however, Peggy and her husband, Bob, were sufficiently determined to go ahead anyway. The journal entry for 30 April 1977 is particularly interesting because it poses the philosophical question that is at the hub of this issue:

> Thirty-fifth birthday coming up next week; haven't got forever to try for another child. If we wait much longer, until our insurance runs out or we're being billed for Andrew's custodial care, we'll know we can't afford another child. Or we won't have the nerve to try again.
>
> We want another child. I'm not going to let Pediatric Hospital [where Andrew was being kept alive against his parents' wishes] destroy our chance to have one. At this rate we'll have neither Andrew nor the next child, who, because of Andrew's extended course, will have lost the chance to exist at all.
>
> Jeff [a junior doctor at the hospital more sympathetic to the Stinsons' views than the other senior medical staff] once said our 'next child' was theoretical, abstract—its interests couldn't be considered. Strictly speaking that may be so, but that next baby seems real enough to me. To Bob too. Decision this week to change that abstraction into a real person before it's too late.

Is the 'next child' an abstraction, the value of whose life cannot be considered before it is born, or even conceived? It is tempting to agree with the advice given to Peggy Stinson: after all, if she had not had any more children, no one would have been harmed by that decision. As things turned out the Stinsons did have another child, a boy whom they named Jonathan; but it would sound odd to say that if their experience with Andrew had dissuaded them from having further children, Jonathan would thereby have been harmed. He simply would not have existed. Can one harm a non-existent person?

Against this conclusion, the Oxford philosopher Derek Parfit has argued that absurd consequences flow from a refusal to consider the value of the lives of the people who will exist if we decide to conceive them. Suppose, Parfit says, that a woman is planning to stop taking contraceptive pills so that she can have a child. Before doing so she is told by her doctor that, because of a temporary medical condition, any child she conceives now will be handicapped. If the woman will wait three months, the doctor says, the condition will pass and any child she conceives then will be normal.

We would all think that in these circumstances the woman ought to postpone her plans to become pregnant. We would think this even if the handicap the child would have is not so terrible as to make that child's life one of unredeemed misery. Suppose that the handicap meant, for instance, that the child would be unable to walk without calipers, but would otherwise be normal. A life of limited mobility with no other handicaps can still be a life very definitely worth living. Yet everyone we have asked agrees that, even if the handicap were of this relatively mild kind, the woman ought to wait three months before she conceives.

Behind this reponse may lie the thought that if the woman were to decide against waiting the three months, she would be needlessly causing her child to have a handicap; but the point to notice about Parfit's example is that if the woman waits before becoming pregnant, the child she will then conceive is a *different* child from the one she would have had if she had not postponed becoming pregnant. Each month a fertile woman produces a new egg, with different genetic material. The child who will be conceived from the egg which ripens in April cannot be the same child as the child who would have been conceived from the egg which ripened in January.

Let us assume that the handicap would have been a relatively mild one, so that the handicapped child would have had the expectation of a quality of life well above the minimal level at which life ceases to be a benefit. Then the woman could not be said to have harmed the child if she had refused to postpone her plans to become pregnant. The child conceived without delay would still have a life which would be a good one for that child; and if the woman had not become pregnant at that time, this particular child would not have existed at all. So if we claim that the woman would be harming 'her child', this claim cannot be true of any particular child which the woman might have. If she does not wait, there will be no child who is harmed by her decision.

It is significant that spelling this out does not lead people to modify their judgement that the woman should wait before becoming pregnant. Since life with this mild handicap would still be good, our judgement cannot be based on the interests of the child who will be born only if the woman does not wait. And we can suppose that the existence of the mildly handicapped child will, on balance, have no adverse effects on the mother or on anyone else. So if we still judge that the woman should wait, our judgement must be influenced by the fact that the child conceived later will have the expectation of a better life than the child conceived immediately. In saying that the woman should wait, we must be taking into account the future prospects of the 'next child' who will be born only if the woman does wait.

Most of us—with the exception of 'right to life' groups and their supporters—think along similar lines when we consider pre-natal testing for abnormalities. It is now routine for doctors to offer special tests to pregnant women who run an unusually high risk of having an abnormal baby. Pregnant women over thirty-five, for instance, are often tested because older women are more likely to have a child with Down's syndrome. If the test shows that the foetus does have Down's syndrome, the woman is able to have an abortion. The same thing happens with women who are shown to be carriers of the gene for haemophilia: the foetus can be checked to see if it will have the disease. If it does, the woman can have an abortion, and then try again, until she has a normal baby.

Why do we regard this as a reasonable thing to do, even when the handicap is one like haemophilia, which is quite compatible with a worthwhile life? As in Parfit's example, we are offsetting the loss of one possible life against the creation of another life with better prospects. Richard Hare, formerly Professor of Moral Philosophy at the University of Oxford, has defended this practice by asking us to imagine a dialogue between a defective foetus with a condition like spina bifida and its as-yet-unconceived possible brother, Andrew. (Since Hare wrote the paper to which we are referring in 1973, his choice of name can have nothing to do with the name of the Stinson's premature son; it is, however, an ironic choice, since one might have imagined Andrew Stinson having a similar dialogue with his as-yet-unconceived possible brother, Jonathan.) Hare asks us to accept that the parents of the defective foetus will not contemplate another child if the foetus survives, but if it dies they will have another child. It is therefore not possible for both the foetus and Andrew to live. The foetus and Andrew try to find a solution which chooses between them on the basis of equal consideration of both their interests in having a happy existence. The dialogue, Hare says, might go like this:

Andrew points out that if the foetus is not born there is a high probability that he, Andrew, will be born and will have a normal and reasonably happy life . . . To this the foetus might reply 'At least I have got this far; why not give me a chance?' But a chance of what? They then do the prognosis as best they can and work out the chances of the various outcomes if the present pregnancy is not terminated. It turns out that there is a slim chance, but only a slim chance, that the foetus will, if born and operated on, turn into a normal and, let us hope, happy child; that there is a considerable chance on the other hand that it will perish in spite of the operation; and that there is a far from negligible chance of its surviving severely handicapped. In that case, I think Andrew, the later possible child, can claim that he is the best bet, because the chance of the parents dying or changing their minds about having another child before he is born is pretty small, and certainly far less than the chance that the present foetus, if born, will be very seriously handicapped.

Hare acknowledges that such an imaginary dialogue can be misleading because it leads us to think of both the foetus and its possible brother as if they were existing beings capable of rational discussion and with desires for continued life. We must always bear in mind that neither the foetus nor the unconceived brother can feel the loss of life, or even the fear of that loss. (Hare qualifies this by admitting that a foetus might be conscious, but adding that the intensity of its feelings would presumably be low.) The essential point of the dialogue, however, is simply that when we contemplate the rights and wrongs of abortion in these circumstances, it is not only the value of the life of the foetus which should be considered. The value of the life of what Hare calls 'the next child in the queue' should not be ignored.

Hare's imaginary dialogue supports the common response to the abortion of abnormal foetuses, and this in turn points in the same direction as our firm conviction that the woman in Parfit's example should wait before becoming pregnant. In each case, we are ready to allow one life to be sacrificed for the sake of the life of an unconceived possible child. We cannot defend such a judgement except by assuming that the value of the life of an unconceived possible child can properly be taken into consideration. 'Theoretical' as such a child may be at the time when it is merely a 'next child', if conception takes place there will soon be an actual living child. When Peggy Stinson was considering whether to bring into the world the child who became Jonathan Stinson, she was right to think that if Andrew's survival would make it impossible for her to have another child, the normal prospects for a good life of this 'next child' should outweigh Andrew's much more limited chances of a minimally adequate life. The life of this 'next child' may have been theoretical at that time, but Jonathan is leading a real life now.

Hare makes it clear that the moral of his dialogue applies as much to new-born infants as it does to foetuses. He suggests that the best chance the foetus has of winning the argument is to say: 'All right, we'll make a bargain. We will say that I am to be born and operated on, in the hope of restoring me to normality. If the operation is successful, well and good. If it isn't, then I agree that I should be scrapped and make way for Andrew.' This compromise, Hare says, gives the best possible chance of a healthy baby, and gives the foetus 'all the chance it ever had of itself being that baby'. The proposal assumes, of course, that infants have no automatic right to life, and therefore infanticide, either active or passive, is permissible. But Hare defends this when he concludes:

I do not think that the harm you are doing to the foetus or the unsuccessfully operated upon newborn infant by killing them is greater than that which you are doing to Andrew by stopping him from being conceived and born. In fact I think it is much less, because Andrew, unlike them, has a high prospect of a normal and happy life.

We have already argued that new-born infants do not have a right to life merely because they are human and have emerged from the womb. Their lives *as persons* have not yet begun. Hare is therefore right to suggest that there is no fundamental moral reason against thinking about new-born infants in the way we now think about foetuses when we allow a woman to abort a defective foetus and try again to have a normal child.

The only significant difference between the foetus and the new-born infant, so far as this discussion is concerned, is that the new-born infant can be given up for adoption, whereas the foetus cannot be, unless the woman is willing to go through with the pregnancy for this purpose—an ordeal which we would not wish to see inflicted upon any woman against her will. If an infant is born handicapped, but with reasonable prospects of a life sufficiently free from suffering to be worth living, and if there is someone willing to adopt and look after that infant, then adoption is better than the pointless destruction of a potentially worthwhile life. After the adoption, the baby's natural mother can have the 'next child' she would not have had if the handicapped child had remained in her care. The interests of the existing handicapped child, and of the possible future child, are then both able to be satisfied.

If, on the other hand, adoption is for some reason impossible, the choice then lies between the life of an existing handicapped new-born infant or an as-yet-unconceived child who will in all probability be normal. In these circumstances it would be quite wrong to ignore the fact that the survival of the handicapped infant will prevent the existence of the possible normal child.

All this raises a further question: to what extent is it desirable by means of adoption, fostering, or institutional care, to relieve unwilling parents of the burden of bringing up a severely disabled child? Can these means be used to avoid the conflict between the value of the life of the 'next child' and the value of the life of a disabled child who still has reasonable prospects of enjoying life? Or is this simply passing over to society as a whole a responsibility which it might be better for it to decline?

The interests of society

Late in 1983, a new 'Baby Doe' case hit the American headlines. This time the patient was a girl, known as 'Baby Jane Doe' and she suffered not only from spina bifida, but also from other problems including microcephaly—an abnormally small head, which is an indication of severe mental retardation. The doctors and hospital supported the parents' decision not to operate on the spinal opening, but Lawrence Washburn, a self-styled 'right to life lawyer' was tipped off about the decision, and brought the issue into the courts. Although the suit was eventually thrown out, the case went through all three levels of the New York State court system. During the controversy, Washburn appeared on 'People are Talking', a San Francisco CBS-TV discussion programme. The interviewer asked him: 'Lawrence, where are you going to be while this family are trying to help this baby lead a full life? How will you be involved?' Washburn replied: 'I probably will not be involved at all.' Washburn's honesty is no doubt commendable, but the question was an appropriate one. If society decides that severely impaired infants must live, is society prepared to take on the task of giving them adequate care?

While the case was before the courts, some American newspapers ran an article describing the life that Baby Jane Doe might face if she survives and is put in an institution. The article featured an institution in Agnews, California, which cares for the profoundly retarded—those with IQs below 35. Agnews appears to be one of the more pleasant of these institutions—it was described as covering '600 sprawling green acres' and the article said it 'could easily pass for a community college' (we assume this refers only to its physical appearance). The institution has 1,080 residents, and a staff of 1000. Some of the patients were described in the article:

Born with a portion of her brain protruding through her nose, Debbie, age 20, will remain forever a child. She is toilet-trained and can feed and dress herself, but little else.

Hugo was born 30 months ago with a portion of his brain protruding through the back of his skull. He lies encircled by mattresses and pillows. An occasional smile comes to his face, and he seems to enjoy attention. But Hugo will never be able to control his body. In all likelihood he will grow up and die without ever leaving Agnews.

The article raised the issue of unexpected future recovery, noting that such recoveries have received much attention; but Dr Karen Kral, medical director of the institution, was cited as saying that such stories 'may be a way of sidestepping more difficult questions'. According to Dr Kral, 'In many cases, preserving life at all costs will translate into trapping these patients forever in circumstances over which they have no control.'

There are, of course, hundreds of 'Agnews' in the United States and other countries which can afford to care for the profoundly retarded. In the past decade, attempts have been made to 'deinstitutionalize' these people, placing them in smaller nursing homes which are supposed to provide a more 'normal' environment. For some this is undoubtedly highly desirable; but unless these smaller homes are exceptionally well-staffed and well-funded, the improvement will not be so great. Even with adequate staff and funding, it is questionable whether the more severely afflicted are able to lead a life that is in any sense worthwhile. When, as is so often the case, staffing and funding are less than adequate, the quality of life for the patients can be very poor. In an American study published in 1973, Ronald Conley stated flatly that 'Living conditions in most public institutions are intolerable.' He added that unless services for the retarded were improved, 'future generations will consider our neglect cruel, incomprehensible, and outrageous. Descriptions of public institutions will fill them with the same horror we feel at the barbarities of the Spanish inquisition and Aztec human sacrifices.'

Conley was by no means alone in his plea for change; yet more than ten years later, it is difficult to note any great improvement. An article on paediatric nursing homes in Massachusetts, published in the *New England Journal of Medicine* in 1983, showed that most of the residents were bedridden and non-verbal, requiring provision of basic care such as feeding, dressing, maintaining hygiene, and sensory and motor stimulation. Three quarters were profoundly retarded and had seizures. About 4 per cent died each year and only 5 per cent were discharged, leaving few beds available for new admissions. The standards of care were described as 'low'. The authors found that the roots of the problem were in 'system-wide deficiencies' and noted that 'These issues will be faced throughout the nation as survival of the multiply handicapped population continues to improve.' The situation in some other states, the authors noted, appeared to be worse: in New Hampshire, for instance, handicapped children were admitted to geriatric facilities, indicating that no regulatory distinction was being made between programmes serving children and those serving the elderly.

The ideal solution to these problems would be for the process of 'normalization' to be carried one stage further, and for handicapped infants to be adopted by willing couples. Unfortunately it is not realistic to expect this to happen. When individual cases of babies being left to die are given wide publicity—as in the cases of

Baby Doe and Baby Jane Doe—some people do offer to adopt the infants whose lives are threatened. These cases are, however, only the tip of the iceberg. Although several couples may be moved to offer to adopt one well-publicized handicapped infant, thousands of others languish in institutions, unwanted. In Britain, newspapers regularly carry advertisements seeking foster parents or adoptive parents for children, some handicapped, others simply in need of a home. Tony Hall, director of the British Agencies for Adoption and Fostering, has estimated that

Of the 120,000 children in care in Britain some 20,000 need a permanent new family of their own . . . Such families do not turn up, at least not in anything like the numbers required to meet the need.

There is a British organization, Parents for Children, which specializes in finding homes for handicapped children. In September 1981 its director wrote to *The Times* reporting on the organization's success:

The chances of adoption for handicapped children are no longer zero. In the last five years this agency alone has placed 22 mentally handicapped and 12 physically handicapped children for adoption.

This is a laudable effort, but even if several agencies are achieving similar success, they will make little impression on the total number of children in care. In saying this, we do not wish in any way to suggest that such organizations should not continue to place as many children as they can—obviously they are helping individual children to lead a better life. Our point is merely that we cannot expect such efforts to result in a substantial drop in the number of handicapped children languishing in inadequate institutions. Quite apart from the numbers involved, some infants are just too severely disabled to be cared for in a normal home.

If the ideal solution of adoption is unrealistic, the next best alternative would be the provision of a substantially larger share of the community's resources to facilities caring for these children. Yet the amount being spent is already significant. The care of patients like Debbie and Hugo at Agnews costs an average of $40,000 per patient each year. Some institutions cost a little less, but this type of care is labour-intensive and hence always expensive. Calls for more money are regularly made, but seldom heeded. Governments always sound sympathetic to the plight of people living in institutions and homes, but the sympathy does not extend to providing all the resources needed.

There is also the question of how much it is realistic to expect a community to spend on this form of care. In the article on the institution at Agnews, Stanford Economics Professor Victor Fuchs was quoted as commenting:

We as a society may decide that preserving life at all costs is a path we would like to pursue, but we also have to recognize that that may not be possible in a world with limited resources.

We are all extremely reluctant to admit that there is a limit to how much we should pay to save a life. We want to believe that a human life is worth more than any amount of money, and we readily agree to sweeping statements to that effect. For instance, in November 1983, a number of major American organizations, representing both medical groups such as the American Academy of Pediatrics, and disability groups like the Association for Retarded Citizens and the Spina Bifida Association of America, met in Washington, DC and agreed to a statement of 'Principles of Treatment of Disabled Infants'. These principles were later quoted with approval by the Department of Health and Human Services in the supplementary information accompanying its 'final rule' on the treatment of handicapped infants. Among the passages quoted was this one:

Consideration such as anticipated or actual limited potential of an individual and present or future lack of available community resources are irrelevant and must not determine the decisions concerning medical care.

But, rhetorical gestures aside, we do limit the amount we are prepared to spend to save lives. We can see this in areas like road safety: does anyone seriously believe that our roads are as safe as money can make them? We know that traffic lights, pedestrian overpasses, and shock-absorbing crash barriers along highways would save lives. So too would a quadrupling of the number of traffic police, or the granting of government subsidies to automobile manufacturers who build their cars to the same safety standards as the latest Volvos. And why stop there? It would probably be rational to spend much more to save lives on the roads than we actually do spend; but eventually there would come a point at which we had put into effect all the relatively inexpensive ways of preventing road deaths, and to save additional lives would cut so heavily into the public resources available for education, the arts, conservation of the environment and so on, that we would not support it. Then we would have reached the limit of what we are prepared to spend to save a life.

In medicine, too, those responsible for setting the health care budget cannot and do not act on the assumption that any expenditure is justified to save a human life. Kidney machines, for instance, are expensive. Even wealthy nations generally do not have enough machines for all who need them. Older patients with kidney disease are being allowed to die for what are, ultimately, economic reasons. In some countries this is also true of younger patients. According to Professor Cyril Chantler of Guy's Hospital, London, about 90 British children develop kidney disease each year, but only 61 were accepted for treatment during 1981. The remaining third go untreated because 'Doctors do not refer children for treatment if the facilities are not there.'

In the United States, a concerted political effort by people with kidney disease led to legislation providing dialysis for all who need it; but in view of the inadequacies of the American health care system, there can be little doubt that others, less well-organized and hence less successful in obtaining public attention and support, are still dying because of lack of funds for health care. Indeed, even in a health care system that was much more adequately funded, this would have to be true. There will always be new, very expensive medical technology. Yesterday's kidney machine is today's artificial heart. No one seriously suggests that we ought to use every dollar of community revenue in order to go as far as we possibly can in the direction of making such costly medical technology available to all who need it. Somewhere, a line must be drawn. With finite resources, we cannot make infinite provision for every life. More money for severely handicapped infants will mean less money for others in need.

This point was forcefully put by Dr Thomas Harris, the medical director of an intensive care unit for new-borns in Salt Lake City. In May 1983, in an open letter to the United States

Surgeon General, C. Everett Koop, referring to the Baby Doe regulations, Dr Harris wrote:

I will take it upon myself after the new federal regulations go into effect to keep you well informed about their impact on our patients and the unit's day-to-day operation.

Periodically, I will send you pictures of the deformed babies we are keeping alive now without sophisticated machines.

You, as a physician, will be able to interpret the computerized tomography scans I will send you showing destroyed brains or lacking organs, such as the kidneys or spleen.

I will also attach the monthly bills we send out to parents, insurance companics, or state Medicare; our average monthly cost for one such patient is approximately $35,000. Finally, I will make copies for you of our logbook documenting times when we have to reject new patient referrals into our regional center due to exhaustion of space, equipment, and personnel—space and equipment taken up in considerable degree by hopelessly damaged or defective children we will now be forced to keep alive at all costs. Remember, our resources are limited and they are becoming increasingly more limited with each passing year the administration you represent reduces the maternal and child health care budget.

That more resources for one group is likely to mean less for another has also been neatly shown by Madeleine Simms, writing in the *New Humanist*. She juxtaposes two events occurring within a year in the London borough of Hammersmith. We have already referred to one of them: the court case concerning baby Alexandra, a Down's syndrome baby with an intestinal blockage born in Hammersmith in 1981. When the parents refused to consent to the operation, the local director of social services took the matter to court, and the upshot was that the Hammersmith Council was granted care of the child and the right to authorize the operation. A year later, the *Observer* reported another case involving a child in the care of Hammersmith Council:

Shirley Woodcock, aged three, died of head injuries while in the care of Hammersmith and Fulham Council, and being looked after by a soldier and his wife . . . the pathologist found about 50 bruises on the child's body . . . The coroner said that social workers had overlooked serious danger signs.

An internal inquiry set up by the Council revealed that no social worker had visited the foster parents for over two months even though the couple were known to be facing difficulties and there was evidence that Shirley had been injured before. In December 1982 it was reported that the director of social services had resigned, saying that 47 children were at risk in the borough because of lack of resources. As Madeleine Simms says:

One must wonder whether this same social services department was wise to insist on taking on additional burdens when it evidently had some difficulty in supervising its existing case load.

These unpleasant economic issues are becoming more urgent for two reasons: the increased costs of some medical techniques, and the increased numbers of infants surviving with severe handicaps.

The cost of some new medical techniques is best illustrated in the case of extremely premature infants. Ten years ago, a baby born 14 weeks premature and weighing less than 1000 grams would have had little hope of surviving. Now many infants weighing between 500 and 1000 grams are surviving, thanks to modern neonatal intensive care. But such care is very expensive. In February 1983 the *Chicago Tribune* ran a series of articles entitled 'Playing God in the Nursery'. The first of these articles described Bobby Lee, a boy born prematurely whose life was saved by intensive care, but whose undeveloped lungs were so badly scarred by the artificial respiration that he may never be able to breathe without the assistance of a machine. His treatment costs $1,500 per day. At the time the article was written, he was 19 months old. It had then cost the community nearly $1 million to save his life. This is an extreme case; but costs in excess of $100,000 are not so uncommon. The six months of treatment for premature Andrew Stinson, whose parents had asked for 'no heroics', ended up costing $104,000—and that was at 1977 cost levels. The *Chicago Tribune* cited a recent study showing that the average hospital bill for a baby weighing under 1000 grams was $40,000. This figure includes, of course, money spent on those who—like Andrew Stinson—don't survive despite all the treatment. A study carried out at McMaster University, in Canada, found that for infants under 1000 grams, neonatal intensive care was costing $102,500 (in 1978 Canadian dollars, or approximately 90,000 1978 US dollars) for each infant life saved. While the costs of medical care were increasing, however, governments were cutting back on the amount they were providing to hospitals. The Illinois State government announced that it would limit the maximum reimbursement to children's hospitals for Medicaid patients to $435 a day, even though intensive neonatal care cost an average of $835 a day. In Florida, when the legislature declared that it would not reimburse hospitals for uncollectable bills, the Tampa General Hospital denied admission to a premature infant. The baby died.

The economic problem is challenging governments in every developed nation. In December 1983 a row developed in Melbourne, Australia, when it was revealed that two premature infants had been flown 700 kilometres to Adelaide, because intensive care units in Melbourne were full. Dr Neil Roy, of the Melbourne Royal Women's Hospital, reported that the number of babies given intensive care at his hospital had more than quadrupled in less than ten years. Professor Peter Phelan, a paediatrician at the Royal Children's Hospital in the same city, was quoted as saying that the cost of saving a baby born 14 weeks premature was around A$50,000, and some of these babies faced long-term problems such as blindness, deafness, and cerebral palsy. He added: 'You could philosophically ask, is it better to spend $50,000 on the small premature infant or tell the parents to go away and have another baby?' Dr Roy agreed that such views had been 'quite strongly put' among doctors.

Improved medical care for extremely premature and severely handicapped infants means that more of these infants survive; and while one might hope that the improved care would also mean that more of them survive without any handicaps, the indications are that the reverse is happening. In July 1983 a study conducted by the Health Policy Program of the University of California at San Francisco indicated that the number of American babies with some physical or mental defect had doubled over the past twenty-five years. It was estimated that about 140,000 babies born in the United States in 1983 will suffer from physical abnormalities, mental retardation or learning problems, compared with about 70,000 in the late 1950s. The proportion of such children has risen from 2 per cent of all new-borns to 4 per cent during this period. The findings in this study paralleled those of a Baltimore study carried out some years earlier. They were also consistent with United States Department of Education figures showing the number of American school-children enrolled in some form of special education had increased by 15 per cent—from 3.5 million to 4 million—between 1977 and 1982.

Not all the reasons for this alarming increase are known. Dr John Marshall, Director of the American National Center for Health Services Research, has suggested that increased cigarette smoking in women, and toxic substances in the workplace, may be among the factors, as may the survival of an increasing number of people with conditions which are inherited by their children. Improved medical technology, however, is undoubtedly one factor; children who a few years ago would have been miscarriages or still births are now surviving, many with handicaps. Dr Godfrey Oakley, Jr., director of the birth defects branch of the Federal Center for Disease Control has said: 'A lot of people are edgy because they feel that the country is on the front side of an epidemic of cerebral palsy and mental retardation associated with the increasing survival of babies of very low birth weight.'

The upshot of all this is clear. There is a limit to the burden of dependence which any community can carry. If we attempt to keep all handicapped infants alive, irrespective of their future prospects, we will have to give up other things which we may well regard as at least equally important. Since most communities appear reluctant to make adequate provision for the needs of the handicapped in their care, it might also be true that the survival of many more severely handicapped infants is not in the interests of those handicapped people already in state care—any increase in the numbers needing care is likely to mean that already stretched resources will have to be stretched even further. We would agree that wealthy societies ought to spend much more on care for the handicapped, but then we also believe that these societies should spend more on welfare services for the poor, and on overseas aid. The amount needed to care for one patient at Agnews, for instance, could be used to save the lives of a score of children suffering from malnutrition in less well-developed countries. Do those who talk of 'discrimination' against severely handicapped infants ever consider the way in which we 'discriminate' against those who happen not to live in our own fortunate country?

It is easy to say that governments should make greater provision for all those in real need. It is much harder to get governments to put this into practice. Unless governments—and the people who elect them—become markedly more generous in their attitudes to all those in need of special help, it does not seem wise to add to the burden on limited resources by increasing the number of severely disabled children who will, if they are to lead a worthwhile life, need a disproportionately large share of these resources.

8 WHO DECIDES?

Decisions about severely handicapped infants should not be based on the idea that all human life is of equal value, nor on any other version of the principle of the sanctity of human life. Such ideas prove, on examination, to lack a sound ethical basis. There is therefore no obligation to do everything possible to keep severely handicapped infants alive in all circumstances. Instead, decisions to keep them alive—or not to do so—should take account of the interests of the infant, the family, the 'next child', and the community as a whole. With this conclusion, we have completed our discussion of the fundamental ethical questions underlying these life and death decisions. There is, however, still a vital practical question to be discussed. It is all very well to state in general terms the interests which should be taken into account; but every case is slightly different. How are these decisions to be taken? Who is to have the authority to say whether a severely handicapped infant should live or die?

Two cases, two ways of deciding

In the United States, the death of Baby Doe brought one answer to this question.

President Reagan instructed his administration to cut off federal funds from hospitals which, in deciding whether to give life-saving treatment to severely handicapped infants, took account of the quality of the lives those infants were likely to lead. By this act, Reagan was attempting to designate the federal government as the ultimate decision-maker in every case; and the federal government's decision was based on its professed belief in the equal value of the lives of all members of our species, irrespective of their life-prospects.

In Britain, the other case with which we began this book has led to a very different proposal. When Dr Arthur was charged with the murder of John Pearson, a group of parents gathered to support him. Many of them had, or had had, severely handicapped children. They thought that their children ought to have been allowed to die instead of being kept alive by all the latest medical techniques. These parents formed an organization called Prospect. One of their aims was to improve support from the caring services for parents looking after severely abnormal children at home; but the parents were also concerned to prevent this situation occurring.

Improved prenatal testing, with abortion available if the tests showed a serious defect, is one means of prevention sought by Prospect; but the other is more controversial. Prospect has sent to all British Members of Parliament a 'Limitation of Treatment Bill'. In essence the Bill provides that if two doctors certify that an infant under the age of 28 days is suffering from a severe physical or mental disability which is irreversible, which no treatment would alleviate, and which is of such gravity that the patient would enjoy no worthwhile quality of life, then, where the parents have given their consent in writing to the cessation of life-prolonging treatment, it shall not be an offence to allow the infant to die. As a safeguard, the Bill stipulates that one of the doctors must be a paediatrician, and both must be doctors of at least seven years' standing.

According to Prospect, 'decisions about severely handicapped babies would be left to parents, guided by the diagnosis and advice of doctors present at the time'. In case this appears to be a radical innovation, we should recall that it is to a large extent the present reality in Britain and many other countries. We have seen that it is quite routine for infants with spina bifida to be selected for non-treatment, and these decisions are made by doctors and parents in consultation. In Britain, these procedures have been officially accepted by the Department of Health and Social Security. In Australia, the Australian Medical Association has said in a recent submission to the Law Reform Commission of Western Australia: 'The dilemma of whether treatment should be given to a grossly malformed child whose expectation of a normal life is nil should be resolved by the family and the doctors concerned.' Sir Douglas Black, President of the Royal College of

Physicians, said as much when, testifying at Dr Arthur's trial, he suggested that in the case of a Down's syndrome child whose parents do not wish it to survive, 'it is ethical to terminate life, provided other considerations are taken into account, such as the status and the ability of the parents to cope in a way that the child could otherwise have had a happy life'.

Is the situation in the United States so different from that in Britain? In terms of the public discussion of the issue, perhaps it is; it would be difficult to imagine an American equivalent of Sir Douglas Black putting the same point so bluntly. But in practice, many American paediatricians adopt the same approach. The differences between John Lorber in Sheffield, and John Freeman in Baltimore were differences of degree, not kind. Both selected some spina bifida infants for non-treatment, with the intention that they should die. Both took this decision in consultation with parents.

In looking at Dr Koop's testimony about the meaning of 'customary care' in the Baby Doe regulations, we have already mentioned some revealing surveys of American paediatricians. These surveys confirm that many American paediatricians and paediatric surgeons give considerable weight to the views of parents in deciding whether to treat a handicapped infant.

The most comprehensive survey was carried out in 1975. Questionnaires were sent to all 400 paediatric surgeons in the surgical section of the American Academy of Pediatrics, and to 308 chairpersons of teaching departments of paediatrics and chiefs of divisions of neonatology and of genetics within paediatrics departments. Nearly two-thirds responded, giving a total of 457 replies. The first question asked was:

Do you believe that the life of each and every newborn infant should be saved if it is within our ability to do so?

Only 18 per cent of those surveyed answered this question affirmatively, the remaining 82 per cent indicating that they did not believe that we should prolong life in all cases.

The second question brought out the extent to which the doctors would go along with parents who refused to consent to surgery to remove a blockage in the digestive system, either when this was the infant's only problem or when it was combined with other conditions. In the classic 'Johns Hopkins' kind of case—where the blockage was combined with Down's syndrome but there were no other abnormalities—77 per cent of the surgeons would not oppose the parents' refusal. The paediatricians were split exactly 50/50 on this case. When heart disease was added to the problems of the baby with the blockage and Down's syndrome, the percentage of surgeons who would acquiesce in parents' decisions rose to 85 per cent, and of paediatricians, to 65 per cent. If the baby with the blockage had spina bifida instead of Down's syndrome, approximately 60 per cent of both groups said they would accept the refusal of consent; 28 per cent stated that they would not accept it, and the remainder did not answer the question.

Not surprisingly, if the baby was born without a brain, an overwhelming majority would accept the refusal of the parents; yet even here one surgeon said he would not accept it, and 3 per cent of the surgeons and one of the paediatricians had answered the entire question by ticking the response 'There is *no* situation in which I would accept such a decision'. Less expected, perhaps, was the response to which Koop alluded—though not altogether accurately—in the testimony we quoted in Chapter 2: when the baby was entirely normal, except for the blockage, 8 per cent of the surgeons and 3 per cent of the paediatricians would still acquiesce in the decision of parents not to allow surgery. The responses to the second question indicate that a majority of the total group—54 per cent—were prepared to go along with the parents' decision against surgery to remove the blockage in all cases except where the infant was otherwise normal.

Another question focused specifically on the case of a Down's syndrome infant with a blockage, and asked whether the doctor would refuse to operate even if the parents had given full consent. Only 1 per cent of the total group said that in this situation they would refuse to operate and would refer the parents to another surgeon.

At the other extreme, if the parents of a Down's syndrome infant with a blockage refused consent to surgery, 16 per cent of the paediatric group, but only 3 per cent of the surgeons, said that they would get a court order directing surgery to be carried out. Twenty-eight per cent of each group would try to persuade the parents to allow surgery, but would not go as far as obtaining a court order; against this, 23 per cent of the surgeons and 13 per cent of the paediatricians would try to persuade the parents *against* consenting to surgery, although they would operate if the parents continued to want it. The remainder would simply give the parents the facts and leave them free to reach their own decision.

If we add together the percentages of those who would not operate even if the parents wanted it, and those who would get a court order to operate when the parents did not want it, we find that only 4 per cent of the surgeons and 17 per cent of the other doctors would, in the end, refuse to go along with the firm views of parents.

The results of these surveys are in broad agreement with those of two more localized surveys of American paediatricians, one carried out in California and another in Massachusetts. In each case, the majority of those responding indicated that they would not recommend surgery for a Down's syndrome infant with a life-threatening blockage in its intestine. All these surveys were carried out before the Baby Doe case and the Reagan administration's attempt to prevent such decisions. It is therefore impossible to estimate how much the situation has changed in the United States. We can be confident, however, that at least until these recent developments, life and death decisions were often being made, in America as well as in Britain, by doctors and parents together. This situation received the endorsement of the Judicial Council of the American Medical Association, which stated in 1982 that 'the decision whether to exert maximal efforts to sustain life (of seriously deformed newborns) should be the choice of the parents'.

We have no doubt that the practice is similar in most nations where modern medicine is practised. (Where there is no modern medicine, of course, the question does not arise, for the severely handicapped infants die anyway.) Our own survey of paediatricians and obstetricians in the Australian state of Victoria revealed that 90 per cent of obstetricians, and 83 per cent of paediatricians had, on at least one occasion, directed that less than maximum efforts should be made to preserve the life of a handicapped infant. Thirty per cent of the obstetricians, and 48 per cent of the paediatricians, said that they had given such directives on several occasions. With the exception of one or two doctors who thought parents should be spared the burden of these agonizing decisions, the doctors said that they consulted with the parents.

Against this background, President Reagan's attempt to take the decision-making power away from parents and doctors might well be regarded as a more drastic move away from present practices than the 'Limitation of Treatment Bill' proposed by Prospect. The Bill seeks little more than the explicit sanction of the law for what is already standard practice in many hospitals.

A middle way

Lying between Reagan's 'government will decide' approach and the 'leave it to the parents and doctors' solution proposed by Prospect, there is also a middle course: an 'ethics review committee' set up within the hospital, to set standards or review particular cases. Such a committee was proposed by the United States President's Commission for the Study of Ethical Problems in Medicine and Biomedical and Behavioral Research, in its 1983 report, *Deciding to Forego Life-Sustaining Treatment*. The idea was taken up by the American Academy of Pediatrics, in its Policy Statement on 'Treatment of Critically Ill Newborns'. An institutional ethics committee, the Academy said, 'preserves the authority of the pediatrician to act as a primary physician' while it also 'allows each case to be judged in all its complexity and individuality without the restriction of simplistic algorithms'.

In its official submission to the Department of Health and Human Services on the proposed Baby Doe guidelines, the Academy made more detailed suggestions about the kind of committees it wished to see instead of the compulsory hospital notices, hotlines, and Baby Doe Squads. The Academy noted that institutional review committees are not a new idea; ten years ago, the United States Congress required them to be set up in all institutions receiving federal government support for medical research on human subjects, following reports of several abuses in this field. Since the 'institutional review boards' had been set up, the problem had, in the view of the Academy, been effectively remedied. Similar boards would, the Academy suggested, be equally effective in matters involving seriously ill infants.

The Academy argued that such committees would have several advantages over the proposed Baby Doe rules: they would assure the confidentiality of medical records; avoid overtaxing the already stretched child protective agencies; provide a comprehensive review of individual, complex cases; develop means of keeping hospitals and physicians informed of the most recent medical information concerning treatment of handicapped infants; and ensure that parents of handicapped infants are given full information on all the alternatives open to them, including adoption and foster care.

The Academy anticipated that some would say it was simply trying to avoid outside scrutiny by setting up an 'in-house' committee consisting only of physicians or hospital staff. The Academy therefore proposed that the 'infant bioethical review committee' would consist of at least the following:

1 a practising paediatrician, neonatologist, or paediatric surgeon
2 a hospital administrator
3 an ethicist or a member of the clergy
4 a lawyer or judge
5 a representative of a disability group, developmental disability expert, or parent of a disabled child
6 a lay community member
7 a member of the facility's organized medical staff
8 a practising nurse.

Such a committee would be equally divided between hospital and medical staff and outsiders.

The proposed committee would have three main functions:

1 providing advice when decisions are being considered to withhold or withdraw from infants life-sustaining medical or surgical treatment;
2 recommending institutional policies for specific categories of life-threatening conditions; and
3 reviewing retrospectively cases in which life-sustaining treatment has been withheld.

The first of these functions—providing advice about decisions for specific living infants—would obviously be the most sensitive. In an appendix to its submission, the Academy stated its views about how the committee would handle these decisions. First, meetings at which these decisions are to be made would be open to 'the affected parties' (presumably this means the parents rather than the infant). The committee must consider the interests of the parents, the physician, and the child. When there is a disagreement about treatment between the doctor and the parents, if it is the parents who desire treatment to be continued, it shall be continued unless it is 'medically contraindicated'. If the doctor wants treatment but the family does not, the committee must decide whether it agrees with the doctor or with the family. If it agrees with the family, treatment will be withheld. If, however, the committee agrees with the doctor, the committee will recommend to the hospital board that the case be referred to the appropriate court or child protective agency. Cases may also be referred to a court even when the doctor and the family agree on withholding treatment, if the committee reviews the case and disagrees with this judgement.

In its 'final' version of the Baby Doe rules, issued on 9 January 1984, the Department of Health and Human Services incorporated a substantial part of the Academy's proposal into the final rule. The Department suggested that hospitals may wish to set up 'Infant Care Review Committees' and it outlined a model committee composition and mode of operation very similar to that proposed by the Academy. (The only difference in the personnel is the elimination of the 'ethicist or member of the clergy'!) Unlike the Academy, however, the Department was not prepared to allow such a committee to exercise the ultimate power of decision. The January 1984 Baby Doe rule leaves the 'hotline' and the Baby Doe squads intact; a hospital which has set up an Infant Care Review Committee in accordance with the Department's model merely has the advantage of the Department's undertaking that the Baby Doe squad will consult with the committee before taking further action. Moreover the Infant Care Review Committees must operate within the rules set by the Reagan administration—that is, they must ensure that severely handicapped infants are given all 'medically beneficial treatment' even if their lives are likely to be miserable. Neither the quality of life of the infant itself, nor the interests of the parents and the community (let alone the interests of the 'next child') are supposed to prevent the provision of such medically beneficial treatment. Only 'medical judgments' about the futility of treatment are acceptable grounds for not treating an infant. Thus the incorporation of review committees into the Reagan administration's Baby Doe rule does not substantially change the centralist approach of earlier versions of the rule.

Choosing between the proposals

We have now looked at three different methods by which decisions about the treatment of severely handicapped new-borns might be taken. If we were to place them on a spectrum according to the size of the group taking the decision, Reagan's Baby Doe rule would be at one end, Prospect's proposal to leave the decision to parents with the advice of their doctors would be close to the other end, and the American Academy of Pediatrics' proposal for infant bioethical review committees in each hospital would be somewhere in the middle. These three proposals therefore cover the field in such a manner that it seems likely that if none of them proves to be ideal, the best solution will be some combination of at least two of the three proposals. But what method of decision-making would be best?

We can start by rejecting the view that the decision ought to be made at the level of national government. All the discussion in this book shows how utterly mistaken the Baby Doe rule is; but it is not only the content of the rule, with its insistence on the supposedly equal value of all human life, which we regard as a mistake. The attempt to lay down the law for all cases, regardless of their individual complexity, is fundamentally wrong-headed. Such attempts can only be made by those who have a dogmatic belief in some rule to the effect that all infants must be treated alike, regardless of their chances of a minimally adequate quality of life. We have seen that such inflexible rules are based on unsound principles like the sanctity of human life. Once we give up such simplistic principles, it immediately becomes necessary to devolve the real decision-making power to smaller groups which can consider the details of individual cases.

Should this smaller group be the parents, acting with advice from the doctors, or should it be some kind of hospital committee? The answer will depend on which decision-making unit is most likely to further the interests of those affected. As we saw in the previous chapter, this means the interests of the child (or, to put it more precisely, the extent to which the child can be expected to have a worthwhile life) and the interests of the family, of the 'next child', and of society as a whole.

How would the kind of committee proposed by the American Academy of Pediatrics stand up against this test? That committee was to be directed 'to ensure that the interests of the parents, the physician, and the child are fully considered'. If we are prepared to stretch our interpretation of the interests of the parents so that they cover the interests of their existing children, we can say that the interests of the family are included in this formula. The interests of the 'next child' have, however, been neglected: an important, if unsurprising, omission. Nor have the interests of society as a whole been mentioned, although perhaps they are partially covered by the inclusion of 'a lay community member' on the committee. Why, however, are the interests of the physician placed so prominently between those of the parents and the child? For the physician, the child will be one patient among thousands seen during a medical career. How can the physician have an interest comparable to the parents or the infant itself?

When the Department of Health and Human Services incorporated the idea of a hospital ethics committee into its rule on the treatment of handicapped infants, it amended the Academy's statement of the interests which should be considered—but it amended them in the wrong direction. Borrowing from a statement in the report of the President's Commission on Ethical Issues in Medicine, the Department specifically excluded 'the negative effects of an impaired child's life on other persons, including parents, siblings, and society'. The Department also effectively excluded consideration of the interests of the infant by not allowing the infant's physical or mental impairment to be the reason for withholding treatment. Suppose, however, that we were to amend the Academy's statement in the opposite direction. The recommendations to the committee might then specify that its decisions were to be based on the extent to which the child can be expected to have a worthwhile life, and on the interests of the family, any possible next child, and society as a whole. A well-informed committee which deliberated carefully and made its decisions on this basis would seem as likely as anyone to come to the right conclusion. Should we therefore adopt the Academy's proposal, with this amendment in the recommendations to the committee?

In an ideal world, this might work well. In the real world, however, we have to look at the composition of the committee and expect that at least some members of it will be swayed by their particular interests or perspectives. For a start, since the interests of the family are so dramatically affected by the decision, why are the parents not full voting members of the committee which decides their future? It is not enough merely to give them the right to be present when the committee meets; if matters come to a vote, they have more right than any others to have their views count in the decision.

We also question the fact that the committee would have a representative of a disability group, or an expert in disability or parent of a disabled child, but no representative of those parents who have had a handicapped child who died soon after birth because treatment was withheld. It could never be easy for the parent of a disabled child to think it would have been better if the child had died in infancy. One might get a very different perspective from the parent of a severely handicapped child who did die in infancy, particularly if the parent has since had other, normal children.

Then there is the stipulation that the committee should include 'an ethicist or a member of the clergy'. We agree that the committee should include someone with a broad knowledge of ethics and with experience in discussing issues in medical ethics. Some experienced ethicists are also members of the clergy, but not all members of the clergy are knowledgeable about ethics. The requirement should therefore simply be that the committee include 'an ethicist'. (Was it a well-founded concern about what an ethicist might say about the whole basis of the Baby Doe rule which led the Department of Health and Human Services to remove this person from its model committee?)

Apart from these defects, the proposed membership of the

committee gives too much power to the institution. The paed-iatrician, the hospital administrator, the medical staff member, and the nurse, are all likely to be working for the hospital. In addition, it will presumably be the hospital board which selects the other committee members. Despite the inclusion of an equal number of 'outside' members, a hospital board with strong views on prolonging the lives of handicapped infants would have no difficulty in ensuring that the committee was composed of people who would make the decisions it wanted them to make.

Finally, we must not forget the inherent clumsiness of a committee system in situations which demand a quick response, without prior notice, at any hour of the day or night. The Academy and the Department of Health and Human Services envisage interim meetings of the review committees taking place within twenty-four hours of a problem arising; the meetings could, if necessary, be held by telephone. That is as quickly as any committee could act; but it conjures up visions of frantic late-night telephoning while doctors try desperately to get sensible responses from committee members who are only half-awake or have been dragged from parties at which the drinks were flowing freely. There are many medical decisions which cannot wait even twenty-four hours. The existence of the committee will then mean that the necessary life-prolonging action has to be taken, so that the committee will have time to meet and discuss the situation. If the eventual decision is that it would be better if the baby died, there may not be another 'opportunity' to allow the baby to die. Of course, if active euthanasia were permitted, such opportunities would not be required—but neither the Academy nor the Department favours active euthanasia.

The alternative to the committee system is to move to a still smaller decision-making unit: to let the decision be taken by those most affected by it. This is the family and the infant. Since the infant cannot take part in the decision, and existing siblings of the infant young enough to be adversely affected would also be too young to grasp all the ramifications of the decision, the primary responsibility would be left to the parents, with advice from their doctors.

There is one simple but very powerful reason for this solution. Peggy and Robert Stinson put it clearly:

We believe there is a moral and ethical problem of the most fundamental sort involved in a system which allows complicated decisions of this nature to be made unilaterally by people who do not have to live with the consequences of their decisions.

Dr Sally Sehring, an American specialist in the care of new-born infants, agrees that it is the parents who are most affected, not the doctors:

It's extremely hard to give up on a baby, but I worry about keeping alive a baby who will impose such a devastating emotional and financial burden on his family that *their* lives are destroyed by it. What right do I have to make decisions like this and then go home at night and walk out of their lives?

In the absence of overwhelming reasons to the contrary, people should be left to make their own decisions about the matters that affect them most. So, if there are no such reasons to the contrary, the life and death decisions that must be made about severely handicapped new-borns should be made by the parents, and not by physicians or by committees. But are there no overwhelming reasons to the contrary? We need to look at two objections which many people do regard as sufficient to override the case for parental autonomy in this area.

Parents as decision-makers

One objection to leaving the decision to the parents is the emotional stress that this places upon them—especially upon the mother, who has just undergone nine months of pregnancy. The birth of a severely handicapped infant is a great shock for couples who have been eagerly anticipating the birth of the usual perfect baby. If a life or death decision needs to be made soon after birth, are the parents in a position to make the right choice? If they act in haste, or under emotional stress, may they not afterwards be crushed by feelings of guilt and remorse?

There are ways in which this emotionally charged situation could be defused. William Silverman, a distinguished American paediatrician, has suggested that prenatal classes for expectant parents should raise, in a routine way, the possibility of the baby's being born with some impairment, or of its being extremely premature and unable to survive without damage.

Couples could discuss this possibility, in a group and among themselves, and clarify their ideas without the stress of having to make a real decision. Unfortunately, Dr Silverman has found that obstetricians with whom he has discussed this idea are reluctant to put it into practice. Apparently they think it mischievous to raise anxieties about such an unlikely event. On the other hand, Silverman says that parents are generally in favour of the idea. 'It is', he says, 'an issue that can't just be swept under the rug.'

Silverman's suggestion is a valuable one. Most expectant parents are already aware of the possibility that their child might not be normal. They may not discuss their fears with their obstetrician, but there can be few couples who do not worry, at some stage during a pregnancy, about the normality of their child. A *routine* discussion of the topic—especially in a group setting—should cause little additional anxiety. The benefits, in the small percentage of cases in which something does go wrong, would be considerable.

In an article published in the *New England Journal of Medicine* in 1973 Dr Raymond Duff and Dr A. G. M. Campbell described their experience of decisions to withhold treatment in the special-care nursery of the Yale–New Haven Hospital. Over two and a half years, treatment was withheld in 43 cases. Duff and Campbell's practice was to discuss this decision with the parent as fully and frankly as possible. Nurses, social workers, physicians, and chaplains were often included in the discussions. At the conclusion of their article, Duff and Campbell have this to say about the ability of parents to make a decision:

Can families in the shock resulting from the birth of a defective child understand what faces them? Can they give truly 'informed consent' for treatment or withholding treatment? Some of our colleagues answer no to both questions. In our opinion, if families regardless of background are heard sympathetically and at length and are given information and answers to their questions in words they understand, the problems of their children as well as the expected benefits and limits of any proposed care can be understood clearly in practically all instances. Parents *are* able to understand the implications of such things as chronic dyspnea, oxygen dependency, incontinence, paralysis, contractures, sexual handicaps and mental retardation.

Perhaps not all doctors will be prepared to put as much effort into discussions with parents as Duff and Campbell did. It is too easy for doctors to assume that they know best, and that the consent of the parents is a formality they must go through. Undoubtedly many parents will simply accept the advice of the doctor, whatever that advice may be—we saw in Chapter 3 that both Lorber and Freeman found that their patients invariably accepted their advice, even though Lorber advised surgery in no more than a quarter of the spina bifida babies he saw, while Freeman thought it best to operate on three-quarters of his spina bifida patients. Nevertheless Duff and Campbell have shown that parents can be genuinely involved in the decision-making process. Ensuring their proper participation should become standard medical practice in this area.

Another commonly heard objection to giving parents the right to decide on treatment for their severely handicapped infants is that there may be a conflict between the interests of the parents and the interests of the person who the child may become. We have seen that this is indeed possible: the infant may be handicapped, but not so severely impaired that life would cease to be worthwhile; yet bringing up the infant might be a considerable burden on the parents, enough to prevent them raising the kind of family they wish to have and living the lives they had planned to live. So the parents might decide to allow the infant to die, not because that was better for the child, but because it was better for them. They would be acting as judges in a case in which they were among the interested parties. Is this not a conclusive objection to giving the parents the final say on whether the infant lives or dies?

We accept that this objection must be taken seriously; but we still take the view that when it is the parents who will be looking after the infant if it lives, it should be the parents who have the principal say in the decision. We take this view, not because parents have any absolute or inherent rights over their children, but because no one else could be in a better position to weigh up all the relevant interests. After all, as we have argued, the decision cannot be resolved by any simple-minded appeal to the right to life of the infant. The interests of the siblings, of any future children, and of the parents themselves are all legitimately taken into account. There is nothing improper in the parents'

giving weight to their own interests; impropriety would arise only
if the interests of the person who the infant may become were not
properly considered because they clashed with the interests of the
parents or of the family as a whole. And who but the parents can
properly judge the other interests at stake? As Dr Michael
Garland, an American doctor, has said:

Only parents can exercise the prudence that weighs the continued life of
the infant against the impact on their family. Physicians should not
substitute their judgment for that of . . . the absent parents.

Nor, we might add, should committees.

The risk of a conflict of interest does exist; but natural parental
affection is a strong safeguard against any widespread neglect of
the interests of the infants by their parents. As Duff and
Campbell have observed:

It is difficult to say when parents endow a fetus with personhood and
cherish him as part of themselves, but they do this almost without
exception before the last trimester of pregnancy whether they wanted the
baby originally or not. Fetal movements and the changing social
relationships prompted by the evident pregnancy create value and an
expectation of more to come. All deaths of potentially viable fetuses
(those born after 24 to 26 weeks of gestation) that we have encountered
have been associated with feelings of acute grief. There has been a death
in the family; that child had become part of the parents and siblings and
will be mourned for weeks or months and on special occasions, like
anniversaries, for years.

Duff and Campbell believe, therefore, that we can rely on the
parents to give sufficient weight to the interests of the person their
child may become. This belief is in line with many other practices
in our society: we are usually content to leave the feeding,
clothing, and general care of children to their parents, assuming
that the parents will be seeking the best interests of their children.

Yet, it must be admitted, there will be exceptions to this
general law of natural parental affection as a sufficient safeguard.
Just as the State accepts some responsibility for seeing that
parents do not abuse or neglect their children, should not the
State accept some responsibility for seeing that children are not
allowed to die when they could have had a worthwhile life?

We believe that the State is justified in intervening when

parents decide for the death of their child, as long as two conditions are fulfilled. The first is that the child has the prospect of a worthwhile life, that is, a life sufficiently free from physical pain and psychological misery to be satisfying for the child. The second condition is that the State must be prepared to accept the responsibility of finding the child a home in which it can enjoy its life to the best of its capabilities.

The reason for the first of these conditions is obvious. It is wrong to preserve a life which will not be a benefit even for the person whose life it will be. The reason we insist on the second condition is that we do not think anyone—doctors, committees, or the State—should say to other people that they must make the sacrifice involved in rearing a severely handicapped child. If couples freely choose to take on this task, and the life is not expected to be a miserable one for the child, there is no basis for objection; but to impose this task on others is wrong. It is wrong for two reasons, each of which would be sufficient on its own.

First, even if parents may on rare occasions be so concerned about their own interests, or those of their existing children, that they disregard the interests of the impaired new-born, it would be at least as likely for doctors, committees, or governments to disregard, or improperly assess, the interests of the parents, existing children, and possible future children. Outside bodies should beware of taking decisions for others, especially decisions which so drastically alter the daily life and long-term plans of families. There are sound reasons for keeping to a minimum State interference in the private lives of individuals. Action by the State to protect a child from death may be justified if it makes it possible for the child to have a worthwhile life; but to override the family's judgement about what is in the best interests of the family as a whole is a different matter. That decision should be left to the family, and if the State believes it must act to protect the infant, it should do so in the manner which will least interfere with the life of the family; in other words, it must see that the child can be cared for outside the family.

The second reason why the State should not impose a severely impaired child on an unwilling family is more pragmatic. A burden we have freely accepted is one thing: a burden that has been placed upon us by others, against our will, is quite another.

A child imposed on an unwilling family is likely to be resented, and resentment is no basis for a happy family life, for the child or for the parents and siblings. Some families may, of course, come to love and cherish the child they at first did not wish to rear; they may even be strengthened by the experience. But the evidence about marriage break-up and family stress shows that this is not the standard situation. Since it is impossible to predict which families will come to accept the task willingly, and which will resent it, it would seem better to find some other means of caring for the rejected child.

A proposal

We are now close to the end of our search. We have seen that when the parents will be the ones who must care for a severely handicapped infant, it is the parents who should have the right to decide whether the infant lives or dies. Sometimes, however, life may be in the best interests of the person the infant will become, but not of the parents and the family as a whole. Then, and only then, the State may step in and say that it will take over the responsibility for the infant, so that the infant can live a worthwhile life without threatening the interests of the family unit.

Our one remaining task is to suggest how this conclusion can best be implemented. Here there may be a role for some kind of institutional review committee. The committee might operate as follows. If parents decide that they do not wish a handicapped infant to live, but the doctor in charge considers that the infant has a reasonable chance of a life sufficiently free from pain and suffering to be worthwhile for that child, the doctor would notify the committee. The first task for the committee would be to check that the doctor's assessment of the infant's prospects is soundly based. If the committee should decide that the infant has no reasonable prospect of a satisfactory life, then no further treatment should be given, beyond what is necessary to make the infant comfortable (we shall consider shortly whether active measures should be taken to end life swiftly). If, however, the committee agrees with the doctor's initial assessment of the infant, the committee should discuss with the parents the possibility of their giving up custody of the infant. Ideally, the committee would have available a list of families willing to adopt infants in these circumstances; if there should not be enough willing families, there should be small, well-staffed, community-based residential units. If the State is not willing to pay for high-standard residential care, then the number of families prepared to adopt severely handicapped infants should set the limit to the number of severely handicapped children whose lives are prolonged after their parents have decided that they do not wish to bring them up. There is no point in keeping handicapped children alive if, despite their potential for a worthwhile life, they end up languishing miserably in totally inadequate institutions.

Assuming that a good home or an adequate level of residential care is available for an infant with a reasonable prospect of a worthwhile life, the parents should be offered the choice of keeping the child themselves or giving the child up to be cared for by others. The parents have a right not to be compelled to take up the burden of caring for the child. They also have the right to ask for a merciful death for a child who, in the opinion of those best qualified to make such judgements, has no reasonable prospect of a life that it will find satisfying. What the parents have no right to ask for is the death of a child for whom others are willing to provide all that is necessary for the child to realize her or his potential for a satisfactory life. It is at this point, therefore, that the State may legitimately step in and say to the parents: 'We will not interfere with your decision against taking on the task of bringing up this child; but at the same time we will interfere if you continue to seek to deny to others the option of caring for the child.'

The possibility of this separation of the interests of the person who the child may become from the vital interests of the parents explains why there is, after all, some basis for allowing women complete freedom to have abortions, but not allowing parents freedom to commit infanticide. The difference is not that during the process of birth, the foetus/infant somehow acquires a right to life which it previously lacked. As we said earlier, the intrinsic moral status of the foetus can hardly be transformed so dramatically by the passage from womb to cot. What has changed is an important, but extrinsic, fact about the foetus.

Unlike the foetus, the new-born infant can be cared for by others without compelling the mother to continue a pregnancy which will result in a baby she does not want. Respect for a woman's sovereignty over her own body requires us to allow women to choose an abortion. If abortion is equivalent to the death of the foetus, then—since the foetus has no intrinsic right to life—respect for a woman's sovereignty over her own body requires us to allow women to kill their foetuses. Once the foetus can survive outside the woman's body, however, the connection between the woman's right to choose and the death of the foetus disappears. We can allow women—and men—maximum sovereignty over their bodies, and still deny them the right to insist on the deaths of their children.

The 'Limitation of Treatment Bill' proposed by the British group Prospect would allow treatment to an infant under 28 days to be stopped, provided the parents consented and two doctors had certified that the infant was suffering from an irreversible disability so severe that the patient would enjoy no worthwhile quality of life. Our proposal incorporates this idea, but goes beyond it by considering what might happen when the defect is severe enough to lead the parents to decide against trying to bring up the child themselves, but not so severe that the child would enjoy no worthwhile quality of life.

Two remaining aspects of our proposal need to be discussed. The first is that we have said that handicapped infants whose parents do not wish to care for them should be kept alive only if adequate care is available for them. The best form of care would be adoptive families, but we would be pleasantly surprised if there were enough families willing to adopt these children. The alternative is high-quality residential care provided by the community. Such care is, as we have seen, quite expensive. Does the community have an obligation to provide residential care for all handicapped children whose parents are unwilling to look after them and who, with good care, can have a satisfactory quality of life? We have seen that the State cannot justifiably insist on keeping such children alive unless it is prepared to pay for the cost of looking after them; but will there come a point at which the community may properly say that infants should not be kept alive, even though they have the potential for a worthwhile life, because it is just too expensive to provide the care needed to realize that potential?

Because we do not think new-born infants have an inherent right to life, we think that a community might properly decide that its resources are more urgently spent on other tasks than caring for handicapped new-born infants whose parents are not prepared to care for them. We stress that in saying this we are not in any way defending reduced spending on the care of those who are no longer new-born and who either are, or once were, self-aware beings with the capacity to have desires about the future. Nothing that we say about new-borns should have any effect on the treatment of persons, in Michael Tooley's sense of the term. It therefore does not pose any threat to the welfare of those who are capable of grasping that their future might in some way be threatened. There are many such people in State-provided residential care in every developed country, and the provision made for their care in quite wealthy countries is often scandalously poor. This, however, is a separate issue from the question of how much should be spent on caring for those who are not and never have been capable of understanding that they have a future at all.

Although a community is not, in our view, obliged to devote extensive resources to the care of handicapped new-borns whose parents do not wish to rear them, some communities will wish to do this, in preference to seeing such infants die. This may be part of compassionate reluctance to allow infants to die just because their parents do not feel up to the task of caring for them. Such a policy is highly laudable, as long as the community has the resources to care for these infants properly without causing greater suffering by taking the resources away from other areas in greater need—for instance, from poorer families who wish their infants to live but cannot afford the medical care the infants need. That is all that we need to say about this issue; the amount allocated by each community will vary according to its resources and to the importance it chooses to place on allowing such new-born infants to fulfil their potential.

The second aspect of our proposal which still needs to be discussed is whether, once a decision has been made that the life of an infant should not be prolonged, a doctor should be allowed to end the infant's life in a swift and painless manner. We saw in

Chapter 4 that there is no real ethical distinction between intentionally bringing about the death of an infant by withholding available life-saving treatment, and intentionally bringing about the death of the infant by administering a lethal injection. Since death as a result of withholding treatment is usually more drawn out than death by a lethal injection, and this more drawn-out death often involves significant suffering, it would seem that any situation which justifies death by withholding treatment must also justify a swifter, more humane means of death.

Some doctors have recognized the need for a change in our laws on this point. One reason for a change is that in most countries the present law is simply unclear about when a doctor may withdraw life support from a severely handicapped or very sick infant: hence doctors are naturally concerned that they may find themselves facing criminal charges as a result of doing what they and the parents believe to be for the best. Apart from this desire for greater clarity in the law, however, some have been concerned about the fact that once the decision for death has been taken, the law forces doctors to allow death to come slowly.

One of the respondents to the American survey of paediatricians wrote that in these circumstances, to give a lethal injection was 'what I would prefer to do but it is illegal under present laws'. Another said that to withdraw all life support, including intravenous fluids, from a Down's syndrome baby with an intestinal blockage, is 'barbaric but best without legal authority' whereas a lethal injection would be 'most humane but illegal'. In our own Australian survey, one doctor wrote:

In cases where maximum effort is not considered and the baby lingers on, active steps are right as a long wait (of between seven and fourteen days) is cruel to the baby and the informed and prepared parents.

Against the obvious desirability of shortening the process of dying, we must weigh the fear that legalized infanticide will be the thin end of a wedge which will eventually destroy our sense of respect for the lives of every member of society. We have already discussed this argument in Chapter 4, where we concentrated specifically on the suggestion that active euthanasia would somehow pave the way for a Nazi-style holocaust. We rejected that suggestion, and we need not repeat our reasons for so doing.

Nevertheless, many readers will wonder how, once we allow infanticide, we can find any morally relevant dividing line beyond which we must not take human life. Birth may not in itself be of great moral significance, so far as the status of the foetus or new-born infant is concerned; but it is at least a visible boundary which can easily be used for the purposes of law and socially accepted ethical standards. The point at which an infant acquires some degree of self-awareness and the capacity to have desires about its future is less clearly defined. In contrast to birth, such a point cannot serve as a useful line of legal demarcation.

That birth marks a clear line, and the development of self-awareness does not, is undeniable. Nevertheless, for legal purposes we can and do draw lines where there is no clearcut natural divide. When does an adolescent acquire sufficient wisdom to be entitled to take part in our society's political processes? At eighteen? At twenty-one? We need some point at which we can allow people to vote, and so we select an age which is in one sense arbitrary—some sixteen-year-olds are better qualified to vote than some thirty-year-olds—but in another sense the line corresponds to our beliefs about when the necessary degree of maturity is likely to be present. We make similar decisions about the age at which people are to be held legally responsible for their actions, the age at which they can drive a car, the age at which they can serve in the armed forces, and so on. Why should we not do something similar with the age at which infanticide is permissible for a severely handicapped infant?

This is just what Prospect's 'Limitation of Treatment Bill' seeks to do in the matter of passive euthanasia. The Bill would set a limit of 28 days after birth during which treatment could legally be withheld. There is, of course, no special significance in the period of 28 days. It was chosen, presumably, to allow adequate time for any defects to be identified and properly confirmed, without extending longer than necessary the period in which the infant lacks the same rights as other members of the community. Early decisions are also desirable because of the emotional strain on the parents, whose affection and bond with the infant will normally be strengthening during the first days and weeks of life.

In allowing a period of time before the new-born infant gains the same protection as other members of the community, the proposed law would reintroduce into our community a concept which, as we saw in Chapter 5, has been understood and accepted in most other human societies. Women of some of the !Kung communities of the Kalahari give birth away from the group to which they belong, and only bring back to the group those infants they plan to rear; the people of Tikopia, like the Japanese of the eighteenth and early nineteenth centuries, killed some babies at birth, but those they chose to rear were as loved and cherished as any Western children. Among both the Netsilik Eskimo and the Ancient Greeks, the infant could be abandoned up to the time at which it had been named, but not thereafter. (Could our present custom of christening also have its origins in the need for a ceremony which shows that the infant has been accepted as a full member of the community?) Even Jewish law, by its stipulation that bringing about the death of an infant less than thirty days old is not murder unless the child is known to have been born after a full nine months' gestation, effectively allows a period of grace before the infant is fully protected.

We are not the first to advocate the reintroduction of such a period before full acceptance of the infant. Glanville Williams, a noted British legal writer, made this proposal in his book *The Sanctity of Life and the Criminal Law*. F. Raymond Marks, a lawyer from the University of California at Berkeley, put the same idea forward at a conference on new-born intensive care, held in California's Sonoma Valley in 1974. Marks there argued for a social policy that would withhold legal personhood from certain categories of high-risk infants until their conditions had been carefully diagnosed and their parents had made an informed decision whether or not they wished to keep and nurture these infants.

The exact time limit is, like voting age, to some extent arbitrary. We think 28 days should be long enough to confirm the presence of most major defects, yet it is well short of the point at which the infant can have sufficient self-awareness to see itself as a being existing over time, and to form desires about its future, as distinct from immediate desires for warmth, food, to suckle, or for the relief of pain. A still earlier time-limit—perhaps as short as seven days—might be preferable from the point of view of parental attachment, but in some cases this would not be sufficient for adequate confirmation of the details of the infant's condition. Much here will depend on the current state of medical science and technology, and any specific proposal should be subject to revision in the light of the state of the art of neonatal diagnosis.

Whatever time-limit is set, there will be some conditions which cannot be detected within that period. If parents are told shortly after the time-limit that their child has serious brain damage, they may feel that the law is unjust, since if the defect had been detected earlier they would have been able to choose a humane death for the child. This could be a most unfortunate situation, but we may have to live with it, just as we live with arbitrary cut-off lines in other areas of almost equal seriousness, such as criminal liability or conscription for the armed services. Perhaps in the long run changes in attitudes about euthanasia in general, rather than infanticide in particular, will lead to some possibility of mercifully ending a life at any age, either at the request of the person whose life it is or, if the person is not capable of understanding such an issue, when an independent panel judges that the life will, for the being whose life it is, be one of unredeemed misery.

Such a line could be drawn by the law and accepted by our society, as it has been accepted by other societies, without proving to be the thin end of a wedge destructive of respect for human life as a whole. The legislation would in no way diminish the status of infants in relation to anyone except their parents. To kill an infant without the consent of the parents would remain as serious a crime as it is now. The change in the law would do no more than allow parents to make, shortly after birth, the decision they are now legally entitled to make before birth: to end a life which has started out with difficulties so great that it is best that it not be prolonged. Indeed, because of what we have said about adoption or other care when the infant's life can be a satisfying one, the parents would continue to have less right to end the life after birth than they now have before birth, in countries where abortion is freely available.

In one respect we do go further than the proposed Limitation of Treatment Bill. For the reasons already given, we would allow active as well as passive euthanasia to be carried out during the period before acceptance of the child into the community. Although no law should oblige anyone to carry out active euthanasia against her or his conscience, we do not believe that the public as a whole sees much difference between denying an infant a life-saving operation because it is thought better that the infant not live, and giving the same infant a lethal injection. To leave infants to die slowly from starvation and dehydration is truly a barbaric way of handling these problems. To force parents to choose whether their infant will live in misery or die in this drawn-out manner is also to place them in an unnecessarily agonizing situation. That we continue to do these things testifies to our inability to free ourselves from the myths of an outdated, authoritarian ethical code. Until we are willing to break with the past and use the most humane ways of ending the lives we have decided to end, the infants drifting slowly towards their pre-determined deaths in our hospital wards will cast a shadow on our claim to be a civilized, independently-minded society.

NOTES ON SOURCES

1 Two babies

1–11 The story of John Pearson is drawn from the transcript of the shorthand notes of the official court reporters, Marten, Meredith & Co. Ltd., 36/38 Whitefriars St, London, for the summing-up by Justice Farquharson in *Regina v. Leonard John Henry Arthur*, 3, 4, 5 November 1981, at Leicester Court, Leicester, England. The 'Arthur Case' is discussed more fully by one of the authors of this book (HK) in an article, 'A Modern Myth. That Letting Die is not the Intentional Causation of Death: Some Reflections on the Trial and Acquittal of Dr. Leonard Arthur', *Journal of Applied Philosophy*, vol. 1, no. 1 (1984), pp. 21–38; sections of this article are reprinted with the permission of the editors.

2 The trial transcript says that Dr Arthur prescribed the dose of DF 118 to be given 'not less than every four hours'. We have been informed by Dr Peter Dunn, in a personal communication, that this is an error, and that the instruction was for the dose to be given not more than every four hours.

10–11 The acquittal of Dr Arthur was reported in *The Times* on 6 November 1981; the results of the opinion poll were published in the same paper on 10 November 1981. For the comments of Dr Peter Dunn and the other doctors, see *The Times* of 6 November 1981. Nuala Scarisbrick is quoted in an article by Jonathan Glover, 'Letting People Die', *London Review of Books*, vol. 4, no. 4 (1982), p. 3.

11 For the medical history of Baby Doe, see the letter to the editor by John E. Pless, MD, of Bloomington Hospital, *New England Journal of Medicine*, vol. 309, no. 11 (15 September 1983), p. 664.

13 The ruling of the Indiana Supreme Court was reported in the *Chicago Tribune* on 17 April 1982. On 18 April 1982 *The Washington Post* reported that a number of families were willing to adopt Baby Doe.

16 John and Susan West's response to George Will appeared in the *Los Angeles Times* on 12 May 1982.

2 Is all human life of equal worth?

18 The quotation of Sanford H. Kadish on the equality of all human lives before the law is found in his essay, 'Respect for Life and Regard for Rights in the Criminal Law' in S. F. Barker (ed.), *Respect for Life in Medicine, Philosophy and the Law* (The Johns Hopkins University Press, Baltimore and London, 1977), p. 72.

19 Rabbi Immanuel Jakobovits is quoted by Cardinal John Heenan, Archbishop of Westminster, in 'A Fascinating Story', in S. Lack, R. Lamerton (eds.), *The Hour of Our Death*, a record of the conference on the care of the dying held in London in 1973 (Chapman, London, 1974), p. 7. Dr Moshe Tendler is cited by Edward W. Keyserlingk, *Sanctity of Life or Quality of Life* in the context of ethics, medicine, and law: A study written for the Law Reform Commission of Canada, Ottawa (Law Reform Commission of Canada, 1979), p. 21. Paul Ramsey expresses his view on the value of human life in his book *Ethics at the Edges of Life* (Yale University Press, New Haven and London, 1978), p. 191.

22 For the 'Baby Doe Guidelines' see Office of the Secretary, Department of Health and Human Services, *Nondiscrimination on the Basis of Handicap*, 48 Federal Register 9630 (1983) Interim Final Rule modifying 45 CFR, para. 84.61.

25 The statements by Dr C. Everett Koop can be found in the transcript of the proceedings before the United States District Court for the District of Columbia, *American Academy of Pediatrics, et al. v. Margaret Heckler*, Secretary, Department of Health and Human Services, Washington, DC, Civil Action no. 83-0774 (21 March 1983), pp. 44–5.

26 For the 'Proposed Rule', see *Nondiscrimination on the Basis of Handicap Relating to Health Care for Handicapped Infants; Proposed Rules*, 48 Federal Register 30846 (1983) 45 CFR, Part 84.

30 Bishop Lawrence Casey gave evidence before the Supreme Court of New Jersey in 1976. An abridged version of the judgement, 'In the Matter of Karen Quinlan, An Alleged Incompetent', is reprinted in *Killing and Letting Die*, B. Steinbock (ed.) (Prentice Hall, Englewood Cliffs, NJ, 1980). Bishop Lawrence's reference to 'extraordinary means' can be found on p. 31.

31 The 12-page *Declaration on Euthanasia* was issued by the Sacred Congregation for the Doctrine of the Faith in 1980. The American Medical Association's reference to 'extraordinary means' is contained in a policy statement adopted by the House of Delegates of the American Medical Association on 4 December 1973. In its entirety the statement reads:

The intentional termination of the life of one human being by another—mercy killing—is contrary to that for which the medical profession stands and is contrary to the policy of the American Medical Association.

The cessation of the employment of extraordinary means to prolong the life of the body when there is irrefutable evidence that biological death is imminent is the decision of the patient and/or his immediate family. The advice and judgment of the physician should be freely available to the patient and/or his immediate family.

32–3 For a good discussion of the distinction between ordinary and extraordinary means of treatment, see the Report of the President's Commission for the Study of Ethical Problems in Medicine and Biomedical and Behavioral Research, *Deciding to Forego Life-Sustaining Treatment: Ethical, Medical and Legal Issues in Treatment Decisions* (US Government Printing Office, Washington, DC, March 1983), pp. 82–9.

33 The quotations are from Gerald Kelly, SJ, *Medico-Moral Problems* (The Catholic Hospital Association, St Louis, 1958), p. 129. That quality of life judgements are at work also becomes apparent in an article by James M. Gustafson; see pp. 546–7 of 'Mongolism, Parental Desires, and the Right to Life' in *Perspectives in Biology and Medicine*, vol. 6, no. 4 (Summer 1973).

35 The remark by Judge John Ferris is quoted in the Report of the President's Commission for the Study of Ethical Problems in Medicine and Biomedical and Behavioral Research, *Deciding to Forego Life-Sustaining Treatment: Ethical, Medical and Legal Issues in Treatment Decisions* (US Government Printing Office, Washington, DC, 1983), p. 84. For the survey of obstetricians and paediatricians, see P. Singer, H. Kuhse, and C. Singer, 'The Treatment of Newborn Infants with Major Handicaps—A survey of obstetricians and paediatricians in Victoria' in *The Medical Journal of Australia*, vol. 2, no. 6 (17 September 1983), pp. 274–8.

36 Robert Veatch calls for banning the words 'ordinary' and 'extra-ordinary means' from further use on p. 110 of his book *Death, Dying and the Biological Revolution* (Yale University Press, New Haven and London, 1976). The conclusion of the Law Reform Commission of Canada that the distinction is too ambiguous to be useful can be found on p. 36 of its Working Paper No. 28, *Euthanasia, Aiding Suicide and Cessation of Treatment* (Law Reform Commission of Canada, Ottawa, 1982). *The Journal of Medical Ethics* discusses the distinction between ordinary and extraordinary means in its editorial, vol. 7, no. 2. The quotation is from p. 56.

36–7 The quotations are from pp. 88–9 of the American President's

Commission's Report *Deciding to Forego Life-Sustaining Treatment.*

39–40 The exchange between Dr C. Everett Koop and Judge Gerhard Gesell is found on pp. 40–5 of the transcript of the 21 March 1983 hearing.

40 Judge Gerhard Gesell's statement that 'there is no customary standard of care' is found on p. 13 of the Judgment in The United States District Court for the District of Columbia, American Academy of Pediatrics, National Association of Children's Hospitals and Related Institutions, Children's Hospital National Medical Center v. Margaret M. Heckler, Secretary, Department of Health and Human Services, Civil Action No. 83–0774 (14 April 1983).

41 For the survey of American paediatric surgeons, See A. Shaw, J. Randolph, and B. Manard, 'Ethical Issues in Pediatric Surgery: A National Survey of Pediatricians and Pediatric Surgeons' in *Pediatrics*, vol. 60, (1977), pp. 588–99.

43 An analysis of the comments received by the Department of Health and Human Services can be found in *Federal Register*, vol. 49, no. 8 (12 January 1984), p. 1623. We are grateful to the American Academy of Pediatrics for sending us a copy of its submission, from which we have quoted the comment of the New Mexico paediatrician. On the size and location of the notice required by the Final Rule, see the above-mentioned issue of the *Federal Register*, p. 1651.

44 Dr Koop's comments at the press conference were issued in written form by the Department of Health and Human Services on 9 January 1984. For the provisions of the Final Rule relating to Infant Care Review Committees, see the *Federal Register*, pp. 1623–5 and 1651. For the rejection of changes to the Department's position relating to the provision of all medically beneficial treatment, see p. 1630.

45 Judge Brieant's decision in the case of American Medical Association v. Margaret M. Heckler, Secretary, Department of Health and Human Services, is reported in 585 *Federal Supplement* (1984), pp. 541–2. See also *American Medical News* (1 June 1984), p. 2. For the earlier case of 'Baby Jane Doe', see 'Weber v. Stony Brook Hospital', New York Court of Appeals, *New York Law Journal*, 1 November 1983, p. 5. For discussion, see Bonnie Steinbock, 'Baby Jane Doe in the Courts', *Hastings Center Report*, vol. 14, no. 1 (February 1984), pp. 13–19, and for a more recent report, *New York Times*, 14 October 1984, p. 56.

47 The amendments to the Child Abuse Prevention and Treatment Act are reported in *Congressional Record*, 19 September 1984, pp. H9805–17. See also *New York Times*, 14 October 1984, p. 56.

3   Deciding when life is worthwhile: the treatment of spina bifida

49 The quotation about the 'traditional' attitude to spina bifida comes from p. 631 of an article by F. D. Ingraham and H. Hamlin, 'Spina Bifida and Cranium Bifidum', which appeared in the *New England Journal of Medicine*, vol. 228 (1943).

50 The influential paper urging immediate operation is W. J. W. Sharrard, R. B. Zachary, J. Lorber, and A. M. Bruce, 'A controlled trial of immediate and delayed closure of spina bifida cystica'. It appeared in *Archives of Disease in Childhood*, vol. 38 (1963).

51 Dr Anthony Raimondi's comments are found in Chester A. Swinyard (ed.), *Decision Making and the Defective Newborn—Proceedings of a Conference on Spina Bifida and Ethics* (C. C. Thomas, Springfield, 1978), p. 117.

51 When outlining the medical bases for treatment decisions, Dr John Lorber was speaking on BBC Radio 3 as one of the participants in a programme, 'The Defect—Part I', transmitted on 18 October 1978. Transcript kindly supplied by the producer, David Paterson.

51–2 Dr John Lorber's quotation is from a conference paper, 'Ethical Concepts in the Treatment of Myelomeningocele', reprinted in Chester A. Swinyard (ed.), *Decision Making and the Defective Newborn— Proceedings of a Conference on Spina Bifida and Ethics* (C. C. Thomas, Springfield, 1978), p. 60.

52–3 For Lorber's summary of the results of treatment, see John Lorber, 'Ethical Problems in the Management of Myelomeningocele and Hydrocephalus', *Journal of the Royal College of Physicians*, vol. 10, no. 1 (October 1975), pp. 47–60.

53 Gerald Leach, *The Biocrats* (Penguin, Harmondsworth, 1972), p. 201. Dr Eliot Slater made this claim in an article, 'From Health Service to Sickness Service?' in the *British Medical Journal*, 4, 18 December 1971, pp. 734–5. John Lorber's figures are found in his article, 'Spina Bifida Cystica—Results of Treatment of 270 Consecutive Cases with Criteria for Selection in the Future', *Archives of Disease in Childhood*, vol. 47 (1972), p. 868.

54 The findings of P. Rickham and T. Mawdsley are contained in their article, 'The Effect of Early Operation on the Survival of Spina Bifida Cystica', *Developmental Medicine and Child Neurology*, vol. 8, suppl. II (1966), p. 20. See D. D. Matson, 'Surgical Treatment of Myelomenyngocele' published in *Pediatrics*, vol. 42 (1968), p. 225.

Robert Zachary's article: 'Ethical and Social Aspects of Treatment of Spina Bifida' appeared in *The Lancet* on 3 August 1968, pp. 274–6.

55 The exchange between Robert Zachary and the other doctors took place in *The Lancet* in 1968 following the publication of Robert Zachary's article on 3 August 1968. The letters are reprinted in *Moral Problems in Medicine* (Prentice Hall, Englewood Cliffs, 1976), on pp. 348–52.

57 The paper in which W. J. W. Sharrard, R. B. Zachary, and J. Lorber jointly take a stand against selection is entitled: 'Survival and Paralysis in Open Myelomeningocele with Special Reference to the Time of Repair of the Spinal Lesion'. It appeared in the journal *Developmental Medicine and Child Neurology*, vol. 9, suppl. 13 (1967), pp. 35–50. The quotation is from p. 49.

John Lorber's comment that he 'almost by accident' took on the role of advocate of selective treatment was made in a personal communication to the authors.

John Lorber expresses his new attitude in his article: 'Results of Treatment of Myelomeningocele', *Developmental Medicine and Child Neurology*, *13* (1971), pp. 279–303. The quotation appears on p. 300.

58–9 The question of possible survival of children not selected for treatment is raised by John Lorber in his article, 'Spina Bifida Cystica—Results of Treatment of 270 Consecutive Cases with Criteria for Selection for the Future', *Archives of Disease in Childhood, 42* (1972). The quotation appears on p. 871.

P. P. Rickham and T. Mawdsley published the article to which John Lorber refers under the title 'The Effect of Early Operation on the Survival of Spina Bifida Cystica' in *Developmental Medicine and Child Neurology*, vol. 8, suppl. 11 (1966).

John Lorber published his analysis of the outcome of 794 unselected cases in 'Results of Treatment of Myelomeningocele—An analysis of 524 unselected cases, with special reference to possible selection for treatment', *Developmental Medicine and Child Neurology*, vol. 13 (1971), pp. 279–303; and 'Spina Bifida Cystica—Results of Treatment of 270 Consecutive Cases with Criteria for Selection in the Future', *Archives of Disease in Childhood*, vol. 47 (1972), pp. 854–73.

The leading article on 'Selection in Treatment of Spina Bifida' appeared in the *Medical Journal of Australia*, vol. 2, 58th year, no. 23, on 4 December 1971, pp. 1151–2.

The Oxford group published its report, co-authored by D. W. Hide, H. Parry Williams, and L. Ellis, in *Developmental Medicine and Child Neurology*, vol. 14 (1972), p. 304.

The Edinburgh group—G. D. Stark and M. G. Drummond—published its report in *Archives of Diseases in Childhood*, 46 (1973), p. 676.

Details of the 295 Melbourne cases were published by G. Keys Smith and E. Durham Smith under the title 'Selection for Treatment in Spina Bifida Cystica', *British Medical Journal*, vol. 4 (1973), pp. 189–97.

John Lorber's reference to selection being the 'least bad solution' is from p. 204 of his article 'Early Results of Selective Treatment of Spina Bifida Cystica', *British Medical Journal*, 27 October 1973.

The article 'Moral and Ethical Dilemmas in the Special-Care Nursery' by R. S. Duff and A. G. M. Campbell appeared in the *New England Journal of Medicine*, vol. 279 (1973), pp. 890–4.

60 *Care of the Child with Spina Bifida* was published by the Department of Health and Social Security in London in 1973.

John Lorber refers to the acceptance of his selection criteria by Spina Bifida Associations in his 'Commentary', *Journal of Medical Ethics*, vol. 7 (1981), p. 121; also in his article 'Ethical Problems in the Management of Myelomeningocele and Hydrocephalus', *Journal of the Royal College of Physicians*, vol. 10 (1975), p. 54.

Selection criteria are spelled out in John Lorber's article, 'Ethical Problems in the Management of Myelomeningocele and Hydrocephalus' in the *Journal of the Royal College of Physicians*, vol. 10 (1975). The quotation can be found on p. 53.

60–1 John Lorber classifies handicaps according to their degree of severity in 'Spina Bifida Cystica—Results of Treatment of 270 Consecutive Cases with Criteria for Selection for the Future', *Archives of Disease in Childhood*, vol. 47 (1972), p. 856. He elaborates on his definition of 'moderate handicap' in 'Ethical Problems in the Management of Myelomeningocele and Hydrocephalus', *Journal of the Royal College of Physicians*, vol. 10, no. 1 (1975), p. 51.

62 John Lorber's comments on mental handicap can be found in his article 'Spina Bifida Cystica, Results of Treatment of 270 Consecutive Cases with Criteria for Selection for the Future', *Archives of Disease in Childhood*, vol. 47 (1972), p. 870. He defends his position in 'Ethical Problems in the Management of Myelomeningocele and Hydrocephalus', *Journal of the Royal College of Physicians*, vol. 10, no. 1 (1976), on p. 54; the statement that no parent had ever wished for an operation after having been given a full account of the baby's condition appears on the same page.

The 'social criteria' for selective treatment are discussed in John Lorber's article, 'Results of Treatment of Myelomeningocele—An analysis of 524 unselected cases, with special reference to possible selection for treatment', *Developmental Medical Child Neurology*, vol. 13 (1971), p. 296.

63 Dr John Freeman made the comment that parents usually accept the doctor's advice in a BBC interview, 'The Defect—Part I', broadcast on Radio 3 on 18 October 1978.

The proceedings of the Montreal symposium have been published in D. J. Roy (ed.), *Medical Wisdom and Ethics in the Treatment of Severely Defective Newborns* (Eden Press, 1978). John Freeman's comments are found on pp. 28–9 in the section entitled 'Ethics and the Decision-Making Process for Defective Children'.

64 The question whether life in a wheelchair is worse than death was raised by John Freeman in the above symposium. It can be found on p. 32 of the proceedings.

65 The present quotation is from Eliot Slater, 'Wanted—A New Basic Approach', *British Medical Journal*, 5 May 1973, p. 285.

John Lorber's comment is found on p. 52 of his article, 'Ethical Problems in the Management of Myelomeningocele and Hydrocephalus'.

66 The grandmother's comments are quoted on p. 18 of 'Severely Handicapped Infants' by Madeleine Simms, *New Humanist*, vol. 98, no. 2 (Summer 1983).

68 The case of the 8-year-old boy is described on p. 311 of John Freeman's article, 'The Short-sighted Treatment of Myelomeningocele: A Long-term Case Report', *Pediatrics*, vol. 53, no. 3 (March 1974).

69 John Lorber outlines what non-treatment means for him on p. 55 of his article, 'Ethical Problems in the Management of Myelomeningocele and Hydrocephalus' (see note to pp. 60–1 above).

Dr Raimondi's comments are found on p. 119 of the conference proceedings. Chester A. Swinyard (ed.), *Decision Making and the Defective Newborn*.

70 The quotation is from R. B. Zachary, 'Life with Spina Bifida', *British Medical Journal*, 3 December 1977, p. 1461.

70 Ian Kennedy's comments can be found on pp. 9–11 of the transcript of the BBC programme.

71 John Freeman's comments appear on p. 9 of the transcript of the BBC programme.

72 John Freeman's article, 'Is There a Right to Die—Quickly?' was published in the *Journal of Paediatrics*, vol. 80 (1972), pp. 904–5; it is reprinted in S. Gorovitz *et al.* (eds.), *Moral Problems in Medicine*, op. cit., pp. 354–6. The quotation can be found on pp. 355–6.

4 Killing and letting die

74 On the 'Johns Hopkins Case', see pp. 198–9 of the report of the President's Commission for the Study of Ethical Problems in Medicine and Biomedical and Behavioral Research, *Deciding to Forego Life-Sustaining Treatment: Ethical, Medical and Legal Issues in Treatment Decisions* (US Government Printing Office, Washington, DC, 1983).

75 The question whether doctors who withhold life-sustaining treatment may in fact be guilty of murder is discussed by Helen Beynon, a lecturer in law at the University of Reading, in her article 'Doctors as Murderers' in *Criminal Law Review*, January 1982, pp. 17–28. For a more philosophical discussion of the moral and legal issues of allowing severely disabled infants to die, see Helga Kuhse: 'A Modern Myth: That Letting Die is not the Intentional Causation of Death—Some reflections on the trial and acquittal of Dr. Leonard Arthur', *Journal of Applied Philosophy*, vol. 1, no. 1 (1984), pp. 21–38.

76 The article by G. Keys Smith and E. Durham Smith is entitled: 'Selection for Treatment in Spina Bifida Cystica'. It appeared in the *British Medical Journal*, vol. 4 (1973), pp. 189–97. The quotation is from p. 197.

77 For our survey of Victorian doctors, see P. Singer, H. Kuhse, and C. Singer, 'The treatment of newborn infants with major handicaps— A survey of obstetricians and paediatricians in Victoria', *The Medical Journal of Australia*, vol. 2, no. 6 (17 September 1983), pp. 274–9.

For the 1975 American survey, see Anthony Shaw, Judson G. Randolph, and Barbara Manard, 'Ethical Issues in Pediatric Surgery: A National Survey of Pediatricians and Pediatric Surgeons', *Pediatrics*, vol. 60, no. 4, part 2 (October 1977), pp. 588–99.

78 The quotations are from pp. 18 and 19 of the Submission by the Australian Medical Association to the Law Reform Commission of Western Australia, June 1982.

79 Robert and Peggy Stinson recorded their experiences in two separate journals. These journals formed the basis for their subsequent book: *The Long Dying of Baby Andrew* (an Atlantic Monthly Press Book, Little Brown and Company, Boston and Toronto, 1983). Peggy Stinson's reflections on Andrew's 'accidental' disconnection from the respirator appear on p. 345.

Herbert Eckstein made these comments in a recorded discussion, reprinted under the title 'Medical Practice—New Horizons in Medical Ethics—Severely Malformed Children' in the *British Medical Journal*, no. 2 (1973), p. 287.

80 The quotations are from pp. 53, 58, and 57 respectively, of John Lorber's article, 'Ethical Problems in the Management of Myelomeningocele and Hydrocephalus', *Journal of the Royal College of Physicians*, vol. 10 (1975).

John Lorber's comment that selective non-treatment is 'another name for letting nature take its course' is from his 'Commentary I and reply' in the *Journal of Medical Ethics*, vol. 7 (September 1981), p. 120.

The statement by Dr Vincent Collins is from p. 390 of his article, 'Limits of Medical Responsibility in Prolonging Life', *Journal of the American Medical Association*, vol. 206 (1968), pp. 389–92.

81 Paul Ramsey's quotation is from p. 151 of *The Patient as Person* (Yale University Press, New Haven and London, 1970).

82 The quotation from H. L. A. Hart and A. M. Honoré's book, *Causation in the Law* (Oxford University Press, London, 1959), appears on p. 33.

John Stuart Mill's comments on causation are found in his *A System of Logic*, bk. III, ch. 5, sect. 3 (Longman's, London, 1959), p. 217.

83 The point that we select different causes for different purposes is made by J. L. Mackie in his book, *The Cement of the Universe* (Oxford University Press, London, 1974). He notes, on p. 35, that in the social context we often want to know what caused a certain event with a view to how it could, and perhaps should, have been prevented.

85 A similar account of why a doctor's deliberate failure to sustain a patient's life is properly regarded as the cause of death is given by Bart Gruzalski, 'Killing and Letting Die', *Mind*, vol. 40 (1981), pp. 91–8.

86 John Lorber's quotations are from 'Ethical Problems in the Management of Myelomeningocele and Hydrocephalus', *Journal of the Royal College of Physicians*, vol. 10 (1975), pp. 53 and 55, respectively.

87 This long quotation is from pp. 55–6 of the same article.

88 John Harris's critique of John Lorber's position is entitled 'Ethical Problems in the Management of Some Severely Handicapped Children'. It appeared in the *Journal of Medical Ethics*, vol. 7 (September 1981), pp. 117–20. In the same issue, John Lorber replies to John Harris on pp. 120–2.

The quotation referring to the 'Johns Hopkins Case' is from an article by Anthony M. Shaw and Iris A. Shaw, 'Dilemmas of "Informed Consent" in Children', *New England Journal of Medicine*, vol. 289:17 (25 October 1973), p. 886.

93 On the Nazi analogy, see also Letters to the Editor, *Pediatrics*, vol. 73, no. 2 (February 1984), pp. 259–63; and the letter of Mrs Alison Davis to the editor of the *Journal of Medical Ethics*, vol. 9, no. 3 (September 1983), p. 181.

   Leo Alexander's article, 'Medical Science Under Dictatorship' was published in the *New England Journal of Medicine*, vol. 241 (1949); the quotation is from p. 44.

94 The quotations from Lucy Dawidowicz are from the symposium 'Biomedical Ethics and the Shadow of Nazism', *Hastings Center Report*, vol. 6, no. 4 (1976), Special Supplement, pp. 3–4.

95 Sam Gorovitz's reply to the slippery slope argument is in the Appendix to the report by the Ethics Advisory Board, Department of Health, Education and Welfare, US Government: 'Protection of Human Subjects: HEW Support of Human In Vitro Fertilization and Embryo Transfer', *Federal Register*, 18 June 1979, pp. 35033–58. *Note:* the written submissions have been published separately as *Appendix: HEW Support of Research Involving Human In Vitro Fertilization and Embryo Transfer* (US Government Printing Office, Washington, DC, 1979). The quotation is from p. 12 of Section 3.

   Grobstein's comments are on p. 71 of *From Chance to Purpose: An Appraisal of External Human Fertilization* (Addison–Wesley, Reading, Mass., 1981).

5 Infanticide: a broader perspective

99–100 See Knud Rasmussen, *The Netsilik Eskimos—Reports of the Fifth Thule Exhibition*, vol. 8 (Copenhagen, 1931), as cited by Asen Balikci, *The Netsilik Eskimo* (The Natural History Press, Garden City, NY, 1970), pp. 148–9.

   On female infanticide among the Eskimos, see A. Balikci, 'Female Infanticide on the Arctic Coast', *Man*, 2:615–25. The story of Ogpingalik is recounted by A. Balikci in his book *The Netsilik Eskimo* (The Natural History Press, Garden City, NY, 1970), p. 149; he refers to Rasmussen's conversation with the mother of Quertiliq on p. 140 of the same book.

101–3 Lorna Marshall's book, *The !Kung of Nyae Nyae* (Cambridge University Press, 1976) gives a good account of the !Kung during the 1951–5 period, when Western influence was still minimal. See also Nancy Howell, 'The Population of the Dobe Area !Kung' in Richard B. Lee and Irven DeVore (eds.): *Kalahari Hunter-Gatherers* (Harvard University Press, Cambridge, Mass., and London, 1976), pp. 137–51. Further references can be found in Mildred Dickeman's article

'Demographic Consequences of Infanticide in Man', *Annual Review of Ecology and Systematics*, vol. 6 (1975), pp. 121–2.

102 Richard B. Lee's account of the life of !Kung women is found on pp. 331–3 of 'Population Growth and the Beginnings of Sedentary Life among the !Kung Bushmen' in B. Spooner (ed.): *Population Growth: Anthropological Implications* (University of Pennsylvania Press, Philadelphia, 1972).

Lorna Marshall mentions the practice of infanticide, and the reasons for it, on p. 166 of her book, *The !Kung of Nyae Nyae*.

103–5 Raymond Firth's comprehensive account of life on the island of Tikopia was compiled in the 1920s, at a time when the inhabitants were still largely untouched by Western influence. See R. Firth, *We, the Tikopia* (Beacon Press, Boston, 1963). Additional references on the Tikopia are found in Mildred Dickeman's article, 'Demographic Consequences of Infanticide in Man' on pp. 123–5.

104 Methods of population control among the Tikopia are discussed by Raymond Firth on pp. 369–75.

The quotation criticizing the influence of Christian morality is on p. 376.

105 Mildred Dickeman reports on the famine in the 1950s on pp. 124–5 of her article, 'Demographic Consequences of Infanticide in Man'.

105–7 On infanticide in Japan, see Mildred Dickeman, 'Demographic Consequences of Infanticide in Man', pp. 125–9; also Thomas Smith *et al.*, *Nakahara: Family Farming and Population in a Japanese Village 1717–1830* (Stanford University Press, 1977). The comment that infanticide was widely practised by the most respectable members of the community is found on p. 83; and the comment that infanticide was a 'normal, even conventional, form of behaviour', on p. 85.

The quotation from I. Taeuber's book, *The Population of Japan* (Princeton University Press, 1958) is from p. 33.

107 Mildred Dickeman refers to Japan's understanding and acceptance of survival imperatives on p. 129 of her article, 'Demographic Consequences of Infanticide in Man'.

For the comparative studies, see C. Ford, 'A Comparative Study of Human Reproduction', *Yale University Publications in Anthropology*, vol. 3 (Yale University Press, New Haven, 1945) and 'Control of Contraception in Cross-Cultural Perspective', *Annals of the New York Academy of Science* 54 (5): 763–8 (1952). See also J. W. Whiting, 'Effects of Climate on Certain Cultural Practices', A. P. Voyda (ed.), *Environment and Cultural Behavior* (Natural History, New York, 1969), pp. 416–50. We owe these references to Mildred Dickeman, 'Demographic Consequences of Infanticide in Man'.

108 The ethnographers' reports are examined by W. T. Divale and M. Harris in 'Population, Warfare and the Male Supremacist Complex', *American Anthropologist*, 78 (1976), pp. 521–38.

Comparisons of murder rates between Japan and other nations can be found in the publication of the Keizai Koho Center, Japan Institute for Social and Economic Affairs, *Japan 1982: An International Comparison*, p. 77. During 1982 the homicide rate in Japan was 1.4 per 100,000 inhabitants; the USA rate was 10.2 per 100,000 inhabitants.

Laila Williamson, 'Infanticide: An Anthropological Analysis' in Marvin Kohl (ed.), *Infanticide and the Value of Life* (Prometheus Books, New York, 1978), pp. 63–4; see also Nancy Howell, 'The Population of the Dobe Area !Kung', pp. 147–8.

109 The passage about the loving concern of the !Kung for their babies is from Lorna Marshall's book, *The !Kung of the Nyae Nyae*, pp. 315–18, and the one about the Netsilik Eskimos from A. Balikci's book, *The Netsilik Eskimo*, pp. 104 and 122.

On the acceptance of children into the community, see Edward Westermarck, *The Origin and Development of the Moral Ideas*, vol. 1 (Macmillan, London, 1906), p. 404; on the exposure of Greek children prior to the Amphidromia see Glanville Williams, 'The Legal Evaluation of Infanticide' in Marvin Kohl (ed.), *Infanticide and the Value of Life*, p. 116.

110 The passage about the importance of naming is from C. Ford, 'Control of Contraception in Cross-Cultural Perspective', p. 765, as cited by Mildred Dickeman, 'Demographic Consequences of Infanticide in Man', p. 115. For Zuckerman's study of baboons, see S. Zuckerman: *The Social Life of Monkeys and Apes* (Kegan Paul, London, 1932).

J. V. Neel is quoted from his article, 'Some aspects of differential fertility in two American Indian Tribes', *Proceedings of the International Congress of Anthropological and Ethnological Science*, 8th, 1 (1969), p. 358, as cited by Mildred Dickeman, 'Demographic Consequences of Infanticide in Man', p. 108.

111 Plato discusses infanticide in bk. 5, sect. 459–61 of *The Republic*. Aristotle's discussion of population questions can be found in bk. 7, ch. 16 of his *Politics*.

On the subject of infanticide as a topic for humour in ancient Greece, see Laila Williamson, 'Infanticide: An Anthropological Analysis', p. 69, n. 44.

Cicero speaks of 'monstrous abortions' in *De Legibus*, iii, 8; Seneca's reference to infanticide appears in *De Ira*, i, 15; and William L. Langer notes Pliny's defence of infanticide as a means of population control in 'Infanticide: A Historical Survey', *History of Childhood Quarterly*, vol. I (1974), p. 355.

112 For the two biblical exhortations to be fecund, see Genesis 1: 28 and Genesis 1: 7. God's promise to Abraham is found at Genesis 22: 17. Reference to child sacrifice is made in Leviticus 18: 21, and, again, in Isaiah 57: 5.

Tacitus is quoted by Salo W. Baron, *A Social and Religious History of the Jews*, 2nd rev. and enl. ed. (Columbia University Press, New York, 1957), vol. 2, p. 219. See also Immanuel Jakobovits, 'Jewish Views on Infanticide' in Marvin Kohl (ed.), *Infanticide and the Value of Life*, pp. 23–31.

113 On the rule that the killing of a new-born child is murder only if the child has been carried a full nine months, see Immanuel Jakobovits, 'Jewish Views of Infanticide', p. 24.

W. E. H. Lecky, from the *History of European Morals from Augustus to Charlemagne*, 11th ed. (Longmans Green Co., London, 1894), vol. 2, pp. 18, 20 and 34.

114 On the decree by Constantine, see William A. Langer, 'Infanticide: A Historical Survey', p. 255.

Paul Ramsey puts forward his view that we are 'stewards and not owners of our lives' in his book, *Ethics at the Edges of Life* (Yale University Press, New Haven and London, 1978), p. 147; see also Thomas Aquinas, *Summa Theologia* II, ii, qu. 64, art. 5; and John Locke, *An Essay Concerning the True Original Extent and End of Civil Government*, pt. II, sect. 6.

115 On the necessity of baptism for salvation, see W. E. H. Lecky, *History of European Morals from Augustus to Charlemagne*, vol. 2, p. 23; and Glanville Williams, *The Sanctity of Life and the Criminal Law* (Alfred Knopf, New York, 1957), pp. 15–16.

For John Noonan's view, see his much-discussed article, 'An Almost Absolute Value in History' in John Noonan (ed.), *The Morality of Abortion* (Harvard University Press, Cambridge, Mass., 1972), p. 51.

St Fulgentius is cited by Edward Westermarck, *The Origin and Development of the Moral Ideas*, vol. 1, pp. 416–17.

116 On St Augustine's views, see *New Catholic Encyclopedia*, vol. 2 (McGraw-Hill, New York, 1967), p. 64.

On medieval laws dealing with the killing of unbaptized children, see Edward Westermarck's comments on the decree of the Council of

Mentz in 852, *The Origin and Development of the Moral Ideas*, vol. 1, pp. 411–12; and W. E. H. Lecky *History of European Morals from Augustus to Charlemagne*, pp. 23–4.

The reference in the *New Catholic Encyclopedia* to the fate of unbaptized children can be found in vol. 2 on pp. 63–4.

6 What's wrong with the sanctity of life doctrine?

120 Joseph Fletcher's article, 'Indicators of Humanhood: A Tentative Profile of Man' appeared in *The Hastings Center Report*, vol. 2, no. 5 (1972).

Michael Tooley develops his position most fully in his book *Abortion and Infanticide* (Clarendon Press, Oxford, 1983), ch. 5.

122 Jane Goodall's observations of chimpanzees are recounted in *In the Shadow of Man* (Boston, 1971). The episodes of Figan and Washoe are described on pp. 107 and 254 respectively.

126 Peter Singer's article: 'Sanctity of Life or Quality of Life?' appeared in *Pediatrics*, vol. 72, no. 1 (July 1983), pp. 128–9; letters to the editor were published in vol. 73, no. 2 (Feb. 1984), pp. 259–61; Peter Singer's reply is in the same issue on pp. 261–3.

Plato's argument against defining 'good' as what the gods approve is in his *Euthyphro*.

127 Bertrand Russell: *History of Western Philosophy* (Allen & Unwin, London, 1961), p. 668.

128 Peter Singer deals with the role of reason in ethics in Chapter I of *Practical Ethics* (Cambridge University Press, 1979). See also his book *The Expanding Circle* (Farrar, Straus and Giroux, New York, 1981), chs. 4–6; and R. M. Hare, *Freedom and Reason* (Oxford University Press, 1963) and R. M. Hare, *Moral Thinking* (Oxford University Press, 1981).

132 John Locke's definition of 'person' is found in his *Essay Concerning Human Understanding*, bk. II, ch. 9, par. 29.

134 The Oxford philosopher Derek Parfit deals with the complex philosophical issues of potential people in his recent book, *Reasons and Persons* (Clarendon Press, Oxford, 1984), part 4.

137 Peggy Stinson's reflections are from p. 46 of the book by Robert and Peggy Stinson, *The Long Dying of Baby Andrew* (Little Brown and Company, Boston and Toronto, 1983).

138 For one example of the view that the killing of severely handicapped infants will pose a threat to severely handicapped adults as well, see Nat Hentoff, 'The Baby Who Was Starved to Death for His Own Good', *Village Voice* (New York, 13 December 1983), p. 6.

Jeremy Bentham's comment on infanticide is from his *Theory of Legislation*, p. 264, and is quoted by E. Westermarck, *The Origin and Development of Moral Ideas* (London, 1924), vol. I, p. 413 n.

7 In whose interests?

141 The case of Shauna Tamar Curlender (*Curlender v. Bio-Science Laboratories*, 165 Cal. Rptr. 447 [ct. App. 2d Dist. Div. 1, 1980]) is discussed by Helga Kuhse in 'The Muddle of "Wrongful Life" and the Limits of "Harm"' in *New Doctor*, no. 24 (June 1982), pp. 9–11. See also George Annas, 'Righting the Wrong of "Wrongful Life"', *The Hastings Center Report*, vol. 11, no. 1 (February 1981), pp. 8–9.

The decision by Lord Justice Templeman was reported in *The Times Law Report*, 8 August 1981, p. 15.

142 John West recounts the aftermath of reconstructive surgery on Brian in an unpublished letter of 30 March 1983 to George Will.

144 Alison Davies's letter was published on p. 181 of the *Journal of Medical Ethics*, vol. 9, no. 3 (September 1983).

145 For John Lorber's question to adult spina bifida patients, see his article, 'The Doctor's Duty to Patients and Parents in Profoundly Handicapping Conditions' in D. J. Roy (ed.), *Medical Wisdom and Ethics in the Treatment of Severely Defective Newborn and Young Children* (proceedings of a symposium held on 18 November 1976, organized by the Centre for Bioethics, Clinical Research Institute of Montreal, Montreal, Quebec, Canada; Eden Press), p. 17.

The letter quoted here is by Tonia Noell Roberts. It is dated 27 December 1982 and was made available to us by courtesy of John and Susan West.

146 The comment by the doctor that it must have 'hurt like hell' each time Andrew drew a breath is found on p. 201 of Robert and Peggy Stinson's book, *The Long Dying of Baby Andrew*.

146–7 The quotation about the problems faced by families with a handicapped child is from a summary of research findings published by the National Children's Bureau Information Service in no. 42 of its *Highlights* series. It is cited by Madeleine Simms, 'Severely handicapped infants: a discussion document', *New Humanist*, vol. 98, no. 2 (Summer 1983), p. 18.

147–8 The quotations are from pp. 69–71 of Charles Hannam's book, *Parents and Mentally Handicapped Children*, 2nd edition (Penguin, Harmondsworth, 1980).

148 Billie Shepperdson's study 'Abortion and euthanasia of Down's syndrome children—the parents' view' was published in the *Journal of Medical Ethics*, vol. 9, no. 3 (September 1983), pp. 152–7.

149 The South Wales study of families of children with spina bifida was conducted by B. Tew, E. H. Payne, and K. M. Lawrence, 'Must a family with a handicapped child be a handicapped family?', *Dev. Med. Child Neurol.*, 16, Supp. 32 (1974), pp. 95–8.

150 For the study of families with Down's syndrome children, see Ann Gath, *Down's Syndrome and the Family: The Early Years* (Academic Press, London, 1978), pp. 61–2.

The effects on siblings of a handicapped child are discussed by Ann Gath in her book *Down's Syndrome and the Family* (ibid.), on p. 69. See also her article, 'Sibling reactions to mental handicap' in *J. Child Psychol. Psychiatr.*, 123 (1974), pp. 161–7.

Stephen Kew discusses his findings in his book *Handicap and Family Crisis* (Pitman, London, 1975). The quotation is from pp. 136–7.

151 The story of Barbara was published in *The Age* (Melbourne) on 16 August 1983.

152 Cliff Cunningham's book, *Down's Syndrome: An Introduction for Parents* was published by Souvenir Press, London, in 1982. The figures quoted are from pp. 19 and 23.

153 Charles Hannam's unspoken words to David are found on p. 46 of his book, *Parents and Mentally Handicapped Children.*

154 President's Commission for the Study of Ethical Problems in Medicine and Biomedical and Behavioral Research, *Deciding to Forego Life-Sustaining Treatment, Ethical, Medical and Legal Issues in Treatment Decisions* (US Government Printing Office, Washington, DC, March 1983). The first quotation is from p. 6; the second from p. 219.

155 The figures relating to mothers who decided against having other children on account of the presence of a retarded child are from p. 52 of S. Kew, *Handicap and Family Crisis*. Stephen Kew cites two studies: K. Holt, 'The influence of a retarded child upon family limitation', *J. of Mental Def. Res.*, vol. 2, pt. 1 (June 1958); and J. Tizard and J. Grad, *The Mentally Handicapped and Their Families* (Oxford University Press, 1961).

156 Peggy Stinson's reflection on the 'other baby' are found on pp. 153 and 266–7 of *The Long Dying of Baby Andrew*.

Derek Parfit outlines these perplexing issues in 'Rights, Interests, and Possible People'. This essay is a portion of an address written in 1973 as a companion piece to R. M. Hare's 'Survival of the Weakest', which was given in lecture form to the London Medical Group. It is reprinted, in part, in S. Gorovitz *et al.* (eds.), *Moral Problems in Medicine* (Prentice Hall, Englewood Cliffs, NJ, 1976), pp. 369–75. For a more detailed discussion of these issues, see D. Parfit: *Reasons and*

Persons (Clarendon Press, Oxford, 1984), pt. 4.

158 R. M. Hare, 'Survival of the Weakest' in S. Gorovitz *et al.*, *Moral Problems in Medicine*, pp. 364–9. For the quotation, see p. 368. This article was first given in lecture form to the London Medical Group.

162 For the article on the institution in Agnews, California, see *The Atlanta Journal*, 11 December 1983, p. 44A.

163 For the comments by Robert W. Conley, see pp. 370 and 372 of his book, *The Economics of Mental Retardation* (The Johns Hopkins University Press, Baltimore, 1973). For the article on paediatric nursing homes, see P. S. Glick *et al.*, 'Implications of the Massachusetts Experience for Residential Care of Multiply Handicapped Children', *The New England Journal of Medicine*, vol. 309, no. 11 (15 September 1983), pp. 640–6.

164 Tony Hall's estimate of children needing a permanent new family of their own appeared in the *Guardian* on 14 October 1981 (as cited in Madeleine Simms, 'Severely Handicapped Infants: A Discussion Document', p. 19).

The letter from the Director of Parents for Children appeared in *The Times*, 25 Sept. 1981.

165 For the quotation from the 'Principles of Treatment of Disabled Infants' see Department of Health and Human Services, Office of the Secretary, 45 CFR pt. 84, *Nondiscrimination on the Basis of Handicap; Protection and Guidelines Relating to Health Care for Handicapped Infants*, Office of the Secretary. Final Rule, *Federal Register*, vol. 49, no. 8 (12 January 1984), p. 1622.

166 Professor Cyril Chantler is quoted in *The Times* (London), 15 January 1982. We owe this reference to Madeleine Simms, *New Humanist*, vol. 98, no. 2, p. 19.

167 Thomas Harris's letter was published in *Pediatric News* (USA), May 1983.

168 The case of Shirley Woodcock was reported in the *Observer* on 18 July 1982 and is cited by Madeleine Simms in her article in *New Humanist*, p. 20.

The articles 'Playing God in the Nursery' were published in the *Chicago Tribune* on 6–10 February 1983; they are also published separately as a booklet by the *Chicago Tribune*, as *Playing God in the Nursery*, 1983.

169 The announcement of the Illinois State government's limit on financial reimbursement was reported in the *Chicago Tribune* of 6 February 1983.

The report on the death of a premature infant denied access to the

Tampa General Hospital appeared in *Sunday Call–Chronicle* (Allentown, Pa.) on 5 July 1981.

The report on the happenings in Melbourne appeared in *The Age* (Melbourne) on 30 December 1983.

The *New York Times* reported on the University of California study on 18 July 1983.

170 Dr John Marshall is quoted in the *New York Times* of 18 July 1983, as is the director of the birth defects branch of the Federal Center for Disease Control, Dr Godfrey Oakley, Jr.

8 Who decides?

173 On the 'Limitation of Treatment Bill', see letter from Catherine Gillespie, Nottingham Representative for Prospect, in *Journal of Medical Ethics*, vol. 9, no. 4 (December 1983), p. 231.

On Prospect's recommendation that decision-making about severely handicapped infants be left to the parents, see Madeleine Simms, 'Severely Handicapped Infants: A Discussion Document', *New Humanist*, vol. 98, no. 2 (Summer 1983), pp. 15–22.

The recommendation of the Australian Medical Association is from its Press Release of 28 June 1982.

174 For the survey of American paediatricians, see A. Shaw, J. Randolph, and B. Manard, 'Ethical Issues in Pediatric Surgery: A National Survey of Pediatricians and Pediatric Surgeons', *Pediatrics*, vol. 60 (1977), pp. 588–99.

176 See 'Treating the Defective Newborn: A Survey of Physicians' Attitudes', *The Hastings Center Report*, vol. 6, no. 2 (April 1976), for the Californian study; and David Todres *et al.*, 'Pediatricians' Attitudes Affecting Decision-Making in Defective Newborns', *Pediatrics*, vol. 60 (1977), as cited in the President's Commission's Report, *Deciding to Forego Life-Sustaining Treatment*, p. 208.

The recommendation of the Judicial Council of the American Medical Association is quoted in the President's Commission's Report, *Deciding to Forego Life-Sustaining Treatment*, on p. 207. The full Statement of the Council is reprinted on pp. 299–300 of the Report.

For our own survey, see P. Singer, H. Kuhse, and C. Singer, 'The treatment of newborn infants with major handicaps—A survey of obstetricians and paediatricians in Victoria', *The Medical Journal of Australia*, vol. 2, no. 6 (17 September 1983), pp. 274–8.

177 The Policy Statement of the American Academy of Pediatrics was

published on p. 5 of the Academy's publication, *News and Comment*, October 1983.

On the kind of committees the American Academy of Pediatrics envisaged, see the Academy's submission to the Department of Health and Human Services, 'Comments of the American Academy of Pediatrics on Proposed Rule Regarding Nondiscrimination on the Basis of Handicap Relating to Health Care for Handicapped Infants', available from the Academy, Washington, DC.

184 The quote from Peggy and Robert Stinson is in 'On the Death of a Baby', *Atlantic Monthly*, July 1979, as cited by Helen Harrison with Ann Kositsky, RN, *The Premature Baby Book* (St Martin's Press, New York, 1983), p. 103.

Sally Sehring is quoted by Helen Harrison and Ann Kositsky in *The Premature Baby Book*, p. 102. Michael Garland is cited on the same page.

William Silverman's suggestion is found in Michael O'Donnell's article on William Silverman, 'One Man's Burden', *British Medical Journal*, vol. 286 (16 April 1983), p. 1291.

185 Raymond Duff's and A. G. M. Campbell's article, 'Moral and Ethical Dilemmas in the Special-Care Nursery' was published in the *New England Journal of Medicine*, vol. 289 (25 October 1973), pp. 885–94.

193 The quote is from P. Singer, H. Kuhse, and C. Singer, 'The treatment of newborn infants with major handicaps—A survey of obstetricians and paediatricians in Victoria'. The quotation is from p. 277.

195 See Glanville Williams, *The Sanctity of Life and The Criminal Law* (Alfred Knopf, New York, 1957), pp. 349–50.

F. Raymond Marks's proposal is discussed on p. 758 of A. R. Jonsen *et al.*, 'Critical Issues in Newborn Intensive Care: A Conference Report and Policy Proposal', *Pediatrics*, vol. 55, no. 6 (June 1975).

SELECT BIBLIOGRAPHY

This bibliography is intended as a guide for those who wish to read more widely on the ethical issues discussed in this book. Hence it includes only those books and articles that are more significant in that respect. There are several items referred to in the text which we have not considered sufficiently central to be listed here. Full reference to such items can be found in the Notes on Sources. Items of a purely medical or anthropological nature have also been excluded.

Books

S. F. Barker (ed.), *Respect for Life in Medicine, Philosophy and the Law* (The Johns Hopkins University Press, Baltimore and London, 1977).

S. Gorovitz *et al.*, *Moral Problems in Medicine* (Prentice Hall, Engelwood Cliffs, 1976).

C. Hannam, *Parents and Mentally Handicapped Children*, 2nd ed. (Penguin, Harmondsworth, 1980).

R. M. Hare, *Moral Thinking* (Oxford University Press, 1981).

H. L. A. Hart and A. M. Honoré, *Causation in the Law* (Oxford University Press, London, 1959).

S. Kew, *Handicap and Family Crisis* (Pitman, London, 1975).

E. W. Keyserlingk, *Sanctity of Life or Quality of Life* in the context of ethics, medicine, and law: A study written for the Law Reform Commission of Canada (Ottawa, 1979).

M. Kohl (ed.), *Infanticide and the Value of Life* (Prometheus Books, New York, 1978).

G. Leach, *The Biocrats* (Penguin, Harmondsworth, 1972).

W. E. H. Lecky, *History of European Morals from Augustus to Charlemagne*, 11th ed. (Longmans Green Co., London, 1894).

J. L. Mackie, *The Cement of the Universe* (Oxford University Press, London, 1974).

J. S. Mill, *A System of Logic* (Longmans, London, 1959).

D. Parfit, *Reasons and Persons* (Clarendon Press, Oxford, 1984).

P. Ramsey, *The Patient as Person* (Yale University Press, New Haven and London, 1970).

P. Ramsey, *Ethics at the Edges of Life* (Yale University Press, New Haven and London, 1978).

D. J. Roy (ed.), *Medical Wisdom and Ethics in the Treatment of Severely Defective Newborns and Young Children*, Proceedings of symposium held on 18 November 1976 (Eden Press, 1978).

Sacred Congregation for the Doctrine of the Faith, *Declaration on Euthanasia*, Vatican (1980).

P. Singer, *Practical Ethics* (Cambridge University Press, 1979).

B. Steinbock (ed.), *Killing and Letting Die* (Prentice Hall, Englewood Cliffs, NJ, 1980).

R. and P. Stinson, *The Long Dying of Baby Andrew* (an Atlantic Monthly Press Book, Little Brown and Company, Boston and Toronto, 1983).

C. A. Swinyard (ed.), *Decision Making and the Defective Newborn—Proceedings of a Conference on Spina Bifida and Ethics* (C. C. Thomas, Springfield, 1978).

M. Tooley, *Abortion and Infanticide* (Clarendon Press, Oxford, 1983).

R. M. Veatch, *Death, Dying and the Biological Revolution* (Yale University Press, New Haven and London, 1976).

E. Westermarck, *The Origin and Development of the Moral Ideas* (Macmillan, London, 1906).

G. Williams, *The Sanctity of Life and the Criminal Law* (Alfred Knopf, New York, 1957).

Reports

Law Reform Commission of Canada: Working Paper No. 28, *Euthanasia, Aiding Suicide and Cessation of Treatment* (Law Reform Commission of Canada, Ottawa, 1982).

President's Commission for the Study of Ethical Problems in Medicine and Biomedical and Behavioral Research, *Deciding to Forego Life-Sustaining Treatment: Ethical, Medical and Legal Issues in Treatment Decisions* (US Government Printing Office, Washington, DC, March 1983).

Articles

R. S. Duff and A. G. M. Campbell, 'Moral and Ethical Dilemmas in the Special-Care Nursery', *New England Journal of Medicine*, vol. 279 (1973), pp. 890–4.

J. Fletcher, 'Indicators of Humanhood: A Tentative Profile of Man', *The Hastings Center Report*, vol. 2, no. 5 (1972).

J. Freeman, 'Is There a Right to Die—Quickly?', *Journal of Pediatrics*, vol. 80 (1972), pp. 904–5.

J. Freeman, 'The Short-sighted Treatment of Myelomeningocele: A Long-Term Case Report', *Pediatrics,* vol. 53, no. 3 (March 1974).

P. S. Glick *et al.*, 'Implications of the Massachusetts Experience for Residential Care of Multiply Handicapped Children', *The New England Journal of Medicine,* vol. 309, no. 11 (15 September 1983), pp. 640–6.

B. Gruzalski, 'Killing and Letting Die', *Mind,* vol. 40 (1981), pp. 91–8.

J. M. Gustafson, 'Mongolism, Parental Desires, and the Right to Life', *Perspectives in Biology and Medicine,* vol. 6, no. 4 (Summer 1973).

R. M. Hare, 'Survival of the Weakest' in S. Gorovitz *et al.* (ed.), *Moral Problems in Medicine* (Prentice Hall, Englewood Cliffs, NJ, 1976), pp. 364–9.

J. Harris, 'Ethical Problems in the Management of Some Severely Handicapped Children', *Journal of Medical Ethics,* vol. 7 (September 1981), pp. 117–20.

I. Jakobovits, 'Jewish Views of Infanticide' in Marvin Kohl (ed.), *Infanticide and the Value of Life* (Prometheus Books, New York, 1978).

H. Kuhse, 'The Muddle of "Wrongful Life" and the Limits of "Harm"', *New Doctor,* no. 24 (June 1982), pp. 9–11.

H. Kuhse, 'A Modern Myth: That Letting Die is not the Intentional Causation of Death—Some Reflections on the Trial and Acquittal of Dr. Leonard Arthur', *Journal of Applied Philosophy,* vol. 1, no. 1 (1984).

J. Lorber, 'Results of Treatment of Myelomeningocele—An analysis of 524 unselected cases, with special reference to possible selection for treatment', *Developmental Medicine and Child Neurology,* vol. 13 (1971), pp. 279–303.

J. Lorber, 'Spina Bifida Cystica—Results of Treatment of 270 Consecutive Cases with Criteria for Selection in the Future', *Archives of Disease in Childhood,* vol. 47 (1972), pp. 854–73.

J. Lorber, 'Ethical Issues in the Management of Myelomeningocele and Hydrocephalus', *Journal of the Royal College of Physicians,* vol. 10, no. 1 (October 1975), pp. 47–60.

J. Noonan, 'An Almost Absolute Value in History' in John Noonan (ed.), *The Morality of Abortion* (Harvard University Press, Cambridge, Mass., 1972), p. 51.

D. Parfit, 'Rights, Interests, and Possible People' in S. Gorovitz *et al.* (ed.), *Moral Problems in Medicine* (Prentice Hall, Englewood Cliffs, NJ, 1976), pp. 369–75.

A. M. Shaw and Iris A. Shaw, 'Dilemmas of "Informed Consent" in Children', *New England Journal of Medicine,* vol. 289, no. 17 (25 October 1973), pp. 885–90.

A. Shaw, J. Randolph, and B. Manard, 'Ethical Issues in Pediatric Surgery: A National Survey of Pediatricians and Pediatric Surgeons', *Pediatrics,* vol. 6 (1977), pp. 588–99.

B. Shepperdson, 'Abortion and Euthanasia of Down's Syndrome Children—The Parents' View', *Journal of Medical Ethics*, vol. 9, no. 3 (September 1983), pp. 152–7.

M. Simms, 'Severely Handicapped Infants', *New Humanist*, vol. 98, no. 2 (Summer 1983).

P. Singer, H. Kuhse, C. Singer, 'The Treatment of Newborn Infants with Major Handicaps—A survey of obstetricians and paediatricians in Victoria', *The Medical Journal of Australia*, vol. 2, no. 6 (17 September 1983), pp. 274–8.

P. Singer, 'Sanctity of Life or Quality of Life?', *Pediatrics*, vol. 72, no. 1 (July 1983), pp. 128–9.

G. Keys Smith and E. Durham Smith, 'Selection for Treatment in Spina Bifida Cystica', *British Medical Journal*, vol. 4 (1973), pp. 189–97.

L. Williamson, 'Infanticide: An Anthropological Analysis' in Marvin Kohl (ed.), *Infanticide and the Value of Life* (Prometheus Books, New York, 1978).

R. B. Zachary, 'Ethical and Social Aspects of Treatment of Spina Bifida', *The Lancet* (3 August 1968), pp. 274–6.

R. B. Zachary, 'Life with Spina Bifida', *British Medical Journal* (3 December 1977), pp. 1460–2.

INDEX